T0347116

THE DECLINE OF JUTE: MANAGING INDUSTRIAL CHANGE

Perspectives in Economic and Social History

Series Editor: *Robert E. Wright*

Titles in this Series

Forthcoming Titles

Energy, Trade and Finance in Asia: A Political and Economic Analysis
Justin Dargin and Tai Wei Lim

Welfare and Old Age in Europe and North America: The Development of
Social Insurance
Bernard Harris (ed.)

Financing India's Imperial Railways, 1875–1914
Stuart Sweeney

THE DECLINE OF JUTE: MANAGING INDUSTRIAL CHANGE

BY

Jim Tomlinson, Carlo Morelli and Valerie Wright

Routledge
Taylor & Francis Group

LONDON AND NEW YORK

First published 2011 by Pickering & Chatto (Publishers) Limited

Published 2016 by Routledge
2 Park Square, Milton Park, Abingdon, Oxon OX14 4RN
711 Third Avenue, New York, NY 10017, USA

Routledge is an imprint of the Taylor & Francis Group, an informa business

BRITISH LIBRARY CATALOGUING IN PUBLICATION DATA

Tomlinson, Jim.
The decline of jute: managing industrial change. – (Perspectives in economic
and social history)
1. Jute industry – Scotland – Dundee – History – 20th century. 2. Jute industry –
Great Britain – History – 20th century. 3. Jute industry – Government policy –
Great Britain –History – 20th century. 4. Great Britain – Economic conditions
– 20th century. 5. Dundee (Scotland) – Economic conditions – 20th century.
I. Title II. Series III. Morelli, Carlo. IV. Wright, Valerie.
338.4'767713'094127-dc22

ISBN-13: 978-1-84893-124-4 (hbk)

Typeset by Pickering & Chatto (Publishers) Limited

CONTENTS

To Alexander and Elaine Wright, Tony and Mary Morelli, Stanley Tomlinson, and in memory of Eileen Tomlinson.

ACKNOWLEDGEMENTS

This book was made possible by a grant from the Leverhulme Trust, and we are extremely grateful to the Trust for their funding.

We are also grateful for initial funding for this project to the Carnegie Trust for the Universities of Scotland, and to the Pasold Research Fund who funded a conference in 2010 on jute in Dundee and Calcutta. We are grateful to all the participants in that conference for helpful discussion.

Researchers on the history of Dundee are extremely lucky to have three excellent archives, at the University of Dundee, the Local History Collection at the City Library, and the City Archives. We are very grateful to the archivists at all three of these for their assistance. We are also grateful for assistance to Julie Millerick at the Verdant Works.

ABBREVIATIONS

Advertiser   *Dundee Advertiser* (merged with the *Courier* in 1926).

Courier   *Dundee Courier* (and *Argus* until 1926, when it merged with the *Advertiser*).

DCA   Dundee City Archives.

DCC   Dundee City Council.

DDUJFW   Dundee and District Union of Jute and Flax Workers.

DSU   Dundee Social Union.

DUA   Dundee University Archives.

DWCA   Dundee Women Citizens' Association.

LHC   Local History Collection, in Dundee City Library.

NAS   National Archives of Scotland.

NLS   National Library of Scotland.

TNA: PRO   The National Archives: Public Record Office (Kew).

LIST OF FIGURES AND TABLES

INTRODUCTION

A central feature of British history in the twentieth century is the long decline of the great staple export industries of the pre-1914 period. These industries were the core of Britain's industrial economy before the First World War, employing huge numbers, and providing the majority of exports which underpinned Britain's extraordinarily globalized economy of that era.[1] At the time of the 1907 Census of Production the four biggest of these staples – textiles, coal, iron and steel and general engineering – employed 25 per cent of the working population and produced 50 per cent of net industrial output. Coal, textiles and iron and steel alone contributed over 70 per cent of total British export earnings.[2] But over the following decades, at varying tempos, they all shrank to a small fraction of their previous size. After the great iron and steel and coal strikes of the 1980s these two industries followed cotton and shipbuilding downwards, with employment in iron and steel going from 186,000 in 1979 to 54,000 by 1990, in coal over the same period from 232,000 to 42, 000. The contribution of these four to British trade had likewise shrunk to insignificance.

The demise of these industries resulted in both their owners and governments facing enormous problems of 'managing decline'. On the employers side a whole range of responses were deployed, usually in combination. These included a diverse set of strategies for increased efficiency (including more effective use of labour and mechanisms for reducing wage costs), technological improvement and new product development; collusive arrangements with other employers; lobbying for protection of markets; and finally, of course, rationalization and exit from the industry. On the government side, the impulse to manage the decline, felt much more strongly in some periods than others, derived especially from the huge concentrations of employment in these industries, usually in particular regions and towns, so that decline threatened mass unemployment and all its attendant evils. The character and degree of success of these governmental attempts at management had huge political a well as economic consequences. The election of the Attlee government in 1945, for example, cannot be understood without recognizing the widespread perception in the 1940s that the interwar Conservatives had mis-managed the decline of the staples; much of the agenda of that Labour government was addressed to avoiding any repeat of those perceived errors. Forty years later, the Thatcher government's approach to the management of decline, especially in coal, was central to both its political outlook and political fortunes.

Jute as a Case Study

This book analyses this process of management by focusing on one example, jute, but treating this as a case study of the wider issues of the approach to and success of dealing with decline in Britain as a whole. There is already a voluminous literature on the staples, much of the best of it concerned with the interwar rather than post-war period.[3] But for all the insights and diversity of this literature, none of it brings together all the elements studied here. These elements are: an understanding of the sources of decline and the approach of employers, government and workers to that decline, and the inter-action of these three agents; the close linking of a specific industry's trajectory to its local economy; and the assessment of how far decline was managed successfully, judged primarily by the consequences for that local economy.

For such a study jute is ideal.[4] Small in relation to the 'big four' listed above, jute was still a significant industry. Employment in the industry reached its peak in 1891 with 49,000 employees, and still had 20,000 by 1948, falling to 8,000 by 1977.[5] Raw jute use peaked in 1902, when 280,000 tons were imported, though the broad picture in the Edwardian period is one of a stagnating trend but with sharp cyclical fluctuations.[6] As these peak dates suggest, the industry was actually a 'pioneer of decline' amongst the staples, its years of maximum prosperity coming around the turn of the century. But, like most of the other staples, the really sharp change in fortunes came after the Great War, when, following a wartime and brief post-war boom in 1919–20, the industry's interwar decline was extremely rapid; it recovered a little in and just after the Second World War, before declining further, especially from the late 1960s, and becoming extinct in the 1990s.[7] In other respects also the industry had a similar character to the pattern for the staples. It was an extreme case of localization, with over 90 per cent of the UK's spinning of the material and over 60 per cent of the weaving in the City of Dundee, and most of the rest in nearby parts of Angus.[8] It thus provides a particularly good case for understanding the impact of industrial decline and its management on a local region.

Jute was also typical of the staples in being highly internationalized, wholly reliant on an imported raw material (grown in Bengal), and selling much of its output overseas.[9] This meant issues of international competition, free trade and protectionism loomed particularly large in the industry's history, and provided one important dimension of industry/government interaction.

In other respects jute differed somewhat from the general staple story. In several cases the staples were the archetypal male manual worker dominated industries – coal, shipbuilding and iron and steel being overwhelmingly of that character. However jute, like cotton, employed large numbers of women, but their role in Dundee was significantly greater even than in the Lancashire industry. In jute women dominated weaving as well as spinning, with men largely confined to supervisory and ancillary activities. This meant that throughout most of its history more women than men worked in the industry, though the proportion fell after 1945, and men outnumbered women by the 1960s. The extent to which this gendered characteristic of the industry shaped the management of decline is an important aspect of our discussion.

Figure 1.1. Closure of the Blackness Foundry, Dundee, 1959. (University of Dundee Michael Peto Collection).

Finally, jute was distinctive in having to contend with the early and substantial impact of imports of Empire produced manufactured products, not just the invasion of its export markets. While imports into Britain were not an issue for cotton before the 1950s, Indian manufactured jute goods first entered Britain in 1885, and were a major cause of contention from the 1890s onwards.[10] Thus managing the decline of jute has to be placed within the complex story of inter-Commonwealth economic and political relations, themselves of course significantly affected by India and Pakistan's independence after 1947.

As always, the case study method needs to be used with discretion. Dundee and jute were not the same as all the other staples, and general conclusions drawn from jute must be appropriately qualified. Nevertheless, it has enough 'typicality' to make the study of its decline, and the management of that decline, a powerful way of examining not only a fascinating individual case, but also a highly instructive example of many wider problems of twentieth century British history.

In analyzing the decline of jute in the context of the bigger British picture there are two perspectives which have been crucial in framing our approach. First we do *not* treat this decline as pathological, as part of some profound failing of British economy and society. This 'declinist' approach to modern Britain, while still ubiquitous, albeit increasingly challenged, we believe to be misleading and unhelpful. Rather than seeing the decline of jute and the other staples as part of a national pathology, we would see it as part of the recurrent history of capitalist market economies, constantly re-shaped by new patterns of demand, competition, and shifts in production technologies. In that context, 'decline' of any industry or set of industries is just part of the warp and weft of modern history, in all capitalist countries. This does not mean the whole process is automatic – it can be resisted or encouraged, and above all it can be managed, well or badly. But in trying to understand it, we should not treat it as a symptom of some profound malaise affecting British society, which tends to lead to moralistic and often unhistorical conclusions.[11]

Second, while we summarize the story of the industry up to 1940 in Chapter 1, we focus the bulk of our attention on the post-1940 period. This is because, while the decline of jute continued in this period, the context in which this was managed was profoundly altered. There was a new 'social settlement' in the 1940s, arising from the war, which pushed the dynamics of managing decline in a new direction.[12]

Central to this new settlement was the production of the White Paper on *Employment Policy* in 1944, which heralded a key political commitment to 'high and stable' employment, however much the precise policy proposals of that Paper were shrouded in ambiguity.[13] In the event, the feared collapse in demand which had so much concerned wartime policy-makers did not occur, so employment policy for the next thirty years mainly had to deal with regional and local unemployment, not a general slump. The key legislation here was the Distribution of Industry Act of 1945, a direct consequence of interwar staple problems, and their high level of regional concentration.[14]

From the 1940s to the 1970s this full employment commitment framed the approach to the decline of the staples. This did not mean no decline took place. On the contrary, after key staples were nationalized in the 1940s, they shed enormous amounts of labour with little resistance.[15] Paradoxically perhaps, nationalization, achieved 'rationalization' of the old staples of coal, iron and steel, and later shipbuilding, in ways which private enterprise had failed to between the wars – and in the 1950s and 60s with much less bitterness. However this decline was now, in large part, deemed tolerable only because overall macroeconomic conditions meant there were alternative jobs for most of those who left the staples – though for many it was still a painful process.

So in the early post-war decades issues of the political tolerability of unemployment were crucial to managing decline in ways which had not existed in the 1920s and 1930s. The context changes again from the 1970s, when, symbolized by Healey's budget of 1975, there began a process of giving a higher priority to defeating inflation and less emphasis on preventing unemployment.[16] But this was by no means an unequivocal and immediate shift, and it was not until the early 1980s that it became apparent that high unemployment was not necessarily politically disastrous for the government, which again altered how far 'decline' was seen as a key problem to address.[17] Our approach, then, treats the 1940s as a watershed in managing decline, but also pays considerable attention to the shifting economic and political context for this management *within* the post-war decades.

Structure of the Book

The book is organized as follows. Chapter 1 analyses the impact on the industry of the combination of foreign (overwhelmingly Indian) competition alongside the decline in world demand for major jute products in the four decades before 1939. It looks at how the Dundee industry responded to this competition, both in changing its own practices, and seeking to change the free trade policy of the government. It suggests that while the industry did alter its behaviour in some regards, for example by installing new machinery and associated shift-working, rapid decline in this period was driven by the overwhelming combination of world trade slump and increased foreign competition, but without any significant willingness on behalf of government to respond actively to the problem. Government involvement was largely limited to the indirect regulation of wages in the industry by Jute Wages Board, and the impact of even this was rather small. Overall, the story of jute (and therefore of Dundee) in the interwar years was one of largely unmitigated depression, with the city suffering probably the highest levels of unemployment of any city in Britain.[18]

Chapter 2 sets out the main elements in the development of the industry from 1939 until its final demise in 1999. It locates Dundee jute in its global context, as the Scottish industry became a minor player in the world production of jute, but was still very much affected by developments elsewhere in the world, both in the jute-growing and jute-manufacturing areas of the Indian subcontinent, and in changing markets for jute products across the world.

Chapters 3, 4 and 5 analyse the various responses to the industry to the postwar challenges, as it sought to 'modernize' itself. Chapter 3 focuses on labour issues. Managing decline plainly involved labour in two senses. On the one hand the response of the industry to increased competition was to seek to reduce wage costs both by cuts in labour employed, and more efficient use of that which remained. The former issue – and the general issue of employment in Dundee – is returned to in Chapter 7, but the latter is focused on in this chapter. The drive to modernization in jute, focusing on more efficient labour usage and higher labour productivity, took place in a national context where such issues had more policy significance than ever before. The impetus to greater labour efficiency resulted in complex attempts at changing patterns of labour usage and wage bargaining, and the industry's involvement in issues ranging from nursery provision to shift patterns, both of which were closely related to the gendered character of the industry's labour force.

Chapter 4 discusses the industry's attempts to defend itself by collusion amongst constituent firms. This was an important aspect of the industry, linked to broader issues of post-war British economic history because of the tensions between competition policy and the desire of firms in many industries to cooperate to achieve their goals – those goals including the 'orderly' management of decline. In the case of jute this issue was especially significant because of its long history of price collusion, which was greatly reinforced by the operation of the Jute Control from 1939. The industry was subject to a landmark Restrictive Practices Court case in 1962, and this is analysed in detail.

Chapter 5 deals with attempts by the industry to reposition itself in the face of competition. These responses included seeking to 'outflank' Indian competition by moving up-market, looking for new uses for jute products, and linked to these changes, searching for new technologies. These responses involved both individual firms and collective bodies, including the AJSM but especially the British Jute Trade Research Institute. An important part of this story is the development of polypropylene as an alternative, synthetic material for sacking and other uses of jute, alongside the development of new end uses for jute, like carpet-backing, both of which had major impacts on the size and shape of the industry.

Chapter 6 focuses upon the industry's multi-faceted attempts to influence government – mainly in London, but also in Edinburgh. The protection issue was transformed in 1939 with the creation of the Jute Control, and thereafter there was an almost continuous dialogue between the industry and London about the future of protection. This dialogue involved an interplay between concerns in London about international commercial policy, which in these years was being driven in a liberalising direction, and Dundee's concerns with employment, an issue on which forces in both Edinburgh and London could be mobilized. This dialogue set the pattern for the broad trajectory of reduction of protection from the 1950s onwards, but within which, at least until the 1980s, fears of unemployment seriously tempered the pace of change.

Issues of gender were also part of the story here, as in the case of jute the threat of unemployment was to a significantly female workforce (though the predominance of women was eroded after 1945), and in a place which had commonly been labelled a 'women's town'. Protection also, of course, meant concerns about relationships with India, a country simultaneously poor and a member of the Commonwealth.

Chapter 7 places the decline of jute in the context of Dundee. How successfully that decline was managed can best be assessed by looking at the economic health of the city, especially in respect of employment. Until the 1970s the decline can be seen as compatible with a degree of economic buoyancy in Dundee, not least because of the successful efforts to encourage multinational manufacturing companies to locate in the city. But from the 1970s these companies began a long retreat, and combined with the sharper decline of jute in the early 1980s, this led to a marked deterioration in the city's economic fortunes.

The conclusion summarizes the major themes that emerge from the book. It emphasizes the considerable degree of success achieved in managing the decline of jute in the two decades after the Second World War. This success rested on internal changes in the industry, but especially on the role of the state both in the broad sense of seeking to use policy to secure full employment, but more specifically protecting the industry in a fashion which encouraged its own efforts to change.

1 THE STORY UP TO 1939

The jute industry in Dundee grew out of the long-established linen industry in the town. Linen continued to be produced in the city until after the Second World War, but increasingly production shifted to Northern Ireland.[1] Jute manufacture expanded rapidly from the mid-nineteenth century, drawing in large numbers of migrant workers from elsewhere in Scotland and from Ireland.[2] By the late nineteenth century Dundee had become 'juteopolis', its local economy extraordinarily dominated by this one industry (Table 1.1), and the industries such as textile machinery or the docks whose fortunes heavily relied upon the local jute trade.[3]

Table 1.1: The importance of jute to Dundee 1881–1931.

	Proportion of Jute Workers in Total Working Population of Dundee (per cent)
1881	49
1911	48
1931	41

Source: A. Carstairs, 'The nature and diversification of employment in Dundee' in S. Jones (ed), *Dundee and district* (Dundee: British Association, 1968), pp. 320, 328.

Expansion was especially rapid in the 1870–90 period, when the number of spindles rose from 94,250 to 268, 165; the number of looms from 3,744 to 14,107; and numbers employed from 14,911 to 43,366.[4] But the pattern of expansion was by no means smooth. Jute was from the beginning a highly 'globalized' industry, greatly affected by events across the world – from regular variations in the Indian monsoon affecting the raw jute crop, the impact of the trade cycle, or one-off events such as the American Civil War in multiplying the demand for jute bags. It was also affected by periodic financial crises, such as the US stock market crash of 1907, which seriously affected its biggest market in the USA.[5] This vulnerability to external forces reflected both the industry's reliance on Bengal for all of its supplies of raw jute, and on export markets for most of its sales. The biggest product of the industry was jute sacks, which, apart from their use as sandbags by the military, were used to transport many of the great staple products of international trade – grains and coal for example. This meant that fluctuations in those trades directly affected Dundee livelihoods.[6]

Alongside these cyclical and 'one-off' factors affecting the industry were long-term competitive pressures, resulting from foreign competition, especially from India. Hand production of jute goods had long been practiced in India, but from the 1850s a machine industry was established and expanded rapidly in the Calcutta area. British, especially Scottish, entrepreneurs played a key role in this expansion, mainly organized around managing agents establishing rupee denominated companies, initially drawing capital resources predominantly from British residents in India. Dundee supplied capital, managers and overseers to Calcutta, along with almost all of its machinery, thus developing an industry which in the long run was to not only surpass but destroy its Scottish competitor.[7]

By the end of the century jute had become one of India's most important manufacturing industries, rivaled in significance only by cotton. There is a very rich literature on the Indian industry, which was in many ways a pioneer of capitalist enterprise in India under the Raj.[8] By the 1890s the Calcutta industry could rightly regard itself as by far the most important in the world, and Dundee as a minor player. However, from a Dundonian point of view Indian competition was becoming the defining issue, Indian jute goods not only capturing British export markets, but beginning to be purchased in Britain. This competition from India was evident from the 1880s, and was combined with the imposition of heavy tariffs on British products in European markets, such as France, Germany and Italy as they built up domestic capacity.[9]

Raw jute use in Dundee peaked in 1902, when 280,000 tons were imported, though the broad picture in the Edwardian period is one of a stagnating trend but with sharp cyclical fluctuations.[10] As these peak dates suggest, the industry was actually a 'pioneer of decline' amongst the staples, its years of maximum prosperity coming around the turn of the century, though with no clear sign of a trend decline before the First World War.

The competitive pressure contributed strongly to the characteristic of Dundee jute as low wage industry, and this was in turn linked to the widespread employment of women and boys.[11]

For the pre-1914 years and down to 1925 we have substantial scholarly work on labour relations in Dundee jute.[12] These studies show a predominantly female and relatively poorly-organized workforce, with trade unions struggling to sustain a strong membership, but by no means entirely placid industrial relations, with periodic if not very sustained disputes in the industry. Women dominated both spinning and weaving, and thus jute notably lacked the core roll of the skilled male spinners in cotton production, who were the foundation of entrenched union strength in that industry.

This female predominance (in 1911 women formed 75 per cent of the jute workforce) had major consequences for the character of the city.[13] Women outnumbered men in the total population, and married women were much more likely to work in Dundee than in other cities, with 86 per cent of Dundee's employed married women in jute.[14] These characteristics led Dundee to commonly being characterized as a 'women's town'.[15] Eleanor Gordon's work is a landmark study of women in Dundee jute before 1914, and she shows that while women's attachment to formal trade union organization was patchy and intermittent, this by no means implies women were passive in their approach to life and work in the mills.[16] Other work has emphasized the highly gendered nature of the organization of work in the industry, with women numerically dominant in the industry, but largely excluded from the better paid jobs commonly characterized as skilled.[17]

Politically, Dundee was a pioneer of labour parliamentary representation in Scotland, but before 1914 labour politicians found it hard to know how to respond to the pressures of Indian competition on the city's biggest industry. Protectionism was not very appealing, given labour's contemporary adherence to the broad tenets of free trade, but also perhaps the evident benefits of that policy in substantially raising the real wage of Dundonians in the late nineteenth century, by providing cheap food, though this trend largely halted around 1900. In Labour and trade union circles there was a focus on seeking to raise labour standards in Calcutta, which reflected in part a commitment to international labour solidarity, as well, of course, as the fact that India was under British rule. But it was not perhaps a very realistic policy in the context of British policy in India, which had to be sensitive to some degree to the interests of major industries and their owners and workers.[18]

On the employers side, jute in Dundee shows evidence of sharing the nationwide swing against free trade, as the turn of the century saw the conversion of many of Britain's capitalists to protectionism.[19] In Dundee there had been such calls as far back as the 1870s, and there was strong support by the time of the Tariff Commission in the early 1900s.[20] (D.C.Thomson, Dundee's 'press baron' also made a rare personal intervention on this matter).[21] But the jute employers were far from unanimous on the issue, certainly before the 1930s. For example, while Sir George Baxter, a linen and jute owner, stood on a protectionist platform in the landmark by-election of 1908, James Caird, another important local jute proprietor, was a key financial backer of free trade propaganda and of the free trader Winston Churchill.[22]

Baxter, who lost to Churchill in the 1908 election, (Churchill was at that time a Liberal), focused his protectionist demands on Germany, rather than India, an Empire country upon which it would be politically very difficult to impose protection.[23] An alternative strategy to protection against Indian jute manufactures was to seek a duty on Indian exports of raw jute going to non-Empire countries, but this too ran up against the complexities of Britain's 'imperial mission' in India.[24]

While political action to protect the industry was part of employers' strategy, this did not exhaust their response to competition. While it is clear that much of the profit made in the industry flowed abroad, especially to North America,[25] this did not mean the owners failed to invest and change the industry itself. The evidence suggests that technical change was pursued by the jute owners, especially when competition increased from the 1890s, and we should not see the industry as passive and conservative as some 'declinist' accounts of pre-1914 British industry suggest.[26] The productivity performance of the industry in this period has led Broadberry to characterize jute as a 'success story', but, as he notes, it was also one where 'technical innovation alone was incapable of changing the fundamental economic position of the industry' in the face of changing international competition.[27]

Before the first war, in a policy structure of free trade and 'cosmopolitanism internationalism' government took little direct interest in the position of specific industries. Neither Conservative nor Liberal governments responded positively to any suggestion of protection for jute. Churchill, the city's most influential MP in the years before 1914 was a resolute free trader and declined to deviate from this position. Late nineteenth century concerns with poverty and the conditions of labour led to official inquiries into wages in jute from the 1880s, but this led to no action. (The most important inquiry of this type was the private, philanthropic work of the Dundee Social Union which formed part of the groundswell of opinion underlying some of the Liberal social reforms after 1906).[28] Before the First World War jute was not subject to 'sweated industry' legislation, which in some other low wage industries led to the imposition of a minimum wage. For jute, laissez-faire remained the rule before 1914.

The War and Interwar Period

1913 was a good year for Dundee jute, and after initial disruption the early years of war brought continuing prosperity as demand for sandbags soared, rising from a quarter of a million per month before spring 1915 to 40 million by December of that year, though freight rates almost quadrupled due to the threat of attacks on merchant ships.[29] The prosperity of the industry coupled with wartime inflation led to significant labour disputes in 1916 and 1917. As across much of the wartime economy, government incrementally built up controls over jute, a task made much easier by the single source of supply of its raw material, and the homogeneity of its output. Because military demand outran the supply of raw material and labour, exports more or less ceased and production for civilian use was severely curtailed.[30]

The war drove up wages in jute, but drove up profits even faster. A sample of six Dundee companies found that their profits quadrupled between pre-war and 1919. As elsewhere in the British economy an immediate post-war 'pause' was followed by a frenetic boom, which in turn collapsed in 1921. For Dundee jute this war and early post-war prosperity was especially misleading as guide to the future. Wartime demand had boosted the Calcutta industry even more than that in Scotland, so once post-war conditions settled down the Indian industry was in a much stronger position to compete, especially at the bottom end of the market where wartime demand had been concentrated.[31]

The war and its immediate aftermath had major significance for the organization of the industry. As across much of British industry, the combination of wartime labour unrest and government control had underpinned the creation of a new employers' organization, the AJSM. This was to prove one of the most important legacies of the war, as the association, aided by the geographical concentration of the industry, organized the overwhelming majority of firms in the industry, and acted as a unified mouthpiece for the industry. However, it was unable to secure the protection of the industry it sought at the end of the war. The Committee that considered this also rejected the workers argument for measures to equalize wages and conditions in Calcutta with Dundee to aid the home industry. The small duties imposed during the War on the export of manufactured jute products (as well as raw jute) from India did little to reduce the competitiveness of its products[32]

The AJSM also failed at this time in its bid to prevent the creation of a Trade Board (Wages Council) in the industry. Initially the creation of this Board looked like a triumph for the workers in the industry, a basis on which they could consolidate wartime gains. But as the tide of prosperity in the industry retreated after the boom peaked in 1920, so did this prospect. From 1921 the Board became the place where the trade unions fought, with only limited success, to minimize the wage cuts sought by the employers, especially after a major unsuccessful strike against such cuts in 1923.[33]

For the rest of the interwar period there was a battle on the Board between employers and unions over wage levels, with variations broadly following the prosperity of the industry after a lag. So after the 1920 peak, rates were cut in 1921, 1922 and 1923; there was a partial restoration of the previous cuts in 1925, a further cut in 1927, and then a reversion to 1925 levels in 1928. Further cuts followed in 1930, 1931 and 1933, with some restoration in 1937.[34]

The new unity of the employers, especially on labour issues, was aided by concentration amongst its constituent firms, especially the floating of Jute Industries Limited in 1920. This company amalgamated seven jute concerns around Cox Brothers, owners of the industry's biggest factory, Camperdown Works in Lochee. Jute Industries became by far the biggest firm in the industry, by the end of the 1930s having twelve manufacturing establishments as well as merchanting interests. A few years after Jute Industries, another major concern was created, Low and Bonar's, which was originally a merchanting company, but after the acquisition of Baxter Brothers in 1924 became the industry's second biggest manufacturer.[35]

The story of Dundee jute between the wars is one of almost unrelieved gloom, a general downward trend being accompanied by sharp cycles of activity. There is no annual data which can wholly summarize the state of the industry, but gross output halved between 1924 and 1933, and over the same period unemployment approximately trebled. After the post-war boom in 1919 to 1920 came the interwar depression, though within this overall trend there were cycles, with notable troughs in the early 1920s and especially in the early 1930s. The main determinant of the prosperity of the industry was exports, and these collapsed in 1921, recovered in the mid 1920s, before collapsing again from 1929, reviving again only slowly after the nadir of 1932. The industry picked up slightly faster from 1937 because of war preparations, but was still operating far below the levels even of the 1920s on the eve of war.[36]

This depression reflected the impact of two forces, both of which operated to a greater or lesser extent on all the staple industries. Characteristic of the interwar period was the failure of the volume of international trade to recover to its pre-1914 peak (it didn't recover those levels until the 1950s). On the other side was increased competition, from new producers or older producers expanding their capacity. In the case of jute, the low levels of international trade fed directly into the demand for the product, so global demand was depressed. There was also the beginning of the long-term process of substitution of other raw materials (eg paper) in the production of sacking, and the use of bulk-handling of grain. Within that depressed global total, India obtained an increasing share. Indian loom capacity rose from 40,554 in 1918 to around 68,000 by 1939.[37] Throughout the interwar years the Indian industry suffered from over-capacity, leading the Indian Jute Mills Association (IJMA) to seek to control output to try and keeps prices up. This was only ever partially successful, in part due to the political dynamics of the IJMA, and collapsed entirely in the 1930s.[38] In consequence of this excess supply, prices in most sectors were impossible for Dundee to compete with, and by the mid-1930s the competitive deterioration of Dundee was manifest in, for the first time, an import surplus with India on jute manufactures. Retained imports of jute goods into Britain (from all sources) rose from 41,000 tons in 1928 to 94,000 by 1938.[39]

While jute employers seem to have been predominantly protectionist after 1918, in line with employers in most British industries, the political circumstances of the 1920s meant little serious inroad was made into the national policy of free trade.[40] But following the introduction of tariffs by the National Government in 1931, coupled with the weakening of the output restrictions in India, pressure for protection intensified and was more or less continuous through the decade. In 1931 the industry received tariff protection against European producers, but despite the Ottawa agreements on imperial preference of 1932, free entry of jute products from India continued. In 1929 a leading figure in the industry, George Bonar had argued for a 'deal' with government by which the increase in European competition of the 1920s would be halted by protection, and in return the industry would put its house in order.[41] But Europe was, in the long run, a side issue. While the European producers had expanded output in the 1920s, they largely served their home markets, so protection against them in the 1930s made little difference to Dundee's plight.[42]

The politics of protectionism in Dundee were complex. By the 1930s employers were generally supportive, and both the AJSM and the local Chamber of Commerce were active in putting pressure on government for restrictions on imports, the forces of organized labour were divided. In the name of international working-class solidarity, plus fear of monopolization of industry behind tariff walls, and the threat of expensive food, both the Labour Party and the Communist Party opposed tariff protection. Their alternative policy was to seek an improvement in the wages and conditions of Indian jute workers so as to create a 'level playing field' with the Dundee industry.[43] Plainly this was not a policy likely to yield immediate relief; as the *Dundee Courier* editorialized on such ideas in 1938: 'The socialist plan is one for postponing the problem till a remote future, while the needs of Dundee are claimant and instant'.[44] Employers also pursued this issue by, for example, in 1935 the AJSM pressing (unsuccessfully) the Government of Bengal to regulate working hours in Calcutta jute mills – but this was much less emphasized than protection.[45]

These pressing needs led to union support for protectionism in the 1930s. Sime, leader of the main jute union (DDUJFW), who had followed the Labour Party line in the 1920s, now joined with employers and other union figures, and Dundee's Lord Provost, in pressing for import controls on Indian goods.[46] Ministries in London were lobbied, and public and private pressure was exerted. The AJSM was especially active, setting up a 'Fiscal Committee' and hiring a Kings Counsel to provide expert support for lobbying.[47] Such pressures led to debates in the House of Commons in 1936 and 1938, initiated by the Dundee MP Frances Horsbrugh. She was Dundee's only ever Conservative (and only ever woman) MP, and the only unabashed protectionist ever elected in Dundee before the Second World War. However, she was not supported by her National Liberal colleague from Dundee, Dingle Foot, nor from the Labour benches, where opposition to actions deemed detrimental to the interests of Indian workers remained strong.[48] The second of these parliamentary debates led to the passing of a motion asking that in the negotiations over trade policy with India, consideration be given to the needs of Dundee both for reasons of unemployment, and because of the strategic significance of jute.[49]

But nothing was actually done to protect the home industry from Indian imports, for reasons which were clear well before these debates. The AJSM had lobbied particularly hard at the time of the Ottawa negotiations in 1932, sending representatives to Canada, but got little response. Its Annual Report lamented that the trade was being sacrificed 'for reasons of Empire politics and the conditions of India', and after a meeting with Sir Horace Wilson, the Government's Chief Industrial Adviser, in late 1932 members of the Association were told: 'the only inference which your representatives could draw from the meeting was that the interests of India must receive first consideration, and the jute industry of this country struggle along as best it could'.[50] That was a fair summary of the political weakness of Dundee in the 1930s and contrasts markedly with its strengthened bargaining position after 1945.

From Dundee's point of view the sad truth was that concerns about India clearly outweighed concerns about the city in the government's calculations. The British government was not concerned directly with encouraging industrial development in India, but it was concerned to maintain the fiscal base of the economy, and to conciliate powerful indigenous interests in the country.[51] The former concern had led to the introduction of the levy on raw jute in 1916 which, despite Dundee protests, had no imperial preference element to aid the Scottish industry.[52] In the 1930s there was generalized discontent in India and growing opposition to British rule, pressures which very much told against the British government seeming to act in favour of British industries at the expense of what was, by then, a hugely important factory industry in Bengal.

In 1937 the *Courier* editorialized that 'nothing could do the Government more damage than a confirmation of the belief that out of a dread of offending Indian susceptibilities and of giving Indian politicians a handle for their propaganda it would permit a native British industry to go to the wall. That is the way to make Empire ideals unpopular'.[53] But such concerns were hardly likely to weigh very heavily in London, where the threat of the loss of the Imperial 'Jewel in the Crown' was likely to trump any worries about the Imperial sentiments of Dundonians.

The dire condition of the jute industry between the wars led, as we have noted above, to substantial wage cuts in Dundee, as the employers sought to cut costs in the most obvious way. However, while these bitter battles over wage levels are an important part of the history of the industry and the city, in the larger analysis two key points about wages in interwar jute should be emphasized. First, while employers did succeed in getting wage cuts in bad times, they did not prevent a floor eventually being put on wages in a way which encouraged the paying of more attention to increased labour productivity as a route to greater competitiveness.[54] Wages relative to those elsewhere in Britain were low in jute, with average adult male earnings in 1938 at 51 shillings and 1 old penny, rates above only those in cotton amongst major manufacturing sectors.[55] But Indian competition could not realistically be met by low wages in Dundee. Lower wages in Calcutta were substantially offset by higher labour productivity in Britain, but it was estimated that in the 1930s total wage costs per unit of output in the Indian industry were still only 70 per cent of those in Dundee.[56]

The second point to stress is that, for most of the interwar period, the aim of the employers to focus on raising labour productivity was little inhibited by union and workforce opposition. A key moment in labour relations was in 1923, when, in the context of bitterness over wage cuts, the union sought to restrict the number of frames worked by spinners. The dispute began in Jute Industries' Camperdown Works, but was responded to by an industry-wide lock out by the AJSM, which, after its foundation in 1918, was largely focused on labour issues, at least until its role in protectionist agitation in the 1930s. It proved very effective in organizing collective resistance to the union, and eventually the employers won the battle. As a result, Walker suggests, 'from 1923 the employers were free to proceed with the modernization and rationalization of the industry secure from effective protest by Sime and the union'.[57]

Changes aimed directly at raising labor productivity included the generalization of two-frame working by spinners, from a level of about 35 per cent in 1923.[58] Also in spinning, substantial new capacity was installed, accompanied by the adoption of two-or three-shift systems. Because of laws restricting the employment of women at night, this shift pattern led to a notable alteration in the gender composition of the work force, with adult males being substituted for women and juveniles.[59] This was to be a trend which continued through to the industry's demise in the 1990s. These changes in work patterns and machinery use help to explain what appears to be significant labour productivity improvements in the industry in the interwar years, perhaps in the 1920s. Relative to a UK index of 100, the US level fell from 200 in 1925/24 to 148 in 1929/30, and 169 in 1947/8. Performance relative to Germany also improved after 1929, with the industries productivity levels being equal by 1947/8.[60] Of course, labour productivity is a function of many forces, and jute had the benefit of perhaps significant Marshallian external economies of scale arising from the tight geographical concentration of the industry in one city, an issue returned to in Chapter 4.

Historically the industry had been dominated by family-owned small scale firms. In the interwar years, in the face of declining overall numbers employed, the average level of employment actually fell, so that according to the Census of production of 1935, the modal size was in the 100–199 employees category.[61]

But, as noted above, after the First World War there were important amalgamations in the industry, most importantly JIL in 1920. This amalgamated the
interests of one the oldest Dundee textile producers, Cox Brothers, with a number of other firms to create what became easily the largest firm in the industry,
by the end of the 1930s having twelve manufacturing establishments as well as
merchanting interests.

This amalgamation took place at the same time as many others in staple trades,
during the post-1918 boom. These often led to significant problems when that
boom collapsed. They were mainly the result of what later generations would
call 'financial engineering' rather that compelling productive logic. This seems to
have been in part the case with Jute Industries, as the amalgamation was carried
out largely by financiers from outside the industry.[62] It is not clear how far the
new company sought rationalization and common production policies, though
it amalgamated the buying of all raw jute early in its existence.[63] JIL continued as
a holding company until 1933, when it became a trading company.[64] In 1933 its
chairman claimed that in the previous 10 years the company had reduced costs
by about 25 per cent, 8 per cent by wage cuts, 17 per cent by 'economies'.[65]

The industry undoubtedly saw significant technical developments in the
interwar years, especially in spinning processes, and this seems to have been especially prevalent in Jute Industries. New, faster, spindles, made up about 40 per
cent of total spindleage in 1938, about a third of these owned by Jute Industries.[66]
These new machines were largely installed in old buildings, the only substantial
new mill built in this period being the Eagle Mill built by Low and Bonar.

While the industry did not endure the depression passively, it seems to have
found it hard to mount a *collective* response, beyond pressure for protection
(where the AJSM focused its attentions) and wage cuts. An attempt to form
a research association not long after the first war 'broke down a result of the
individualism of the manufacturers'.[67] Equally evidence of a lack of collective
will, it has been suggested, was the failure of the Chamber of Commerce to gain
enough support to justify acceptance of Government's offer of space in the British section of the New York World's Fair of 1939.[68]

In 1948 the Working Party on jute obtained information from firms with 95
per cent of the industry's spindles and 80 per cent of the looms about profitability in the 1930s. The data showed a rate of return on capital falling sharply from
5.2 per cent in 1934 to 0.8 per cent in 1938, with average profits in spinning
significantly above those in weaving. This pattern is, perhaps, surprising, given
the revival of output in the late 1930s, and the Working Party offers no explanation of this pattern.[69]

In the short run such investments in machinery were only likely to add to the
unemployment problem that the jute depression brought to Dundee. According to Beveridge, jute had the worst official unemployment rate of any industry

in Britain by 1937.[70] The official rate, based on national insurance records, may have significantly underestimated the problem because the Anomalies Regulations Act of 1931 disqualified large numbers of married women from claiming benefits, therefore adding to the hidden unemployed.[71] The result of this for Dundee was devastating; the City's condition was comparable with that of Jarrow as a 'town that was murdered' because of the interwar slump.[72]

Apart from the impetus given to pressure for protection given by this unemployment, it did also galvanize action for measures to boost the economy, especially through local authority housebuilding, where Dundee was a pioneer, and requests for central government funding of a road bridge across the Tay, opening up Dundee's links with Fife, and along with a Forth Road Bridge, to Edinburgh.[73] But this transport development did not happen until the 1960s.[74]

There was widespread recognition of the gloominess of the industry's future in the interwar years, and one response was some attempts to attract new industry in 1930s. Unfortunately for Dundee, the Special Areas which were created in 1935 did not embrace the city. Alongside pressing for inclusion in these Areas, the council and the Chamber of Commerce established a Dundee Trade Development Committee which pursued the idea of establishing a site company to encourage 'new' industries to come to Dundee.[75] This was an idea which, after the 1945 Distribution of Industry Act provided significant central government funding, was to prove hugely important in improving Dundee's economic fortunes.

Writing in 1939 for the British Association about conditions in jute, J. Eastham wrote:

> 'At present the industry feels itself precariously balanced on the edge of a precipice and, if it falls over, the city of Dundee will be largely dependent on Unemployment relief'.[76]

Fortunately, no such fall took place because the war brought a quite new context for the industry to work in, a context which was to shape the industry's future long after the war had finished.

2 DE-GLOBALIZATION AND DECLINE, 1939–99

In the sixty years after the introduction of Jute Control in 1939 jute manufacture in Dundee declined then disappeared entirely.[1] This chapter provides an overview of that period, concentrating upon the interwoven processes of de-globalization and decline.

Table 2.1: Employment in Jute 1901–99 (thousands).

	MALE	FEMALE	TOTAL
1901	12*	28*	40*
1924	13	28	41
1929	12	27	39
1933	12	23	35
1938	11	17	28
1948	8	12	20
1954	9	12	21
1959	8	9	17
1964	9	9	18
1969	9	7	16
1974	6	3	9
1979	5	2	7
1982	3	1	4
1991	1	0.3	1.3
1999	0	0	0

* Census figure: likely to be a significant underestimate: see W. Walker *Juteopolis: Dundee and its Textile Workers 1885–1923* (Edinburgh: Scottish Academic Press, 1979), p. 86.
Sources: 1924–82: *Ministry of Labour/Department of Employment Gazette,* various issues. 1901, 1991: Census.

Historically jute was a classic 'globalized' industry, its fortunes intertwined with the international economy like so many of Britain's staple industries which flourished before 1914. As outlined in Chapter 1, for jute this intertwining was especially prominent because of the combination of total dependence on imports for raw material, heavy reliance on exports markets for finished products, and also the role of Dundonian capital and management in the development of the rival industry in Calcutta. In the interwar period this globalized nature of the industry underpinned its disastrous experience of output collapse and mass unemployment. From the Second World War the reliance on imported raw jute continued, but in other respects the international dependence and connections withered. Hence we can sensibly talk about a process of 'de-globalization' of Dundee jute in the last six decades of its existence. The first part of this chapter examines this process, while the second explores the interconnected issue of decline.

The Global Jute Manufacturing Industry from 1939

Immediately prior to the Second World War the world jute industry was slowly recovering from the depths of the early 1930s depression, which hit the industry particularly hard because its fortunes were so closely attached to fluctuations in the volume of international trade, which fell even more than world output in that depression.[2] By 1939 the resurgent Indian industry (where capacity had continued to expand in the 'twenties and 'thirties, even as output stagnated or fell) easily dominated the world, with well over half of all loom capacity.[3] The war generated strong demand for some jute products, including sandbags, camouflage and hessian coated with bitumen for temporary road surfaces. But output was constrained by the diversion of jute-growing land to rice production, transport difficulties and re-allocation of factory space and labour to other uses. Global output therefore fell during the war, though production by non-belligerents increased.[4]

Because the sub-continent was by this time the overwhelmingly most important producer of both raw jute and manufactured jute goods, Partition between India and Pakistan at the time of Independence in 1947 had an immensely disruptive influence on the industry across the world. At Partition the new Republic of India inherited all of the jute manufacturing capacity built up under the Raj, but 76 per cent of the acreage devoted to growing jute (and 80 per cent of the raw jute output) was in Pakistan.[5] For a short period after Partition a free trade agreement allowed the industry to function largely as if these new national borders did not matter (though Pakistan put an export tax on raw jute in November 1947), but by 1949 deteriorating relations between the countries, and especially the effects of the devaluation of the Indian Rupee in line with Sterling, hit the jute trade very seriously. Pakistan did not devalue its currency, raising the export price of raw jute by over 30 per cent, but India refused to accept this sharp deterioration in the terms of trade, and a trade war ensued. No raw jute moved from Pakistan to India from September 1949 for over a year.[6]

In the short run these events were extraordinarily disruptive of all jute activity in the subcontinent. As the IJMA newspaper, the *Indian Jute News,* remarked 'the two limbs of what was once amongst the most highly integrated industries in the world were torn asunder'.[7] In the longer run they spurred major expansions of the industry, as India sought to replace raw jute imports from Pakistan, and Pakistan built up its own manufacturing industry. Under the aegis of the state-owned Pakistan Industrial Development Corporation the first manufactured jute goods were produced in 1951, and by 1953 the industry was producing all the country's domestic needs and entering into the export market.[8] Under successive Five Year Plans capacity was increased, so that by the late 1950s Pakistan had overtaken Dundee as a producer, and by the mid-1960s was producing a third as much as the Indian industry.[9] Pakistan's position relative to India was aided in the 1950s by the latter's drive to become self-sufficient in the raw material, achieved in 1959.[10]

In the 1950s and 1960s Pakistan and India dominated competition in the expanding world market for jute goods, an expansion that meant that by the mid-1950s total world consumption had surpassed immediate pre-war levels. (Table 2.2) This expansion was geographically uneven, with post-war growth especially rapid in Asia, the centrally-planned economies and the USA. While growth in the first two of these was largely in the 'traditional' areas of jute use in sacking and packaging, the growth in the USA was striking because it combined a *declining* share of the market in these areas, more than offset by rapid growth in a variety of industrial uses, but above all in carpet-backing.[11] These new uses gave a substantial and unexpected boost to the industry.[12]

Until the 1930s the USA had been the world's biggest market for jute products because of its huge role in trade in agricultural products, especially grains, flour, sugar feeds, oilmeals and potatoes. But from that decade onwards these goods were increasingly moved either in paper rather than jute sacks, or by bulk-handling methods. In the post-war period these trends accelerated, so that, for example, between the mid-1950s and mid-1960s the proportion of US commercial feed shipped in jute bags halved, as bulk-handling expanded. By contrast, the growth of tufted-carpet use was very rapid indeed in the USA in the 1950s, with the proportion of all carpets made in this way leaping from 9 per cent to 90 per cent.[13]

Table 2.2: Apparent world consumption of jute manufactures 1937–63/5 (1,000 metric tons).

	1937	1953/5	1958/60	1963/5
W. Europe	562	517	557	556
USA	458	303	351	469
Asia	455	429	574	804
L. America	203	235	220	256
Africa and N. East	191	200	266	284
Centrally-planned economies	85	288	467	696
World total	2,095	2,116	2,609	3,225

Source: International Bank for Reconstruction and Development, *Indian Exports of Jute Manufactures: Problems and Prospects* (IBRD: Washington DC, 1969), Table 10.

While the USA was a pioneer both in substituting for jute in traditional uses, and developing new uses, both these trends spread across the globe after the Second World War. Of course, both substitution against and new uses for jute were in part a function of relative prices, and this meant arguments about the future of the industry could become strongly contested, especially because of disagreements about how far substitution could be halted or reversed by more favourable price trends. Such arguments were especially evident in India because for that country jute exports were so important for the whole economy, usually being the biggest single export product and earning 20–5 per cent of total foreign exchange.[14]

Concerns about the strength of global demand for jute were reinforced by the slowing down of that demand in the late 1960s, which continued in the 1970s, as shown in Table 2.3. In the 1970s what was particularly striking was the decline in sales in the rich industrial counties, especially North America, traditionally a hugely important market (consumption had peaked in the USA in 1965). In developing countries the pattern was different because there 'jute products are mostly employed in packaging, (and) the growth of output and trade of agricultural products, as well as of other packageable commodities such as cement and fertilizers, continued to be the major source of underlying strength to jute market's development'.[15]

Table 2.3: Apparent consumption of jute and allied fibres 1969/71–1979/81 (thousands of metric tons).

	1969/71	1979–81	Growth rate (per cent) 1969/71–79/81
Developing countries	1,747	2,613	4.1
Industrial Countries	1,525	1,004	-4.1
(of which) North America	515	240	-7.3
World	3,272	3,617	1.0

Source: M. Thigpen, P.Marongiu and S. Lasker, *World Demand Prospects for Jute* (Washington DC: World Bank, 1982), p.5.

Two new developments from the 1960s acted to further increase competition to the use of jute. One was containerization, containers being one of those simple technologies which revolutionize economic activity, in this case especially by taking out huge amounts of labour costs from the process of transhipment of goods. Across the world, beginning in the rich countries, dockworkers lost their jobs in their thousands from the 1960s as products like grain, fertilizers and chemicals were increasingly moved in containers.[16]

Second, jute was hit by the rise of polypropylene as an alternative fibre.[17] Polypropylene had originally been developed in Italy in the 1950s, was first produced commercially in 1957, but came into widespread use from the 1960s.[18] Polypropylene proved an immensely important competitor for jute partly because its relative price compared with jute fell sharply from the 1960s, but also as an alternative fibre it could replace jute in all its uses, including in the 'new' areas of carpet-backing as well as the traditional areas of bagging and packaging.[19]

As early as 1967 jute producers were seriously concerned with the possible impact of polypropylene, and the Food and Agricultural Organization (FAO) produced a study in 1969 which sought to assess the problem. The study focused on demand in rich industrial countries, and found that while demand for jute as bagging was decreasing sharply, that for carpet backing was rising rapidly.[20] But the second of these trends slowed markedly in the 1970s, as economic growth slowed and in particular the 'fitted-carpet' revolution ran out of steam. In Western Europe demand for jute in the 1970s held up even less well, total consumption roughly halving in that decade.[21]

The relative price or availability of jute goods was affected by tariff and other protective policies. As discussed in Chapter 6, Britain used the Jute Control to limit imports from 1939 until 1969, and thereafter tariffs. After 1971 the EEC reduced its tariffs, these going down to zero in 1981, though this was only agreed for as long as Bangladesh and India restrained their exports. After 1983 all restrictions ended.[22]

The fact that jute and jute products throughout this period were overwhelmingly produced by poor countries (especially India and Pakistan to 1971, India and Bangladesh thereafter) meant that concern with economic development inevitably led to a concern with the fate of the industry. In 1982, under the first International Agreement on Jute and Jute Products, UNCTAD created the International Jute Organization, with headquarters in Dakka. This organization encouraged the development of both raw jute and jute manufactures. It focused its attention on Research and Development projects, market promotion and cost reduction, but did not attempt measures of price stabilization.[23]

By the 1980s global demand for jute products was still rising, but much more slowly than previously, and wholly through expansion of markets in the developing world. Between the mid 1960s and mid-1980s the developed world's share in global consumption of jute fell from 48 per cent to 20 per cent, as its total consumption more than halved. The share of imports taken by rich industrial counties fell less dramatically (from 69 to 42 per cent) as they also saw their domestic production shrink.[24] From the mid-1980s onwards there was evidence that the fall in consumption in rich countries was tailing-off, but by this time these countries share of world use of jute products had fallen to only around 16 per cent. But total world consumption was continuing to grow, especially because of demand in India and China.[25]

The picture of a sharp divergence in the trends in the use of jute products between rich and poor countries, notable from the 1960s, is accurate, but that is not the whole story. Developing countries were by no means willing to allow the developed countries to monopolize polypropylene use and production. By the 1980s 'recognizing that plastics play a useful role in agricultural and industrial development, many developing countries have already undertaken, or are in the process of undertaking, ambitious projects for production and consumption of thermoplastics including polypropylene', and by 1987 production capacity in these countries had reached 1.2 million metric tons.[26]

While throughout this period India and Pakistan/Bangladesh sustained their role as the world's biggest jute manufacturers, production did expand in other countries. In the early post-war years the most rapid expansion was in Thailand, but later China grew fast and indeed by the mid-1980s produced almost as much as Bangladesh.[27] In Western Europe there was also expansion in the immediate aftermath of the War. As in Britain, output in France and Germany peaked in the mid-1950s, while in Belgium expansion was sustained into the 1960s. Because of this pattern, the Belgian industry briefly rivalled the British in size in the early 1970s, but in that decade the industry declined in all countries in this region.[28] By the early 1980s Western Europe as a whole was a minor contributor to world production, with just 2 per cent of the total.[29]

Changes in the volume and pattern of international trade in jute goods obviously followed the shifting balance between output and consumption in individual countries. Most importantly, India's share of total world trade diminished as growing demand at home out-paced domestic production. Just after the war India accounted for almost 90 per cent of world exports, but by the early 1960s this had fallen to two-thirds, and by the 1980s to 27 per cent. The biggest gainer has been Bangladesh whose share rose to over 40 per cent in the 1980s.[30] The import market for jute goods has grown across much of the developing world, but also in the developed world where from the 1970s the decline in production out-paced the fall in consumption.[31]

By the early 1990s total world production of jute goods was reaching its peak, as demand even in developing countries stagnated, while that in developed countries declined further. The biggest exporter, Bangladesh, suffered particularly sharp output declines around the turn of the century, but in India, the biggest producer, and China, output also stagnated. By 2000 India was producing 1,621,000 tonnes of jute goods (62 per cent of world output), Bangladesh 630,000 (24 per cent), China 176,000 (7 per cent).[32]

Raw Jute

As a relatively unsophisticated manufactured product, around half of the total selling price of jute goods was made up of the costs of the raw material.[33] Buying jute at the best possible price was thus a key part of the industry's operations, and fluctuations in the raw jute price a key determinant of profitability. In Dundee the local newspapers carried news of the raw jute price on their front pages, reflecting its crucial role in the prosperity of the city's key industry. Historically, all jute imported into Dundee had come from Bengal. This tied the jute price to a number of factors operative in the jute growing areas of that part of India, especially monsoon conditions and the relative price of competing crops, particularly rice.[34] Prices were also much affected by speculative activity in the market.[35] Before the Second World War the international trade in raw jute was almost entirely in the hands of British companies, but from 1941 the Jute Control became the sole purchaser of the Indian product. Export quotas were also in use from 1944.

From the mid-1930s the Government of Bengal attempted to restrict the supply of raw jute by a propaganda campaign. This was largely ineffectual, and in 1941/2 compulsory restrictions were brought in. Over the next few years the actual crop grown fell below the maximum permitted by these restrictions, as high rice prices attracted growers into that food crop.[36] However, from 1948 output expanded, above all because of India's desire to replace imports from Pakistan. Indian production grew approximately five fold in the fourteen years after Partition (1947/8 to 1961/2), from 1.7 million bales to 8 million bales, and imports were almost insignificant by the early 1960s.[37]

From a Dundonian point of view the early post-war years were characterized by high and fluctuating raw jute prices. In the war rising prices led to the Government of India imposing price controls, and after these were abolished in 1946 prices rose to four to five times those of pre-war.[38] Prices were further enhanced once Pakistan came into being and imposed an export tax on raw jute. While Indian output expanded, Pakistan's production was well below pre-war levels, so total output hovered around the pre-1939 level into the 1950s. In addition, more of the Pakistan crop was being used at home which further limited the quantity entering world markets.[39] Even worse than high and fluctuating prices were interruption to supplies, which occurred at the time of Partition (and was to occur again at the time of the Indo-Pakistan dispute of 1964/5 and when Bangladesh was created in 1971). The Korean War also had a radical impact, sending prices up to £275 per ton, compared with £100 in 1948.[40]

One response to this problem was to look elsewhere for raw jute supplies.[41] After 1945 the growing of jute expanded in a number of countries, notably Brazil Formosa and Nepal, but these countries contribution to the world total remained marginal. In the face of this, in 1952 Dundee jute spinners and the Ministry of materials contributed £60,000 each to finance the British Guiana Fibre Research Company 'to investigate the possibility of growing jute on a commercial scale in British Guiana'. In 1956 the company was wound up without having found a way to make jute growing in Guiana a viable proposition.[42] So Dundee remained dependent on the sub-continent (overwhelmingly Pakistan, later Bangladesh) for its raw material, albeit small quantities were brought from Thailand and Burma at the peak of the crisis surrounding the creation of Bangladesh.[43]

Some sense of the vulnerabilities involved in this dependence is given by the experience of the end of the 1950s, when then price of raw jute delivered in the UK rose almost three-fold in a year, before subsiding almost back to its previous level.[44]

While such fluctuations were obviously highly disruptive to jute manufacturing, their impact on the Dundee jute firms profitability was much more complex, as commonly the manufacturers also traded and speculated in raw jute, activities which could yield substantial profits if predictions about prices proved accurate. After private trading was restored in 1954, this activity resumed.[45]

In the late twentieth century the relative price of raw jute rose compared with polypropylene, but fell relative to products competing for land, above all rice. This combination had enormous implications for Bangladesh, where raw jute production has been contracting on trend since the 1980s. Production in India over the same period has been more stable.[46]

Dundee and the World

Jute Control was introduced in 1939 because jute was considered a strategic material. The output of the industry contracted during the war as labour and factory space were 'Concentrated' into fewer factories, with fifteen establishments closed and 1.7 million square feet of space given up. Output was directed towards war-related uses, so that, for example, supplies to the carpet industry fell by 90 per cent.[47] Exports also fell very sharply, by between 80 and 90 per cent depending on slightly different calculations.[48] At the same time imports increased, rising to around 60 per cent of British consumption of jute goods by the end of the war.[49]

In the post-war period Dundee was a minor player in the world jute industry. In 1960, measured by looms, she had 7 per cent of the world total, with India having 57 per cent.[50] But presenting the figures in this way is in many ways misleading, because the outputs of jute manufacturing are not homogenous, and a key feature of the jute industry in post-war Dundee was its movement 'up-market' in an attempt to reduce direct competition with Indian imports. Thus we can see Dundee producers following a 'twin-track' policy in relation to import competition: campaigning for the continuation of the protection initially granted by the creation of Jute Control in 1939 (discussed in detail in Chapter 6), while also shifting output into lines where India's competitive advantage would be smaller.

The jute manufacturers did not begin their move into more sophisticated products in the post-1945 period. Unrestricted competition in the 1930s had led to mass unemployment in Dundee, but it did help to reinforce already existing trends to move away from the products where Indian competition was most acute. In fact Dundee producers had been moving away from low grade sacking and bagging for coarse heavy bags, and also making more of the wider hessian cloths, where India specialized in the narrower, standard 36-45 inch widths.[51] As a result, before Jute Control was introduced, the Dundee industry was able to supply, for example, the whole of domestic demand for yarn for the backing of carpets and yarn uses such as twines and cordage, whereas in bags home production accounted for only a third of consumption. Similarly, the home industry supplied almost all the demand for backing for linoleum, which was made from wide (72 inch or more) hessians.[52]

This process of moving up-market was halted and even reversed during the war, as the boom in demand for basic jute goods such as sacking and bagging, meant production was tipped back towards these cruder products. But the Working Party was clear that the future lay in further developing more sophisticated products, which it saw as one of the remits of the new British Jute Trade Research Association (BJTRA).[53]

The continuation of Jute Control after the War protected Dundee against Indian competition, but in a fashion which did not stop the drive towards producing more sophisticated products. Most generally this may be seen as a result of the fact that protection always had an air of being temporary, given the unwillingness of any post-war government to give the kind of pledge suggested by the Working Party that the industry would be sustained in perpetuity (see Chapter 6). More specifically, the structure of protection was such that products in the cruder areas gained less immunity from competition than those higher up, so there was a strong incentive for Dundee producers to reduce import competition by production of the more sophisticated goods.

Unfortunately, simply moving upmarket did not guarantee buoyant demand for Dundee's products. Most importantly, the linoleum-backing use of jute, which had begun before the war, and grew rapidly after 1945, peaked in 1955 and after 1960 fell rapidly to a marginal source of demand by the end of the 1970s. This was due primarily to an overall decline in the popularity of linoleum as a floor covering, exacerbated by the replacement of jute by bituminized paper as backing for the reduced volume of lino sold.[54] However, as Howe remarks, 'the situation was saved' by the rise of jute for carpet backing, which demanded the wide widths of cloth which Dundee produced, and which initially found not only a rapidly expanding demand at home but also an export market before Asian producers moved into this market.[55]

An optimistic review of the state of the industry in 1960 emphasized the lack of overlap between the products of the Dundee and Asian jute industries, suggesting that 'only about ten per cent of Dundee output is directly competitive with India'. The authors of this assessment suggested that this very limited significance of Indian import competition meant that the extensive public discussion in Dundee of protection was 'misplaced', as only perhaps 10 per cent of employment in the city was in the production of common hessians, the one sector which relied on protection for survival.[56]

The data in Table 2.4 enables us to examine this issue in more detail, by looking at the pattern of import penetration in the industry. These figures would support a qualified version of the view that by the 1960s protection was not the crucial issue in the survival of the industry, as when protection began to be eroded from 1957, and especially from 1963, there was no overwhelming inrush of imported products. In yarn there is no clear trend in import penetration, while in cloth import penetration does increase from the mid-1960s, but at a relatively slow rate. The key problem for the industry was the fall in total home consumption. The peak in the absolute volume of imports was in the late 1940s; even in cloth, where import penetration rose, as shown in the table, from 36 per cent in the mid-1960s to 66 per cent in 1976, absolute volumes fell by more than a half over the same period.[57]

The implication is well summarized by McDowall, Draper and McGuinness: 'It is apparent that a major technological shift has taken place, severely reducing the demand for UK jute goods. Cheaper imports have not taken the place of home-produced jute manufactures'.[58]

This is not to suggest that protection didn't much matter to the fate of the industry. Higher prices for jute goods which followed from protection must have speeded up the processes of substitution of paper and polypropylene, thus decreasing the size of the total market for jute in Britain. There were also, of course, knock-on effects on consumers of jute goods who faced higher prices than would have been the case under free trade. Conversely, the imposition of protection enabled the Dundee industry in the two decades after 1945 to restructure and modernize itself around a strategy of finding new, more sophisticated products. This strategy worked, but only as long as polypropylene and other jute-replacing technologies were limited in impact. In particular, the rapid displacement of jute by polypropylene as carpet backing, rising from 10 to 95 per cent of the market between 1967 and 1974, was crucial to the contraction of the home market.[59] The problem for jute was that this contraction was added to by the more or less simultaneous reduction in protection, but it was the former factor that mattered most.

Table 2.4: Import penetration in jute (imports as percentage of home consumption) 1955–76. (Three year moving averages).

	Yarn	Cloth
1955*	2.1	49.4
1963**	2.7	41.8
1964	3.1	37.6
1965	3.4	37.5
1966	2.9	40.7
1967	1.9	47.3
1968	1.5	49.8
1969	1.5	50.5
1970	1.8	51.8
1971	2.4	54.0
1972	2.6	56.3
1973	2.4	57.3
1974	1.3	58.9
1975	1.5	62.5
1976	2.7	66.3

Source: S. Howe, *Dundee Textiles Industry 1960–1977, Decline and Diversification* (Aberdeen: Aberdeen University Press, 1982), pp. 60–1.
*   1955 saw the post-war peak in the industry's output.
**   1963 was the beginning of much faster decline in the industry's output.

Nevertheless, the view that the focus on protection in Dundee was at times disproportionate to its direct economic significance for the industry's prosperity seems correct. However, as always, arguments about protection are never straightforwardly economic, an issue returned to in the concluding chapter.

After 1945 the Dundee jute industry was 'deglobalized'. The industry became more domestic in orientation as the proportion of its output exported shrank, with yarn exports varying between 3 and 6 per cent of total production, cloth between ten and twenty per cent.[60] As we have seen, what mattered to the industry's prosperity in the 1950s and 60s was not primarily what was happening in the global market for jute goods (though trends and cycles in the world raw jute market were of course still hugely important), but what was happening to the markets for jute products in Britain. While much of the decline of the industry prior to 1939 has to be explained in a global context, the relative success of the industry for twenty years after the war, and its crisis from the mid-1960s, is largely to be explained by events within Britain, rather than without.

De-globalization also involved an untangling of many of the threads that had historically tied together the Dundee and Calcutta industries. As outlined in Chapter 1, the establishment of the Indian industry was in significant part the result of Dundonian capital and companies.[61] By 1939 a complex arrangement had grown up whereby British managing agencies like Thomas Duff still had an important role in the industry, but did so by controlling rupee companies that increasingly had majority Indian shareholding.[62] But in the 1930s these agencies had been powerfully challenged by the rise of Marwari-owned jute manufacturing companies, which grew out of a long-established role in jute trading and speculation.[63] Why these new companies were so effective in competing with the expatriate companies is much debated, but Tomlinson emphasizes the linkages they were able to make with local 'up-country' merchants, bankers and credit suppliers, networks foreign-controlled companies found it difficult to penetrate.[64]

This summary of shifts in the ownership and control of Indian jute manufacturing makes it clear that Independence in 1947 was not the sharp divide it might be thought; 'Indianization' was well underway in the last decades of the Raj. Conversely, some residual role for the agencies in the industry was sustained into the 1960s and 1970s.[65] In addition, the development of jute machinery manufacture, a sector traditionally dominated by Scottish products imported into the sub-continent, was almost entirely dominated by Scottish companies in the mid 1950s.[66] Despite these continuing ties, the significance of Indian jute trading and production for Dundee's prosperity was, by the time of Independence, far less than it had been up to the end of the 1920s, and destined to decline markedly further over the next thirty years.

Decline and Declinism

There is no doubt about the long-run applicability of the term decline to Dundee's jute industry in the post-war period. While it should be emphasized that the industry's post-1945 peak in output and employment was in the mid-

1950s, and that rapid decline was not evident until the second half of the 1960s, its trajectory thereafter was clearly one of accelerating decline towards extinction. Complete extinction such as in jute is unusual in an industrial sector, but major decline has been a common fate of many of Britain's industries since the Second World War. This was clearly what happened to all the other old, nineteenth century, staples such as coal, cotton, shipbuilding and iron and steel. But decline has also occurred in many newer industries, across almost the whole range of manufacturing. We know that manufacturing as a share of employment peaked in the 1960s, and we have subsequently seen a process of de-industrialization, such that by the end of the twentieth century under 15 per cent of Britain's working population were employed in sectors deemed industrial.[67]

For much of the period since the 1950s, and accelerating when de-industrialization took hold in the 1970s, these declines have commonly been treated as evidence of a profound pathology, what was often called 'the British disease'. In such accounts the decline of any sector was analysed not as a normal part of the dynamics of competition in a market driven, capitalist economy but as evidence of of fundamental failure. Such diagnoses were usually accompanied by accounts of the alleged causes of decline, and a pointing of the finger at the culprits, who varied according to ideological taste. Over time the rhetoric surrounding such 'declinist' narratives shifted, and different suspects accused of culpability, but the theme, by drawing support across the political spectrum maintained central to much of both popular and 'elite' understanding of the post-war British economy.[68]

By the end of the twentieth century the tide was beginning to turn as these 'declinist' narratives came under increasing criticism.[69] At the most general level, it is important to emphasize that de-industrialization, defined as the share of industrial output and employment in the total economy, has been the common fate of the OECD world since the 1970s. The pace of this in the UK was faster than the OECD average in the 1970s and 1980s, but the end result has been broadly similar; manufacturing employment in 2003 was just below the OECD median of around 15 per cent.[70] It is worth noting that this declining *share* has been accompanied by a *trend* rise in the absolute value of manufacturing output since 1970, albeit this rise has been slower in Britain than most OECD countries.[71]

Of course, these broad patterns conceal as well as reveal. The particularly sharp declines in industrial output in the 1970s, and especially the 1980s, fell very hard on places, such as Dundee, where reliance on such activity was proportionately high and replacement types of employment slow to grow. In Chapter 7 we show how hard de-industrialization hit Dundee in these decades, combining, as it did, a sharp decline of jute with major contractions of other industrial sectors.

Much of the more serious declinist literature concentrates on explaining Britain's poor industrial performance in the 1940s down to the 1970s, in the belief that thereafter performance improved.[72] However, as is now well-established, much declinist literature on these early post-war decades (both contemporary and historical) does not take account of the hugely significant fact that much of the relatively slow growth of the British economy in the 1950s and 1960s reflected the 'catching-up' by other Western European economies of the higher levels of income per head Britain enjoyed at the beginning of the post-war years.[73]

Those who construct a narrative contrasting performance before and after the 1970s usually put a lot of emphasis on competition as a key issue. In these accounts, import restrictions inhibited productivity growth, while industrial concentration and cartels limited innovation.[74] Such limits on competition clearly existed in jute. The Jute Control tightly restricted imports, albeit the level of protection diminished from the early 1960s. By the early 1960s jute was also a relatively concentrated industry, which helped to underpin the price-fixing which is discussed in Chapter 4.[75]

Do these features of the industry support a pathological interpretation of jute's post-war history? As already noted, protection had a number of impacts on the industry, but it does not seem to have inhibited a drive towards innovation and modernization. In Chapter 5 we also suggest that the concentrated and cartelized nature of the industry, while complex in its effects, cannot be seen as leading to a cosy life for the jute companies in the post-1945 years.

There is no one agreed measure of performance that can be applied to an industry like jute. On innovation, Carter and Williams suggested that:

> 'In the jute industry, the greater security given by import controls and by Government purchasing has freed managers from the immediate struggle for existence, and they have been able to give attention to the introduction of new equipment which has been developed in other industries'.[76]

On productivity, the work of Howe suggests that, perversely, if one focuses on the links with competition, labour productivity performance was much better in the 1950s and early 1960s, and deteriorated later, precisely at the time the industry was more exposed to competitive pressures.[77] Such figures may reflect in part the focus on *labour* productivity, at a time when investment was high and technological change was labour-displacing. Also, it is common for labour productivity to be closely linked to the path of output, and it was in the late 1960s that jute's contraction gathered pace.

It is an important indication of the changed context of the post-war industry that productivity comparisons with India rarely figured in discussion. Stretching back into the nineteenth century, Dundee's jute employers had used the strength of Indian competition as an argument for both minimizing wage increases and maximizing productivity enhancement, when negotiating with their workforce.[78] The Working Party *Report* put a lot of emphasis on the need to increase labour productivity, especially because, it argued, this had reduced over the war years.[79] In calculating relative costs in Dundee and Calcutta the Working Party made no explicit calculation of labour productivity, but did assume significantly higher levels in Scotland, without suggesting that there was any prospect that this difference could offset the gulf in wage levels. It was the implausibility of that difference significantly diminishing which led to the strong call for protection.[80] In the period after 1948 the wage gap between Calcutta and Dundee seems to have increased markedly, as producers in Dundee sought a 'high wage, high productivity' strategy to accompany their move up-market.[81]

The story of jute after 1939 is not a tale of pathological failure. Without counter-posing a Panglossian view to such a pathology, we argue that the decline of jute is a story of serious attempts to escape the historical legacy of decline so dramatically evident in the 1930s. These attempts embraced strategies of both political campaigning and economic 'modernization'. In the long run neither of these strategies could avert decline. But in the short and medium term they achieved a measure of success. An understanding of how these strategies were constructed and pursued, and how, for a while, they achieved a measure of success tells us much about the economics and politics of post-war Britain.

3 THE INDUSTRY AND ITS WORKFORCE

The Working Party *Report* published in 1948 became a key reference point in post-war discussions of the jute industry, and the need for its 'modernization'. The establishment of this Working Party was one important sign of a major new *national* emphasis on industrial efficiency which began during the war and was strongly pursued by the Attlee government after 1945.[1] In many respects this shift was a straightforward consequence of wartime Britain moving from a labour surplus economy, suffering mass unemployment, to one in which labour was in short supply, and therefore had to be used more efficiently. While the emphasis on efficiency led to national initiatives on everything from Research and Development to investment to training, at the centre of much of the argument was labour; 'higher labour productivity' became a key aim, and in many analyst's and policy-maker's views this was to be achieved by direct action on labour usage and labour effort.[2]

Working parties were set up by the Labour government for a range of industries with a similar remit, which in the case of jute was to:

> Examine and inquire into various schemes and suggestions put forward for improvements of organization, production and distribution methods and processes in the jute industry, and to report as to the steps which should be taken in the national interest to strengthen the industry and render it more stable and more capable of meeting competition in the home and foreign markets.[3]

The establishment of these bodies was controversial, because many employers saw them as unwarranted interference in the affairs of private industry, interference all the more pernicious because the government insisted upon a significant trade union presence.[4]

In the wake of Labour's election victory of 1945, and widespread perceptions of the need for industrial 'modernization', employers in the affected industries could not wholly reject the Working Party initiative, but the FBI coordinated efforts to minimize the 'threat' posed to employer interests by their activities. Employer resistance was very effective in preventing these working parties evolving into permanent tripartite development councils, as advocated in many of the

Reports (including that on jute). While Labour put great emphasis on these councils, in the end they were established in only four industries, not including jute.[5]

Indicative of employer views in jute was William Walker's (Jute Industries)
comment at a Federation of British Industry meeting that 'The Trade Union
members had been able to make no constructive suggestions. They possessed
limited technical knowledge and were interested only in welfare and wages'.[6]
Despite such views, there is no evidence of much dissent on the conclusions of
the Jute Working Party *Report*.

The *Report* mirrored many of those written on other industries (except on the
protection issue), in advocating grouping and reorganization of the industry in
pursuit of economies of scale, and the exploration of new uses for jute products
and the use of jute machinery for other fibres (see Chapters 4 and 5). Further, it
was argued, the industry should have a major drive for capital re-equipment linked
to raising both recruitment to the industry and output per worker. On labour,
the specific recommendations were 'That the industry should improve working
conditions; review the wages structure; and further harmonious relations between
management and workers'.[7] This chapter looks at each of these aspects of the initial
post-war agenda in turn, before looking at how the much more troubled times for
the industry from the late 1960s impacted on its labour force.

Interwoven with all these issues was that of gender. Women numerically
dominated the jute workforce down to the late 1950s. Women also played a
prominent part in union activities in the industry, dominating the management
committee, although it was only in 1971 that Margaret Fenwick became the
first General Secretary of a British trade union when she took on this job in the
DDUJFW.[8] Her own union career illustrates some of the complexities of gender
in the jute industry in these years. On the one hand, she was clearly discrimi-
nated against, as when in 1950 she was rejected by the management for a role
as shop steward as 'she was the mother of a young family and could not hope
to carry through the duties of a shop steward in a manner that a single person
would'.[9] On the other hand, as shown below, she seems to have acted on occasion
to reinforce gender stereotypes in her approach to labour deployment in jute.

Improving Working Conditions

The first of the Working Party's recommendations reflected the fact that jute
had undergone a particularly radical turnaround in its labour supply position
across the war years. The excess supply of labour which had been extraordinarily
large in the 1930 was reversed from 1942, as the industry was concentrated into
fewer factories whilst many other war-related jobs became available. From 1943
labour supply was falling short even of the concentrated industry's demands, and
despite the use of an Essential Work Order restricting worker's ability to leave the

industry, and other measures, decline continued until July 1944, by which time numbers had fallen to 44 per cent of the 1939 level.[10] Thus, paradoxically for an industry widely regarded as 'in decline', in the early post-war years jute was suffering a major problem of labour recruitment, especially down to the mid-1950s.

This problem was particularly acute in the case of women. Between 1939 and 1947 the numbers of women in the industry fell by over 6,000, the number of men by just under 4,000.[11] Even before the war there had been a long-run trend for the proportion of men to rise (see further below) but still in the 1940s twice as many women as men were employed, and in the early post-war years, and up to the mid-1950s, the industry saw itself as suffering from a major shortage of women workers. This problem was driven by a range of factors, including the attractiveness of alternative employments, especially in the new light manufacturing companies such as Timex and NCR, and supply factors like the rise in marriage and birth rates (in a climate where men's wages were more able to support a family).[12] The jute employers successfully lobbied to slowdown the influx of new companies to try and restrict loss of 'their' workers.

Figure 3.1 Low and Bonar, East Port Works, Dundee. Bag-sewing department, circa 1950. (University of Dundee Archive Services).

A report from a 'special correspondent' in the *Scotsman* suggested that while the jute industry welcomed the first recommendations of the Working Party *Report*, that the trade would be assured protection against Indian competition, there were also 'plenty of people in the business in Dundee who taken the view that an even more pressing need is assurance of protection against industries which are being introduced to the city as a matter of Government policy'.[13] It was felt that such industries were being 'subsidised from the public purse' and 'denuding the jute mills of much wanted labour'. Recruitment to the jute industry which it was estimated required a further 'six or seven thousand workers' was proving 'very difficult' because of 'full-blooded propaganda about "dark satanic mills"'. Thus it was argued that the 'psychological disturbance' of the new industries was 'great'. Tom Cook MP argued that the 'jute industry was vital not only for Dundee, but for the country itself' with it being 'necessary to keep it fully alive and at peak production'.[14] The main concern was that 'once people left and got other jobs they were lost to this vital industry'.

By 1950 the directors of the Dundee Chamber of Commerce were in support of the jute industry and the British Jute Trade Federal Council in its request in a letter to the President of the Board of Trade that 'from the labour point of view, no further new industries should be located in Dundee at present'.[15] It was felt that the 'programme had already passed the danger point'. Mr William Walker of Jute Industries agreed, suggesting that the introduction of new industries to Dundee had prevented 'the rehabilitation of the jute industry after its drastic war-time concentration' and were, in 1950, 'on a scale out of all proportion to the labour available'.[16] Walker also suggested that 'the serious and ever-increasing shortage of labour' in the jute industry hindered the expansion of production for sale in home and dollar markets in spite of attempts at capital investment to improve the productivity of the industry. He hoped that government spon-sored bodies and official would 'take action before the situation deteriorates further'. These statements proved prophetic with a special meeting being held of the Dundee and District Local Employment Committee in April 1950, at which representatives from the Board of Trade in Scotland, the Board of Trade and the Ministry of Labour were all present. The necessity of a 'master plan' for Dundee's future was considered, with considerations including the 'up-grading of labour by training', the provision of additional opportunities for part time work as well as improving transport facilities.[17] At this meeting it was found that although jute was 'no longer the dominant source of employment in the city' with nearly 'one in five' of the working population being occupied in jute it was 'still the main factor' in the city's prosperity. It followed therefore that 'any future assessment of labour requirements in Dundee must be greatly affected by the needs of the jute industry'. Thus the Board of Trade ruled that no further new industrial developments will be allowed to take place in Dundee.[18] Even taking these recommendations into account the government departments concerned felt that there would still be a shortage of labour in Dundee which could 'only be overcome by the importation of additional workers' although it was 'not easy to see where the additional population is likely to come from'.[19] But, alongside this campaign, and as the Working Party recommended, jute employers also sought to make the industry more attractive to potential workers.

Married women continued to be an important source of labour in post-war Dundee. As a result, Dundee Corporation, in an attempt to facilitate the return to work of married women, continued public provision of nurseries, which kept the same hours as the jute works. It also subsidized workplace nurseries. This policy was in contrast to patriarchal attitudes concerning opposition to married women working voiced by local politicians, who argued that Dundee should be concentrating on improving male employment prospects while women should be in the home caring for their children and homes.[20] Accompanying this at a national level, the Ministry of Health would not support the Corporation's nursery building programme in the early 1950s.[21] However, the Corporation continued to lobby for nursery expansion in Dundee to enable married women to return to work, in jute and in the new industries locating in the city.

Several companies also established nurseries. Low & Bonar were the first to do so in 1947 with Jute Industries opening a nursery at its Camperdown Works a year later at a cost of £4,200 and at its Manhattan Works in 1950.[22] Jute Industries gave three reasons for the establishment of nurseries; the recruitment and retention of working mothers, to prevent absenteeism among working mothers, and the fact that public provision was full and had long waiting lists.[23] The provision of the nursery at Camperdown ensured some measure of success for Jute Industries. In August 1948 13 workers had taken advantage of the nursery facilities, six full time workers, two part-time workers and importantly five workers who intended to return to work. It was also expected that ten evening shift workers would change over to full time work.[24] A month later it was reported that the opening of the day nursery had resulted in '835 hours of additional work being obtained at Camperdown Works'[25] Indeed Jute Industries felt that the provision of day nurseries would be 'the main factor likely to help recruitment of women workers, particularly the type of productive workers likely to be in demand and in short supply'.[26]

However the private company nurseries were rarely full to capacity. As early as 1905 Dundee employers helped to fund four crèches in the city, but these were also underused by the women that they were aimed at. Women may have preferred to use the 'child-minding services of neighbours', thereby resisting philanthropic provision characterized by 'regulation and social control'.[27] In the post war years this may also have been true; women did not wish to use the facilities offered by their employers, although they were willing to use local authority nurseries. Yet it may be more likely that women did not want to use nurseries if avoidable, as all nurseries incurred financial expense whereas informal arrangements with neighbours and friends could be less costly. In addition many women may have preferred to exploit opportunities available to work part time. The jute industry did not offer part-time work, which was surprising given the rise in part-time working among women in the post-war years at a national level. In contrast the Lancashire cotton industry, which was also keen to attract more women, offered part-time work and was therefore more flexible in terms of taking into account the 'double burden' of women's work in the home and workplace.

Historically women's work in jute was deemed almost entirely 'unskilled'.[28] Women had little opportunity for vertical mobility, and there was also little option of horizontal mobility for female workers with the boundaries between the weaving factory and spinning mill being clearly drawn. As Margaret Fenwick suggested: 'a weaver widnae, a weaver couldnae go across the mill and work'.[29] This division of labour mapped on to powerful social and cultural distinctions outside work. As a result weavers were 'often accused of regarding themselves as a 'cut above' the spinners' and were described as 'toffs'.[30] Oral history evidence confirms this with one respondent stating that 'the weavers aye said they were better than the spinners .. 'cause they made their ane pey, but we only had a set pey'.[31] Contests over whether spinning or weaving was the more difficult work abounded.[32]

Training was another route to try and improve the attractiveness of working in jute. In 1947 Jute Industries established a training scheme to 'make the Jute Trade as attractive as possible to juveniles', which involved the provision of lectures in rove spinning from specially trained instructors as well as 'Industrial Courses' at the technical college in Dundee.[33] In 1949 Jute Industries held talks with other companies who wished to institute similar training due to the 'increasing demand for Male Sliver Spinners owing to the starting up of new machinery throughout the Trade' and the 'need to attract young workers'.[34] Boys were the target of such training. Like apprenticeships, training was not offered to girls working on the older spinning frames. Again the masculine character of skill was apparent in this decision, the provision of training for boys of school leaving age provided the position of spinner with a qualification thus making it a credible or respectable prospect. Men were not expected to return from war and replace women in the jute industry as was the case in other industries, as jute continued to be seen as predominantly 'women's work' in the post-war years, although Jute Industries provided training for ex-servicemen who wished to train as rove spinners.[35]

The majority of organized training offered to jute workers in the post-war years was aimed at the male occupation of tenter, which was seen as a 'skilled' occupation.[36] Such classes were held at the technical college in Dundee and the Scottish Power Loom Tenters Society was intimately involved in determining the programmes of teaching as well as which workers qualified for admission to these courses. Moreover it was argued that 'in light of the high wages which skilled tenters could earn' it was 'only reasonable to expect that they should be reasonably skilled to achieve such earnings'.[37] Thus apprenticeship schemes of three years were seen as essential for tenters. This training undoubtedly elevated the status of the (male) occupation of tenter within the industry.

Notwithstanding this continued concern with women workers, the industry as part of post-war 'modernization' saw a marked shift towards employing proportionately more men, as noted in Chapter 2. This process had begun in the interwar years, as many jute firms moved to a double shift system. 'Protective' legislation prevented women from working at night, therefore increasing numbers of men were hired to work nightshifts.[38]

In the immediate post-war years Jute Industries employed increasing numbers of men especially to extend night shift working and the double day shift. In 1946 a night shift was introduced at Walton Works with the explicit purpose of 'absorbing male spinners' and 'building up' the labour force for the introduction of a double day shift.[39] The company attempted to organize night shifts at all of its works, yet there was difficulty in fully staffing these shifts with advertisements being placed in the local press for more workers.[40] A double day shift was also introduced in Caldrum Works in February 1947 with it being stated that this would be comprised of '100% men', with female breaker feeders to be replaced by men also.[41] Similarly Low & Bonar established a night shift 'with purely male labour' in 1947 which it argued had been a successful 'practice' in operation up till the outbreak of war.[42]

Alongside shift patterns deemed male, women workers were also discouraged by other methods used to raise productivity in the industry, notably getting workers to work at more machines simultaneously. The major companies made attempts to combat the labour shortage in the industry through capital expenditure on more efficient machinery in order to lower labour requirements. As the retiring president of the AJSM, Mr J. Raymond Scott, argued in 1950 there seemed no prospect of increasing the present labour force but there was 'every reason to hope for greater production with existing labour'.[43] In the post-war years many innovations were made, first in spinning and then in weaving. In spinning automatic followed by high speed sliver spindles were introduced, while in weaving individual electric motors, circular looms for bag making, wide looms and automatic cop loading were all introduced.[44] In both processes plant and equipment were modernized. Jute Industries were one of the first companies to invest in a policy of 'progressive modernization' in spinning which included the installation of sliver spinning machinery with 'considerable progress' being made in 1949 with regard to the development of automatic weaving.[45] Mechanical developments were slower in automatic weaving as the quality and preparation of the yarn had to be of the highest possible standard and this required experimentation. In contrast by September 1950 it was estimated that 73 per cent of the spindles in the jute industry were high speed or sliver which compared favourably with the 1939 figure of 39 per cent.[46] However Howe argues that by the early 1960s the industry had 'certainly passed the peak of its new capital expansion rate'.[47] In addition while Jute Industries, Low & Bonar and other industry leaders modernized in this manner such innovations were not adopted equally across the industry.

Margaret Fenwick also stated that women left the jute industry as the machinery became 'more difficult for the women to handle' and the 'machine charges got greater'.[48] She suggested that as the companies made attempts to increase labour productivity in weaving, the number of looms each woman had to operate increased, and while automation was introduced to make the job easier, 'it never ever really wis successful'. One participant in the in the oral history project on jute, Bella Keizer, reported that she was annoyed by the fact that while the jute trade 'wis heavy physical manual work' which 'took yer bloody guts out' women were employed and 'when they automised the bloody looms they put men in'.[49] In addition as wider looms were introduced to produce the wide cloth required for carpet backing Fenwick argued that the stretching involved for women resulted in 'miscarriages .. cervical cancer, this sort o' thing'. Thus 'women werenae able tae cope, ye know, so more and more men were trained intae the industry'. As she stated 'the heavier the machine wis eh it wisnae a womans job anymore, ye know, ... It wis a mans job'.

Indeed in 1961 these issues were considered by the AJSM as a result of complaints made by Mrs Fenwick to the industrial consultants, AIC Ltd, hired by the AJSM on behalf of the jute industry (see next section on role of AIC). One of those consultants, Mr Perry, stated that in a meeting with DDUJFW officials Fenwick had suggested that five yard loom weaving and above should be 'a male responsibility' as it was 'outwith the capabilities of a woman'.[50] It was also suggested that women should not work on batching or in the movement of full drawing frame cans over long distances. On this occasion Perry had noted the fact that the suggested change over from female to male labour would 'cause a complete upheaval' in 'wide loom development' as male labour was not available. Perry also stated that as the industry was not expanding, a large number of women would be made redundant as a result of this proposed change. He confirmed that Union officials were 'prepared to accept the redundancy of women if men were used for the wide looms' and that the union was not interested in 'male rates for female operatives on five yard looms' or in batching or drawing occupations.

Mr Strachan, the Chairman of the Industrial Sub-committee of the AJSM, stated that they could not accept 'an arbitrary statement' that five yard looms and over were 'too heavy' for female operatives. Instead he maintained that 'each situation required to be considered on its merits'. Mr Perry 'felt that the majority of factors involved' in women operating wide looms could be 'measured and compared' with national levels. Mr Reid, also of AIC Ltd, stated that there was a 'top limit' of physical effort applicable to women and irrespective of the amount of compensating relaxation allowance they could not handle in excess of that limit'. In this sense the points put forward by the Union were considered 'valid' and 'certain occupations' would require individual consideration. Thus Perry suggested that medical advice should be sought on 'the stretching question'. A follow up meeting was held in which the AJSM expressed its 'sympathy with the Union's aims' and 'agreed to co-operate in exploring the subject further'.[51] Discussion centred on the likelihood of obtaining a grant to conduct and investigation and which experts should be consulted.

The AJSM was opposed to changing wide loom weaving to 'a man's job' while the Union demanded this, even at the cost of female redundancy. It was perhaps the case that female workers themselves felt that these jobs were 'outwith their capacity' but it is doubtful that they would have been accepting of redundancy. The DDUJFW refused to even consider accepting male wages for women engaged in wide loom weaving, it simply wanted the position designated as 'male'. Therefore, in this case, the union may have contributed to the declining numbers of women employed in the jute industry.

As the machinery installed became more sophisticated and demanding, and eventually jute companies began to specialize in woven plastics, some jobs in the jute industry were designated as requiring greater skill and men were employed to do these jobs. Such a 'reworking of the gendered division of labour' enabled men to gain higher-status 'skilled' positions.[52] In addition the extension of the double shift system throughout the industry resulted in an expansion of the numbers of men hired to work night shifts deemed unsuitable for women in general, and mothers in particular. The differential in wage rates between male nightshift workers and the female day shift was attributed to the fact that men on average operated more machinery and were therefore seen as more productive. As Fenwick stated in relation to male weavers 'it wis amazing once they did get used tae it they made damn good weavers, they made good weavers, Eh, Eh must say that'.

The jute companies also sought to attract labour by improved 'welfare facilities' such as canteens, lockers, washing facilities, improved toilets and heating as well as the provision of drinking fountains and 'forenoon tea' for workers.[53] Some companies were more ambitious. Jute Industries made its own arrangements to improve its 'labour position'. In 1953 Dundee Corporation announced plans to build an 'extensive new housing development' on the 'northeastern parameter of the city' which Jute Industries stated was 'moving the population further and further away from our present manufacturing premises'.[54] The company's solution was to acquire 21 acres of ground in an area intended for industrial development in the centre of this new housing. This move was justified by the fact that it had been noted that there was 'an increasing tendency for workpeople formerly employed by 'new industries'' to apply for work with Jute Industries. It was later announced in 1955 that even though the company's existing sliver spinning establishments were running two or three shifts per day, it was 'still unable to meet demand'.[55] Consequently it was decided to construct a new spinning mill to be called Douglasfield Works on this land which would be 'strategically sited for labour recruitment'.[56] Yet the company continued to draw attention to the 'shortage of certain types of labour in Dundee' in company reports in the 1960s.[57]

Concern with 'Human Relations' combined with the growth of more complex, multi-divisional company structures led to other changes. Howe suggests that the employers 'changed attitude' was also 'accompanied by a genuine concern for employees' and evidences this by stating that 'an estimated two thirds of establishments in the industry had a personnel officer by the mid 1950s'.[58] Jute Industries appointed its first 'welfare supervisor' to serve all of its works in December 1944 with its personnel department being expanded later in the decade. In his annual statement in 1949 Mr Cox, chairman, suggested that the company had been 'greatly assisted' by its personnel department. This was due to the fact that labour was 'not a commodity' but consisted of 'individuals with feelings, ambitions and ideas'.[59] The problem of the employer was to 'harness these individuals into a team which will give of its best for the benefit of the company, community and nation' with care being taken to ensure that 'friendly and informal contact' is established between employer and workers. In instituting a personnel department Jute Industries' object was to establish a 'sufficient, efficient and contented labour force' as 'the best advertisement for any company is a satisfied and contented worker'. Moreover Cox suggested that the improved working conditions within the company 'compared favourably with any new industry in Dundee' and that the new 'canteens, first-aid rooms, facilities for social clubs' and the day nursery in Camperdown, which was 'of the very highest standard' went to prove that the company 'recognises the value and merit of the human factor in industry'.

Further evidence of employers' changed attitude may also include the formation of a company newspaper for staff. In 1966 Jute Industries launched *JIL News* with the Chairman stating in the introduction that he looked forward most to reading about the 'people of our works and offices' and hearing about their 'hobbies, views and interests'.[60] However as well as articles on staff, their hobbies and involvement in local sporting activities the newspaper was also used by management as a forum to discuss such issues as labour productivity and absenteeism. For example an article in September 1966 entitled '19,000 Tons and You' discussed the importance of the 'carpet business' for 'jute men' as it was 'by far our biggest customer for yarn and cloth'.[61] It stated that 'irregular yarn full of thicks and thins can spoil an expensive woven carpet. Bad jute cloth for tufted carpet backing can deflect the needles of the tufting machine which injects the tufts of pile into the backing'. Therefore although 'we all make mistakes' reader were encouraged to read a further article by Stanley Godsall, 'one of the men at the receiving end of J.I. yarn', in order to 'learn how your work affects him'. This article was obviously an explicit attempt to inculcate a sense of responsibility in the jute workforce and ensure less mistakes and a higher quality of yarn and cloth.

Into the mid 1960s the AJSM continued to discuss the improvement of the conditions of employment in the jute industry. Jute Industries initiated this discussion as it felt that 'further concessions' should be made in the industry in order to attract and keep workers, but this raised problems about movement of workers *within* the industry. The other employer representatives in attendance were not convinced as the trade unions involved in the industry had not requested all of the measures proposed by Jute Industries. One of Jute Industries' main suggestions was to increase premiums for shift working to encourage individuals into the industry. However the general view of the other companies represented was that while this 'might have the desired effect in certain areas' this might attract labour away from other jute establishments operating on day shift only, thus causing a labour shortage in some firms. Such representatives were not convinced that these concessions would attract workers into jute from other industries in the city. It was therefore argued that 'it would be useful to await the outcome of the present Review of Wages Structure' before making any concessions in rates of pay. The Chairman in summarizing the meeting suggested that although 'there seemed to be general sympathy for a scheme to improve general labour conditions', at the same time 'it would not be desirable if additional labour was attracted to some Jute establishments at the expense of others'.[62]

As 'no decision could be reached' at this meeting another was scheduled, with the industrial consultant hired by the AJSM giving his opinion on how to attract labour to the jute industry.[63] Mr Perry did not support Jute Industries suggestion of increased shift premiums, arguing that this would in his opinion 'result in more active competition for labour within the industry itself'. Instead he suggested that to make shift work more attractive other methods could be employed such as three weeks working followed by one week off. Perry felt that unless the concept of shift work was altered 'the proposals did not hold much bargaining power in themselves'. Mr Walker of Jute Industries stated that it was 'essential that the Industry be more competitive for labour' and he felt that 'the unpleasantness of shift work was not being fully recompensed by the present differentials over ordinary day shift earnings'. It is notable that as one of the leading jute companies, Jute Industries were willing to offer workers increased wages to ensure that it had the required number of operatives on its shifts, which was important in ensuring the maximum productivity of the machinery in which it had invested significant amounts of capital. Other companies in the industry may not have been in the same financial position and were clearly concerned that their workers would leave to work for Jute Industries if the latter offered increased wages outside of the industry agreements. Walker therefore re-emphasized the need to raise the level of double day shift premiums in order to 'operate modern machinery during the maximum number of hours possible'. He also stated that 'where instances had arisen where double day shift working had been made more attractive the migration of labour had been reduced'. Walker's attitude would suggest that Jute Industries were unwilling to back down, the company needed more workers on its shifts and was intent on attracting additional labour. The other companies represented at the meeting remained unconvinced by Walker's arguments with the Chairman expressing his concerns relating to competition for labour within the industry and he stated that the proposals discussed being 'unlikely to attract labour from new industries'.

Yet there were some gains to be made by women remaining in the jute industry as male employment increased. As Table 3.1 illustrates, overall, the gap between male and female hourly earnings, as measured by the ratio of male to female wages, declined between 1960 and 1977 from 1.47 to 1.13, although there were substantial fluctuations during this period. As Howe argues women in the industry therefore 'significantly improved their earning position' and this did not 'appear to have been as a result of overtime working'.[64]

Jute Wages Structure

The Working Party's call for a review of the wages structures was taken up by the unions in late 1948.[65] In 1949 this pressure led to the AJSM debating and then somewhat reluctantly agreeing to call in 'Associated Industrial Consultants' (AIC) to do a Work Study as the basis for such a new structure.[66] Work Study can be traced back to F. W. Taylor's 'scientific management', from which developed the idea that work tasks could be allocated a 'scientific' value, providing an objective basis for wage determination. Work Study had found some favour in Britain before the 1940s (especially in the First World War), but became very popular in the drive for industrial modernization and increased labour productivity after 1945.[67] Employers combined wariness about its possible implications for wage levels, with a keenness to 'rationalize' wage systems, but even more to gain the productivity benefits which advocates of Work Study said could be gained from the labour re-deployments that such Study would facilitate. In jute the more positive assessment led the employers to agree to the process in October 1950, making the industry a pioneer in the application of job evaluation.[68]

The first stage involved allocating a points value to all jobs, overseen by a joint employer-union committee. This stage of the process proved largely uncontroversial, with agreement reached by March 1951.[69] Unsurprisingly, allocation monetary values to these jobs proved more contentious.

The jute wages structure was fairly controversial among workers in the jute industry in 1952 as negotiations were often used by the AJSM to rebuff applications for wage increases, this being the case in relation to one of the few wage claims made by the Union of Power Loom Tenters.[70] While Smith of the AJSM industrial committee suggested in September 1956 that the wages structure agreement had assisted greatly in increasing the effective use of manpower, 'a number of firms had not yet adopted the principles of this agreement and consequently there was still scope for improvement'.[71] Under the wages structure all occupations within the industry were evaluated on a merit basis and from this scale a basic pay was derived. An opportunity to earn a bonus was also included which was dependent on 'work loading and effort'.[72] At its company meeting in March 1953 Jute Industries stated that although similar wage structure had been adopted by large companies or branches of industry, the wages structure in jute was 'the first time that this had been worked out on an industry-wide basis'. One of the results of the structure was to standardize wage rates across the industry for each job and position and thus prevent competition between companies for labour and ensure labour productivity throughout the industry. If the agreement was not implemented universally across the industry this may have caused workers to continue to 'shop around' for the best wages.

The DDUJFW were very involved in negotiations concerning the jute wages structure. In 1961 the AJSM again employed AIC to consult with employers and trade unions to 'ascertain their views on the Pink Book'. Mr Perry of AIC stated that the main point raised by the employers was that there appeared to be insufficient weighting given to responsibility in respect of new and wider looms. Mr Lumsden of the AJSM agreed that as a result of the increasing number of automatic and wider machines operatives had greater responsibility for material and equipment and he felt this was 'not recognised nor allowed in the present values'. Thus though the 'operatives might have less work' they had 'greater responsibility'. Mr Halley of the AJSM also spoke against the payment of reduced wages for new machinery because even although they 'were easier to operate' failure to increase wages 'built up barriers against the introduction of further new machines'.[73]

While the DDUJFW had strongly pressed for a formal wages structure agreement and endorsed the accompanying work study, the latter remained controversial among workers in the jute industry.[74] Indeed in March 1956 Mr William Walker, chairman of Jute Industries, argued that there was 'still a tendency for some of our workpeople to resist modern methods of work evaluation and redeployment'.[75] He suggested that 'by doing so they are denying themselves the opportunity of earning a higher standard of living and are also, in the long run, making the jobs of those in this and in other industries less secure'. Unlike the DDUJFW, the AEU never accepted Work Study. In 1957, five years after the implementation of the wages structure agreement, AEU members stressed that Work Study had been introduced into the industry in 'direct opposition to the Union wishes' and his members had 'unanimously agreed to oppose the introduction of such schemes'. The AJSM also held negotiations with the Associated Blacksmiths' Forge and Smithy Workers' Society and the National Union of General and Municipal Workers (NUGMW). Mr Morton of the former opposed the introduction of incentive schemes based on scientific work measurement as members of his Union were 'firmly opposed to this principle'. His members were 'in favour of piece work prices as agreed by shop committees' but 'opposed to similar targets based on work study'. Morton pointed out that in the jute industry 'members of his Union were in the main of a high age group, and consequently these men were not in favour of accepting any scheme which would harass them in their work'. Mr Strachan of the AJSM in response stated that 'there was no question of harassing people' and that incentive schemes were 'merely a means of arriving at accurate standards similar to those which appeared to be acceptable under the piece work system'. The NUGMW was similarly opposed to the introduction of incentive schemes.[76]

Harmonious Relations

The Working Party's call for 'more harmonious relations' in the industry partly reflected the common view amongst most policy makers and opinion formers in the 1940s that the post-war era would be one in which more co-operative industrial relations would be crucial to raising productivity. The contemporary focus on improving 'human relations', was linked to a widespread assumption that institutionalized collective bargaining between unions and employers would be a key part of improving those relations. Of course, such a social democratic view of the world was not embraced by everyone, but it did have significant impact, including in jute.

In the post war years the DDUJFW seems to have regained some ground in the industry, though never came any where near organizing a majority of the workers (we do not have systematic data on membership).[77] Howe suggests expansion was as a result of the 'new approach' taken with regards to employee relations by the 'new, younger group of owners emerging among the larger businesses' in the industry.[78] Such individuals possibly viewed trade unions as a partner in ensuring the industry's efficiency and in helping increase labour productivity. This approach is most evident in the introduction of the new wage structure outlined above. As we have seen, the DDUJFW was highly instrumental in the acceptance by most, though not all, workers of Work Study and the reformed wage structure.

Generally the approach of the DDUJFW supported a 'harmonious' attitude to industrial relations. While in Dundee generally, and the AEU in particular, the Communist Party was an important post-war presence, it never seems to have gained much amongst the jute workers. This is suggested by the recurrent votes on whether the ban on CP members being proscribed from election to the management committee; in these votes the ban was consistently and overwhelmingly supported.[79] More broadly, a reading of the union minutes suggests the activities of its officers were predominantly 'fire-fighting' in relation to disputes, rather than encouraging militancy. This is not to say the union was passive in its attitudes to employers. For example, in 1961 it organized an overtime ban and work to rule to fight for a higher wage increase from the Wage Council, though even in this case there is evidence the other unions wanted a more militant posture.[80] One factor underpinning this 'moderate' stance was perhaps the unity with employers over the issue of protection, with the union strongly supporting the protests of the AJSM at the time of the emerging attempts to reduce this protection in 1963 (see below, Chapter 6, on this issue).[81]

The extension of the double day shift system in the post war years was problematic for the trade unions in the jute industry. The Tenters' Union and the DDUJFW began voicing their concerns in April 1954 with Mr Macbeth of the former stating that 'considerable opposition to the continuance or extension of shift working had been expressed by the union members'.[82] Given the labour shortage in the industry in the 1950s this was obviously a troubling development for the employers. Interestingly the main concern of the Tenters' Union, the members of whom were all men, was the inconveniences of double day shifts for married women, a position shared by the DDUJFW, whose members were mostly female. Macbeth argued that the 'odd hours' of the double day shift 'upset normal domestic arrangements, made transport difficulties greater and caused considerable upset to mothers who had young children to look after'. He therefore suggested that it would be necessary for the employers to 'consider the position of day nurseries', as discussed the larger jute employers had already began providing such facilities.

Thus the concerns of the two unions very much focused on the predicament of working mothers. Macbeth also suggested that the members raised 'strong objection' against the late finish at night. Such shifts, he suggested, caused 'dangers to health from overstrain' as women had to leave their work at 11pm and were also 'required to take up domestic duties after that time'. In addition such an individual 'would not get a reasonable amount of rest as 'she would be required to be up in the morning to see to her family, prepare breakfast, dinner, etc before starting her afternoon shift at 2.30pm'. Macbeth argued that this 'was a community problem' with double day shift working 'disrupting community life'. Moreover he suggested that if shift work continued 'arrangements would required to be made regarding transport, shopping and so on'. He stated that 'there had been considerable agitation against this type of working by women members'.[83] Notably the division of labour in the home was not questioned by either union, women were to continue to take responsibility for most of the domestic duties regardless of the fact that they were working double shifts. The solution was to dispense with the double day shift or make it easier for women to work the double shift and complete their domestic duties. An alternative where fathers may take a share of such duties was not envisaged by either the largely male Tenters' Union, which is not surprising, nor the DDUJFW. The acceptance of women's roles in the home as a restriction on their ability to work shifts by the women members, or at least the trade union representing them, was notable as an acceptance of the status quo in gender relations in post-war Dundee.

The AJSM responded by re-iterating the employers' concerns with ensuring 'higher production be obtained in view of the vast amount of expenditure incurred by the Industry in installing new machinery'.[84] The employers stressed that it was essential that this machinery 'be kept running as long as possible dur-

ing the 120 hours of the five day week', anything less being 'uneconomic'. While
the Chairman 'fully appreciated' the points brought by the Unions he argued
that the industry and 'indeed the country' called for 'maximum production
and highest efficiency in order to maintain survival'. He further elaborated on
the changing conditions of Jute Control as of February which left the industry 'in no doubt that it was required to operate at the highest level conductive
to efficiency in order to obtain the production which was the very life of the
whole industry'. Thus 'if opposition was to be made to current conditions, all
the efforts of the industry to help itself would be brought to nothing'. While
the AJSM and employers firmly denied the union's requests, this did not prevent further delegations from the textiles unions concerning the problems of the
double day shift. Transport difficulties continued to be a prominent issue, with
the unions stating that as operatives were now living on 'the outskirts of the city'
as a result of Dundee Corporation's building of peripheral housing estates and
high rise developments travel to work for the early morning shift was especially
problematic.[85] Although special buses were arranged to bring workers into the
city centre where they could catch trams to work, the trams often left before the
buses arrived. The AJSM agreed that it would hold meetings with the transport
manager to discuss the matter.

Two years later the matter of the double day shift was revisited by the textile unions. On this occasion Mr Duffy of the Tenter's Union stated while the
members continued to be opposed to the double day shift, the management
committee of the union on the other hand 'had realised it was inevitable'.[86] To
this end he proposed that a solution to the problem would be a reduction in
the shift from forty to thirty-seven and a half hours. Duffy stated that the present shift was causing 'considerable frustration, particularly in the relationship
to married women and their children' as children were collected after eleven pm
and then taken home, 'in many cases to outlying parts of the town'. Mr Doyle of
the DDUJFW supported Duffy emphasizing 'the position of married women
and the effect the present hours had on children' even although 'a great deal had
been done in the industry to cater for children'. Again it was interesting that
both unions chose to appeal to the employers in terms of the effects that mothers' work had on their children. Perhaps on this occasion responsibility for child
welfare was partially placed in the hands of employers as it was noted that 'a great
deal had been done in the industry to cater for children' but 'in many instances
difficulties remained'. Mr Duffy suggested that if women finished their double
shift at 10 pm such inconvenience to children would be reduced.

The Chairman responded by expressing his sympathy but also pointed out
that in his opinion 'working two and a half hours less would not help married
women to any appreciable extent'. Mr Duffy was not satisfied, he argued that
the AJSM should consider 'the position of a family over a period of a fortnight
where it was possible for a married women to be working a range of hours starting at 5am and finishing at midnight' and stated that this 'imposed tremendous

difficulties to the women concerned'. Duffy then restated his case for a shorter working week. Again the Chairman did not concede arguing that the 40 hour shift working was 'essential for the well being of the trade'. He also argued that the labour position in the trade was 'reasonably satisfactory' which allowed employees to have 'a wide choice of hours offered by different firms', thus women employed on the double day shift could change their employment to the single shift if they desired 'but many found the shorter hours for the same pay on the double shift more attractive'. The Chairman added that if the Union's demands were conceded then the 'difficulty of family life in the City' would be increased as more married women would be attracted by the better conditions on the double day shift, therefore 'defeating the object of the Union's claim'. The two sides had reached a stalemate. Duffy responded by stating that as automation became more widespread in the industry, double day shift would become more pronounced and therefore it was 'important that the workers have this incentive to accept double day shift'. The matter remained unresolved.[87]

The trade unions in the jute industry therefore represented the views of their members in the adoption of the wages structure, but also in voicing opposition to aspects of the working of the work study measures. In addition the extension of the double day shift was also problematic for unions, especially the DDU-JFW, in terms of the burden placed on women's responsibilities in the home. Yet the unions were not very successful in influencing the AJSM and industry wide policy and ultimately all of these measures were introduced and extended throughout Dundee's jute companies.

Of all the unions represented in the jute industry, the Amalgamated Engineering Union (AEU), small but well-organized (and overwhelmingly male), was the most vocal in bringing wage claims before the AJSM, largely as a result of national engineering wage agreements. In February 1952 for example the AEU requested at a recent engineering wages award be applied in the jute industry at the full rate of 11/- as opposed to the 5/- offered by the employers, a month later the AEU accepted the employers offer with the concession that the national award be extended to apprentice mechanics.[88] Yet in January 1953 there was a strike of mechanics throughout the jute industry with workers claiming that they had been 'done out of 6/d per week'.[89] A month later Mr Brown stated that the district committee of the AEU had recommended that its members return to work. Although he did argue that while many of his members received a wage of approximately £7.10/- 'these men would have been better off had they been tied to engineering awards'.[90] While he referred to the 'friendly atmosphere during the negotiations' with the AJSM he suggested that in the Caledon ship yard mechanics were earning £8 per 44 hour week and the new industries in Dundee paid even higher wages with more overtime opportunities than were available in jute.[91]

In April 1955 the AEU made a similar request for an increase of 15/- for all grades of workers as 'it cost the same for the necessities of life to all of them' with the claim being based on 'the prosperity and efficiency of the Jute Industry' as production 'gone up' with increased profits.[92] The AEU 'expected an increased standard for their members'. The response of the Chairman of the AJSM negotiations subcommittee argued that the industry was not prosperous as 'jute prices had fallen rapidly and employers had very thin order books'. Such negotiations continued throughout the remainder 1950s and 1960s with similar arguments being made on both sides. By April 1957 mechanics in the jute industry were earning £9.15.7d for a forty-five hour week, Mr Petrie of the AEU argued that this 'compared unfavourably with rates being paid to similar classes of workpeople employed in other industries in Dundee'. He stated that maintenance men in Caledon Ship Yard received £10.5.8d for a 44 hour week and that Timex and National Cash Register were paying £11.14.8 and £11.16 respectively for a 44 hour week. This he felt justified an increase for his members in jute of £2 per week. This pattern of negotiations and disputes led Mr Strachan of the AJSM to state at a meeting of the Industrial Relations Department, Ministry of Labour in Glasgow, to argue that while most of its negotiations with trade unions associated with the jute industry were conducted 'on a basis of trust and understanding', there was 'a lack of such a spirit in dealings with the AEU'.[93]

The AEU seems to have been the only union in jute to use the 'male breadwinner' argument in its negotiations. In October 1958 the AEU brought a wage claim justified by increases in the cost-of-living, including higher rents, rates and national insurance contributions, but also argued that Union members 'presently received no more than allowed them to maintain themselves under current costs' and 'any luxuries which might be obtainable were mainly due to the wives of his members also working to provide such additions'.[94] Similar arguments were deployed in 1961, when the AEU argued that 'the skilled man in jute was badly enough off with £11.3/- but the unskilled operative with his wife and family required overtime to live and where there was no overtime his wife had to find a job'.[95]

While the AEU focused on increasing the wages of its members the other trade unions represented in the jute industry concentrated on improving the working conditions of the jute factories and mills. Yet one issue that was a priority of all of the trade unions was the demand for a 40 hour week, with negotiations with the AJSM beginning in August of 1959.[96] Mr Macbeth of the Scottish Union of Powerloom Tenters spoke first for the unions, arguing that the I.L.O. Geneva had made a recommendation for a five day, forty hour week in 1938, which had been adopted by the 'unions of this country'. Further Macbeth suggested that the trade unions had 'co-operated in the full to get the best out of' the new machinery and processing techniques introduced as a result of the Jute Working Party *Report*. However he argued that there were 'other problems which had not received the same consideration'. While the employers had focused on increasing 'the tempo', greater operator work loads, intensified concentration and higher output, this had resulted in 'increased labour fatigue'. Macbeth stated that a reduction in the working week would 'considerably decrease that fatigue'. He supported his claim with statistics relating to labour productivity noting that before the Second World War 7.48 tons of jute were produced per operative with the rate being 8.35 in 1957. Lord Dundee, a senior figure in the AJSM, had also stated that the jute worker had 'increased his production by 45 per cent and the *People's Journal* had reported a 37 per cent increase in productivity in the industry with a 54 per cent increase in spinning departments. Thus the machines produced more but in Macbeth's view was that the operator also required to work harder and quicker. He also suggested that although the reduction of the working week from forty-eight hours to forty-five hours had resulted in a drop in production the unions 'would not agree there would be a parallel today'.[97] Instead Macbeth argued that a 'shorter working day would result in an alleviation of industrial fatigue' and thus production would not fall. Moreover he suggested that 'there was no question as to whether the industry could afford the alteration or not' as 'it had to'. This was because the numbers employed in the industry was declining due to 'the increased tempo required from modern production methods' with the labour turnover in the jute industry being 'the highest in all textiles in the country'.[98]

Mr Brown of the AEU spoke second, arguing that production 'should not be taken as the only yardstick' as the introduction of new machinery and processing techniques undoubtedly increased output per man.[99] He suggested that as technical developments continued, in spite of the contraction of the industry, output per person was increasing and this was the 'real basis on which to advance their claim'. In addition he suggested that as the 'increased tempo was too high' there was more absenteeism, a shorter working week would solve this problem. Mrs Geddes of the DDUJFW also suggested that the shorter working week would benefit the women in the industry as 'they had to bring up a family' and 'the strain today was too great'. Again the acceptance that it was a woman's responsibility to raise the family was notable. Although Geddes did qualify this statement stating that a reduction in the hours of work would give women 'some time for their family' but also time for 'social life and recreation'. As she stated the jute industry depended on middle-aged women 'who today had to take time off which they could ill afford because of the strain'.

The DDUJFW were also particularly concerned with its place within the jute industry and its ability to fully represent its members. In the late 1950s it began demanding 'a clearer and better understanding between management and the workpeople' which it felt would be aided by the re-establishment of the works' committees which had operated in the jute industry during the Second World War.[100] Admittedly the union felt that these committees had 'never functioned satisfactorily' due to the lack of union members who served on them, accompanied by the fact that a 'great deal of time' was spend discussing absenteeism and ways and means of reducing it. Thus the DDUJFW envisaged a system based on work's committees but which would involve the election of 'work's delegates' to represent the interests of the workers on the shop floor. Mr Doyle of the union suggested that while a 'friendly relationship' existed at the 'top level' this was 'non-existent' at floor level due to the 'lack of recognition of delegates'. Moreover he argued that a good relationship had only existed due to the conditions of full employment and 'poorer worker management relationships' might be anticipated in 'these leaner times'. Doyle stated that at a shop floor level there were people 'more capable than himself' in negotiating the minor everyday problems of the workers', however at the moment workers 'did not know with whom to negotiate at shop floor level'. This was because there was a confusing array of 'managers, foremen, personnel officers, work-study men, industrial consultants, white coats, grey coats, and brown coats'. Thus managers were 'only a cog in the management function and had to confer with some specialist or other before giving a decision'.

Accompanying the demand for work's delegates the DDUJFW also argued that 'to avoid real trouble' employers should encourage all of their workers to join the trade union. Mr Doyle acknowledged that 'employers might have good reasons for opposing this suggestion' especially in view of 'what had appeared in the press in respect of shop stewards and others or fellow travellers of the Communist Party' who were 'trying to tell management how to run their business'. However he assured the AJSM that 'such would not be the case in respect of the jute industry'. Indeed the DDUJFW had drawn up conditions which ensured that the union would only recognize individuals who were members of the union and would remove any delegate who 'caused trouble or stoppages not recognized by the union'. In addition 'communists or fellow travellers' would not, under any circumstance, be elected as delegates as they were not recognized or accepted by the union. Finally the management would be consulted to ensure that the delegate appointed was 'acceptable'. Mrs Fenwick also added that the main consideration in appointing a delegate was that the workers 'should have full confidence in their representative'.

In response the Chairman of the Negotiations Sub-committee of the AJSM, Mr Strachan on this occasion, stated that he could not agree that 'the specialist was usurping the authority of the manager'.[101] He also felt that 'it had never been the function' for employers to encourage or discourage Union membership. Strachan also argued that 'history had shown' in regard to delegates or local representatives that the main problem was 'the apathetic attitude of members on appointment'. Mr Urquhart stated that in his establishment delegates on work's committees did not have to be union members and emphasized that 'no politics' were allowed at these meetings. In addition Mr Cunningham made the point that 'they would never tolerate delegates usurping the authority of the foreman'.

The representatives of the DDUJFW then outlined the benefits for management of works' delegates in order to persuade the AJSM of the merits of their envisaged scheme. Mrs Geddes of the union stated that as a shop steward before the war she had 'averted many stoppages'. She suggested that the worker on the shop floor 'would not always accept something from management but would accept it from the shop steward or delegate'. One company she worked for introduced a 'Wages Structure scheme' which the workers refused to accept. She approached management and asked them to permit a stop during working hours in order to call the workpeople together, she then explained the scheme to the workers who in turn accepted it. Geddes suggested that from that date 'they had a closer relationship between management and workers in that establishment'. Mr Doyle also suggested that the appointment of works' delegates would prevent 'the common practice of people coming out in sympathy with someone who had been dismissed' as management would make the delegate aware of the reasons for the individual's dismissal which the union would then 'transmit' to the workers. He also suggested that as a result of unemployment in the industry 'tempers were on occasion frayed' and delegates would be in a 'better position to obtain the facts from both sides and could clear up any misunderstanding far more quickly than if the Union Secretary was called in'.

In order to gauge industry views on union representation at a shop floor level the AJSM circulated a questionnaire round its members. The response was not favourable. The questionnaire found that members were 'satisfied with present methods of communication'.[102] As a result the AJSM 'found it difficult to make specific recommendations'. It was also established that 'about one third' of establishments already had works' committees with one member establishment stating that 'much time was wasted at meetings of these committees with little constructive benefit'. Furthermore 'approximately two-thirds' of these establishments 'permitted negotiations on domestic problems between works management and individuals through a union or employee-approved representative'. It was felt that there was 'no evidence' that any of the methods employed in such establishments 'did not work satisfactorily'. Some establishments also indicated that they 'assisted the Union in their activities' by providing permission to collect dues during working hours and making premises within the works available to union officials to conduct union business.[103] The respondents also felt that it was 'unwise' to deliberately encourage union membership. The AJSM argued that 'from information available and experience gained', in the long run, such encouragement 'might perhaps lead to 100 percent membership' which may in turn give opportunity of a closed shop. This it was suggested 'could well be used to the disadvantage of the Employers' and was therefore 'strongly opposed' by all respondents. Thus 'no assistance' was to be given to unions in terms of recruiting members from among the jute workforce. In conclusion it was found that thirty-one members declared themselves opposed to the appointment of official union delegates at a shop floor level. However the AJSM decided that 'certain recommendations' could be made to member firms 'for declining to fall in with the Union's official suggestion'. This involved 'inviting' members to 'set up clearly defined channels of communication' for considering workers' grievances with this being 'made known to the workers' though publication on notice boards or inclusion in booklets relating to working conditions. Thus an attempt was made to address the DDUJFW's concerns.

The AJSM presented its findings to the DDUJFW in June 1959 with the chairman stating that the 'Association was unanimous in not desiring to disturb the excellent relations which pertained in the Trade' and were therefore 'practically unanimous in opinion that shop floor delegates could do no more harm than good'. This included 'the nomination of fiery heads who might be bent on trouble, quite irresponsible as to the interest of the trade and undo much of the good will which both sides had built up over the past decade or two'.[104] Unsurprisingly Mr Doyle was 'not at all satisfied'. He reiterated his points relating to union delegates and their 'mutual benefit' to both employers and employees. Doyle also maintained that a number of work study schemes would not have been introduced without assistance from the union and again stated that only persons approved by the union and acceptable to the employer would be elected as a works' delegate. The Chairman simply stated that with regard to delegates while 'some of them might be good' the effect of shop stewards on industry nationally 'was generally known'. Mr Doyle and Mrs Fenwick contested this statement, with Doyle suggesting that although the union 'might include hot heads' they 'would not be permitted to take office'. Fenwick added that she herself had been 'victimized' on two occasions for 'going through the proper channels' and therefore did not think that the current system employed in the industry worked. Mr Doyle therefore concluded by stating that it was the union who wished to 'further happy relations' as the industry was experiencing 'small strikes through introduction of new ideas, the fear of unemployment and redundancy'. He argued that while the union 'endeavoured to prevent stoppages' it could not 'be blamed' under the present arrangements, adding that he did not feel that the present suggestion would solve the problem. It was debatable as to whether this was a thinly veiled threat or rather a prediction of trouble to come.

Following the AJSM's reluctance to appoint works' delegates strike action in jute establishments appears to have intensified. In August 1962 the workers of Hillbank Works threatened to strike. At discussions held between the Negotiations Subcommittee and the union Doyle stated that the DDUJFW's[105] Management Committee had 'never been satisfied' with the Association's decision in 1959 but 'now his members were pressing the matter'.[106] The DDUJFW had 100 per cent union membership in eleven firms in the jute industry, but while the union was recognized at Association level this was not the case on the shop floor. The members were pressing for such recognition as well as works' delegates and the right of the trade union to collect Union contributions during working hours. In addition the DDUJFW's members in Hillbank works were refusing to work with non-trade unionists. Consequently Mrs Fenwick clearly outlined that while the union had been 'very patient' the members were now demanding a closed shop in the jute industry. Workers in Hillbank and Caldrum works, owned by Scott and Jute Industries respectively, were threatening strike action but Fenwick expected such demands to 'spread further' as the union had 'contacts in every works in Dundee'. She confirmed that their works' delegates would have no authority to decide on stoppages of work and also stated that the union would expect a new employee to joint the union within 14 days, with it being expected that management would discharge workers who did not join as 'otherwise the other ninety-nine per cent of the workforce would strike'.

It was clear that the matter of the appointment of shop floor representatives had escalated into demands for a closed shop from the union and its members, this being supported by threats of strike action. The AJSM's response was to firmly oppose membership of the trade union being a condition of employment as it 'believed in the freedom of the individual'.[107] Mr Strachan, in his role as chairman of the Negotiations Subcommittee, stressed that it was 'most essential at the present time and in the difficult years to come that the two parties should work together'. Thus by way of concession, and to avoid strike action, the AJSM now accepted 'the principle of recognition of works delegates'. Strachan also stated that the AJSM had no objection to 100 per cent union membership but maintained that 'such could not under any circumstance be achieved through assistance from or pressure upon employers'. Mr Doyle stated that while the principle of communications 'might be satisfactory as between the Association and the union', the workers 'had to be convinced' as 'the communications channels did not operate lower down'. He also reiterated that works' representatives would be 'a responsible type of worker' rather than a 'trouble maker or ringleader'. As such 'no member of the communist party or any proscribed organization would be eligible for office of any description'.

Strachan and the AJSM seemed more concerned with the public image of the industry. He argued that it was 'essential to have a period of peace in the industry'. He also 'hoped the union would do everything possible to keep jute out of the headlines, as considerable harm could be done from which perhaps recovery would be difficult'. Mrs Fenwick stated that the Union also 'did not want stoppages' but rather acknowledged that 'it was essential to work together with the forthcoming Common Market and other difficulties ahead'. She added that they 'fully realised their responsibilities' and as such would recommend to the Hillbank members that they continue working, although she foresaw difficulties as their members were categorically refusing to work alongside non-union workers. The dispute rumbled on as it emerged that the cause was five men who worked the night shift 'steadfastly' refusing to join the trade union, while the remainder of the unionized workforce demanded 100 per cent membership.[108] The negotiations continued in the same vein, with the AJSM stating its belief in the 'freedom of the individual to choose' whether or not he wanted to join a trade union and the representatives of the DUJFW stating that their members 'had thrown down the gauntlet' and would not accept anything less than 100 per cent membership. As a result there was an 'impasse' with '500 workers idle' as a solution could not be found or agreed upon. The Association and Messrs Scott

& Son claimed that they 'were powerless' and urged the union 'to do something and use the responsibility vested in them to get production going again'. Doyle blamed the five men holding out against membership of the union although stated that it was not their wish for the men to be discharged although they 'had no sense of loyalty even to the firm' and were 'not desirable'. Mrs Fenwick simply stated that 'this situation might never have arisen had works representatives been in operation earlier'. Moreover she confirmed that the Union would 'have to' support workers' demands for a closed shop in other establishments even if this resulted in strike action. Strachan, the chairman, concluded the meeting by reiterating the AJSM's concerns relating to the 'customer impression and public opinion' with 'this war of attrition' being 'bad for the trade'. The outcome of the dispute is unclear, however it is highly unlikely that the AJSM accepted the principle of the closed shop and more likely that the workers returned as improved conditions for works delegates and shop floor representation were negotiated and secured. However this dispute does illustrate the power that strike action held in the jute industry as the concern with the public image of the industry coupled with losses in production meant that the industry was keen to settle such disputes quickly with concessions being made in this case.

In the sense of avoidance of major conflict, the Working party's aim of 'harmonious relations' in the industry could be said to have been achieved in the post-war industry. In its survey of the jute industry's history in 1981, the *Evening Telegraph* recalled that when the UJFKTO celebrated its centenary in 1956 its then leader, John Duffy, 'proudly recalled one had to go back to 1923 for the last major stoppage in the industry'.[109] There were no sector wide strikes in jute after 1945, though in 1961 there was a widespread but very short-lived cessation of work to enable workers to lobby the Jute Wages Council meeting which was considering the union's 15 per cent wage claim. 8,000 were said to have attended the resulting demonstration, and an overtime ban and go-slow prolonged the issue until February the following year. But perhaps more accurately symbolic of industrial relations in the industry was the tributes paid by the employers to the last major Jute union leader, Margaret Fenwick. When she retired in 1978 the AJSM was happy to say that 'she has kept the interests of the jute industry very much to her heart and it is to a great extent thanks to her that industrial relations have on the whole been so good throughout the trade'.[110]

Coping with Decline

For almost twenty years after the 1948 Working Party Report the 'labour' agenda it had laid down was pursued. In the face of labour shortage, and especially competition from the new multinational corporations, wages went up. Conditions of work also improved in many respects, though shift-working greatly increased, and for many the intensity of work rose. The wages structure was radically revised in the early 1950s, and this underpinned generally more 'harmonious relations' with the most important union, the DDUJFW. Combined with the other aspects of modernization, and within the protection given by jute control, these changes could be seen as in many ways successful up to the 1960s. But from the middle of that decade the interwoven conditions of that success started to unravel.

The wage structure agreement in jute was hugely important as part of the 'modernization' of the industry. But it was only partial in its coverage and also bound to come under scrutiny as the industry evolved.[111] The limited coverage of the agreement partly reflected the refusal of the AEU to have anything to do with the notion of Work Study. While the proportion of the workforce who were members of this union was small, it was as we have seen well-organized and relatively powerful in its negotiations with jute employers. The agreement also excluded many of the least skilled and lowest paid in the industry, whose wages, down to the late 1960s, continued to be regulated by the Wages Council.

The existence of this Wages Council was a legacy of immediate post-1918 circumstances, when the industry was seen as lacking a well-established collective bargaining system, this absence being the key reason why legislation affecting wages was deemed necessary. In the interwar period the unions had seen the Council as some kind of defence against wage cutting, though wages had been cut down to the early 1930s. In the changed labour supply conditions after 1945 the unions gradually came to the view that the workers in jute should rely on their own collective bargaining strength rather than on the state in the form of the Wages Council.[112] Paradoxically, perhaps, the Wage Council minimum wage increasingly exceeded the base rates laid down in the Wage Structure, but the addition of substantial bonuses to the latter raised actual pay above Council minima.[113] One of the problems for the union in developing a strategy for the industry was that the wage structure agreement was made with the AJSM, but the actual implementation of the agreement was reliant on individual company's decisions. This was one reason why the agreement's coverage was partial; some companies chose not to be involved. By the early 1960s the union view was that they should press for a review of the wages agreement, with the idea of pressing for all jute companies to embrace the revised provisions.

By this time the AJSM too was looking for revisions, and linking this to the desirability of making its coverage more comprehensive. One reason for revision was a desire to move to Measured Day Work, a popular form of wage payment in much of British industry in the 1960s, which largely replaced individual bonus systems. The Association was keen to make the agreement more comprehensive, because it believed the limited coverage provided a mechanism for the unions to play off one employer against another in the pursuit of higher wages.[114] But while unsurprisingly keen to keep their wage bills in check, members of the AJSM in the early 1960s also thought some 'rationalization' of the structure might encourage redeployment in the context of continuing introduction of new machines, and also stabilize some wages whose current instability deterred recruitment in what was still a tight labour market.[115]

Negotiations about a revision began in early 1965, again employing the consultants AIC. These discussions ranged far and wide, covering issues from industrial diseases, to the capabilities of women, and with the aim of reducing the striking complexity of the 1952 Agreement.[116] But the main issue pressed by employers was what was initially called 'secondary redeployment', which meant situations where improvements in machinery generated higher labour productivity, but where by the conventional standards of work study none of this improvement involved greater labour effort to justify higher pay. The employers were willing to offer a payment to such workers to discourage the view that all the benefits of 'modernization' accrued to employers, and this payment eventually took the form of a 'Production Improvement Allowance'.[117]

While discussions about amending the Agreement were going on, the AJSM and unions agreed to press for the abolition of the Wages Council once alternative bargaining machinery was established, with the employers also asking for a single union body to negotiate with.[118] The unions had withdrawn from the Council in 1965, and eventually a joint application for abolition was made in 1969, after two Joint Industrial Councils for the industry had been established, one for Dundee and one for surrounding areas.[119] A detailed study of the consequences of this abolition suggested that it was effectively replaced by the new Joint Councils, so that wages in the sector in the ten years after 1969 were higher than those in Wage Council industries, though continued to be below other textile industries.[120]

In August 1966, marking agreement with the unions on a new structure, the AJSM offered a 5 per cent wage increase, alongside a reduction in hours of work.[121] But even as this deal was being finalized (it was delayed by the Labour Government's incomes policy) evidence of the impending sharp deterioration in the environment in which the industry operated was becoming clear. At the key meeting of August 1966 the Chairman of the committee negotiating the agreement noted that 'great care would be required in the handling of the present situation, particularly as talks on the protection review were likely to commence soon although the level of protection would not alter until September 1967'.[122] As noted in Chapter 2, this review would in short order lead to the abolition of Jute Control and the significant reduction in protection. Even more ominously, at roughly the same time the issue of polypropylene was beginning to be recognized as a major new issue. By 1967 the Association was seeking to contain any impact on the wages structure from the growth of polypropylene by arguing that the working of the new material could be assimilated to the job structures of jute.[123] But this position quickly came under pressure, initially it would seem because firms introducing new polypropylene looms wanted them to be maintained by mechanics, rather than the tenters who had traditionally done this job in jute.[124]

On the employers side, the AJSM had been acutely conscious from the late 1960s that polypropylene was becoming increasingly important to its members. Through the 1970s it sought to embrace manufacturers using this new material within the Association, but while existing members who moved wholly or partly from jute to polypropylene stayed in the body, new polypropylene manufacturers did not join. In 1971 they formed their own grouping, the British Polyoeflin Textiles Association.[125]

It became increasingly difficult in the 1970s to speak of a 'jute industry', and the diversification of the industry obviously had major consequences for the workforce. Most obviously, labour intensity in the working of the new materials was very much lower than in jute, so diversification meant job losses. Despite this, the unions always seem to have taken a supportive approach to these changes, and at the same time to have developed no structure for formally negotiating redundancies.[126]

Diversification also meant the applicability of the Wages Agreement declined. One result of this was to add to the problems of the unions. Obviously as employment in the industry fell their membership followed, but in addition the centralized bargaining with the old jute companies which had been at the core of their activities also fragmented. The unions had never been strong at company and plant level, so the decline of centralized bargaining was a heavy blow.[127] The Jute and Flax Workers merged with the Dyers and Bleachers in 1979, but by then the unions were too weak to mount much resistance to decline and fragmentation.[128]

The consequences of industrial decline for wage levels were complex. Initially data on the jute industry included polypropylene, so the higher wages in the latter suggested that despite the decline in numbers employed, earnings did quite well. This reflected that fact that polypropylene production tended to be higher skilled and with more intensive shift systems, and so yielded higher earnings than jute processing.[129] But this, of course, was a statistical artefact as those still engaged in jute processing saw their relative wages being eroded.[130]

The accelerating decline of jute in the 1970s, and the general weakening of labour demand in Dundee did not necessarily solve the 'labour problems' perceived by employers. The unattractiveness of work in jute is shown by continuing vacancies in the industry even as unemployment edged up.[131] Turnover remained high, especially in spinning mills, with in 1977 the AJSM reporting that while recruitment had become easier there was still a retention issue. Around the same time employers were continuing to complain about the perennial issue of absenteeism, with 'Saint Monday' still said to be widely celebrated amongst jute workers.[132]

For women workers in the industry, the decline of jute was complex in its effects. Most importantly, the total number of jobs fell faster than those for men, and after 1962 women's numbers fell continuously. But the relative position of those women who remained improved, as Table 3.1 shows.

Table 4.1: Male and Female Hourly Earnings 1960–77.

Ratio – Jute Industry – Men/Women	
1960	1.47
1961	1.44
1962	1.40
1963	1.45
1964	1.41
1965	1.43
1966	1.44
1967	1.48
1968	1.45
1969	1.45
1970	1.61
1971	1.37
1972	1.40
1973	1.33
1974	1.26
1975	1.23
1976	1.12
1977	1.13

Source: Howe, *Dundee Textiles*, p. 128.

One external factor which played some part in the position of women was the legislation on equal pay at the end of the 1960s. The implementation of this policy was debated in the joint negotiating machinery established in the late 1960s, with the union pressing for rapid implementation. This was resisted by the employers, an AJSM leader noting in 1970 that 'the industry was specially vulnerable in that its wages structure facilitated the application of equal pay and that a high degree of militancy had been expressed in connection with the claim'.[133] By 1975 full equality was recognized by the ending of separate pay for women in the Wages Structure.[134]

Overall, the relative position of women in jute seems to have been inversely related to their significance to the industry. As they increasingly became a minority from the 1960s, their earnings both relative to men in the industry and to other manual occupations improved, so as the industry's decline accelerated it meant a significant loss of well-paid jobs for Dundee's women.[135]

A report on labour in the industry in the late 1970s concluded ominously:

'the run-down of the traditional sector of the industry was recognized by the unions as unavoidable, and their policy has been to actively encourage the restructuring of the industry, through mechanization and diversification, to ensure the long-term survival of an industrial textile industry in the region. This policy of co-operation in the restructuring process has by no means always been rewarded by the creation of new employment opportunities in Dundee: many of the jute firms have diversified not only into other industrial textiles but also into new industries and activities, but in these cases the firms have almost always developed these interests outside Dundee...'[136]

Epilogue

In the years immediately after 1979 these processes of restructuring accelerated, but the economic context in which they operated sharply deteriorated. Under the policies of the Thatcher government elected in 1979 the exchange rate rose with unprecedented speed to a level which undermined the competitiveness of large parts of British industry. For jute the specific damage was especially through the cheapening of imported carpets, undermining the demand for what had become a key use of jute as a backing for the domestically-produced product.[137] (This also hit hard at the market for polypropylene, as this was also used extensively in carpets). Also in the early 1980s the restrictions on imports of jute goods from South Asia imposed in 1980 came to an end, so there were no protected niches for the Dundee industry any more.

1979–80 saw the biggest ever proportionate fall in numbers employed in Dundee jute, which went from 8,100 to 5,600. 1981 saw the fall continue, with the highly symbolic closure of Camperdown Works at Lochee, once the largest jute works in the world. While at its end the Works only employed 340 workers, it had received £2million of investment in the late 1970s in an attempt to build of production in jute wall-coverings, but it could not cope with the slump of the early 1980s.[138] Another historic event for the industry in 1981 was the near demise of the AJSM, which lost its role as the employers negotiating body for what was left of the industry. Wages and conditions were now dealt with by a newly-created East of Scotland Textile Employers Industrial Association, the AJSM living on in a much reduced form largely as a lobbying organization. The Association's shrinking membership had led it to search for a new structure since the early 1970s, but its attempts to embrace the new polypropylene producers had failed, and by 1981 it was reduced to two spinner members, one manufacturer and six joint producers.[139]

Employment in the industry fell to 2,000 by 1986, and 1,200 in 1987; thereafter the pace of decline slackened as the economy generally expanded, but the trajectory was clear. There were occasional concerted but unsuccessful efforts to pressure governments to protect the industry, unions and employers combining with local government to petition authorities in London and Edinburgh.[140] There were also occasional small-scale reversals of this downward trend, such as the expansion of Victoria Spinners which quadrupled its workforce, albeit from only thirty-five to 127, in the early 1980s. But they too in the longer run contracted especially because of falling carpet sales.[141]

The Decline of Jute

In 1994 Sidlaw Industries (successor to Jute Industries) sold off its last jute interests, effectively ending jute weaving in the city. The last jute was spun in 1999, the last company, Tay Spinners, closing with the loss of eighty jobs in the spring of that year. The equipment from this factory was then dismantled and shipped to Calcutta.[142]

4 DEFENDING THE DOMESTIC INDUSTRY

The historiography of the jute industry discussed in Chapter 1 identified the era marking the end of the nineteenth century through to the First World War as the high point for the industry. This historiography faces a paradox; as an industry of the first industrial revolution, one in which technological change was limited or transferable between competitors, and an industry that saw rapid international competition leading to mass unemployment in the 1930s, it is quite remarkable that jute in Dundee not only continued but thrived into the post-war years. The explanation for the longevity of the jute industry requires a detailed explanation. A significant part of that explanation, as this chapter seeks to demonstrate, lies with the ability of the industry to successfully regulate market conditions. The invisible hand of market forces was partly displaced by the visible hand of firm level co-ordination and government regulation of competition and prices. In Chapter 3 we highlighted the degree to which the industry collectively managed labour supply, labour costs and the labour process. As this chapter now examines, management of the industry on a collective basis extended further than simply the question of labour and extended into all aspects of its commercial relationships. That collective approach included co-operation and regulation both vertically between firms within the supply chain and horizontally between competitors within each sector of the industry. Industry regulation thus played a significant role in a range of areas that are essential to understanding the longevity of the industry after 1945.

This chapter examines the nature of this coordination and highlights the ways the firms within the industry proved capable of regulating new entrants, entry of new products into existing markets and the extent of price competition within existing product markets. At the heart of this process of regulation was a series of what became known as 'Gentleman's Agreements', whose interdependence provided a complex set of relationships between ostensibly competing firms and whose maintenance brought the jute industry into a direct relationship with the government through the Board of Trade.

Aoki *et al*'s interpretation of transaction cost analysis places an emphasis upon the firm as a co-ordinating mechanism between markets and hierarchies.

In this approach many transactions maintain features of both market and firm level co-ordination.[1] The firm as a 'nexus of contracts' then becomes a looser co-ordinating structure permitting an extension of control beyond the boundaries of the firm. In many ways this is a useful interpretation of the pattern of development for the jute industry in the decades after 1945.

Prior to the Second World War a process of concentration had occurred with two dominant firms emerging in Low & Bonar Ltd. and Jute Industries Ltd. as described in Chapter 1. Despite this growth of concentration, the jute industry was considered in Evely & Little's 1960 study of concentration ratios to be only a medium concentrated industry, with the three largest business units responsible for 38 per cent of employment and 42 per cent of net output.[2] The industry therefore continued to consist of a range of different producers and merchants; specialized spinning or weaving firms operated alongside combined spinning and weaving producers. These manufacturing firms also developed vertical integration strategies and created merchanting divisions such that the whole of the jute trade consisted of a multitude of overlapping enterprises, with interests stretching across the full range of functions within the industry. Thus, in the case of Low and Bonar Ltd and Jute Industries Ltd both firms contained purchasing functions for the acquisition of raw materials, a full range of manufacturing capabilities in spinning and weaving and marketing and distribution networks both within the United Kingdom and internationally.[3] In the case of Low and Bonar by 1950 their marketing and distribution networks were extensive, consisting in North America of the Canadian Bag Co., the Economic Bag Co., the Gifford Warehouse Co. and the Thomas Bonar & Co (Canada), while in Africa they included the African Oilskin Industries, the DJKS Co. Ltd, Hardware Buildings Ltd, and the South African Canvas Ltd.[4] In the case of Jute Industries, while the original amalgamation had concentrated upon the manufacturing end of the industry, it had by 1949 nevertheless also developed distribution networks in both North America and Australia.[5]

It was this market structure that became the focus of attention when the Working Party enquiry into jute took place in 1948. The Working Party *Report* with respect to changes in labour was the focus of attention in Chapter 3, here we focus upon the industrial structure and market competition aspects of the *Report*. The *Report* documented the perceived wisdom within the industry as one of falling demand and product market competition brought about by substitution effects, increased international competition within jute products and a geographical concentration with a consequential impact of high local unemployment.

The Working Party was always going to produce a report which was sympathetic to the plight of the industry given its tripartite representation of equal membership of the industry, trade unions and Board of Trade appointed independent representative, and unsurprisingly, the *Report* concluded with a need for government support and protection for the industry. The Government's implicit price to be extracted from the industry for such protection was to be the further concentration of the industry, with specific proposals for the re-organizing of the industry into groups with a minimum of 100,000 spindles of which a minimum of 15,000 spindles were required to be the faster sliver spinning type.[6]

Despite the Working Party's inherent sympathy for the industry it was nevertheless difficult to refute the evidence from the interwar industry. The most optimistic assessment suggested that even if the industry could achieve output levels of 247,000 tonnes of jute products and cloth, equivalent to total home demand excluding the low cost bag product market satisfied by Indian imports, then, assuming the use of modern sliver spinning machines working double shifts, approximately only 11,000 workers would be necessary.[7] This corresponded with the private estimates produced by the Board of Trade in 1943 which suggested that while an initial 25,000 workers might be employed during the restocking boom within five to ten years this figure would fall to no more than 10,000.[8] Yet employment in the industry in 1947 was at 17,000, despite being considerably down from the 32,600 workers in 1936, over 50 per cent higher than the accepted estimates for future labour demand.[9]

Thus the consensus within government, and shared by both the employers and trade unions, was that the economic pressures which led to a fall in establishments from 85 to 66 between 1935 and 1946 would soon reassert themselves. After a temporary period of buoyant demand the contraction that would emerge had to be managed to encourage rationalization of producers, with the exit of many, and the development of efficiencies through economies of scale and investment in higher productivity machinery for those that remained. Government protection was the key assumption underlying the *Report*. The continuation of protection was required in order both to facilitate these changes and provide a level of social stability to the city that had been so clearly absent from the interwar years.[10] As the *Report* unequivocally stated 'without protection, however, we see no possibility of a healthy home industry and contraction is inevitable'.[11]

The favourable macro economic conditions that persisted into the long boom of the 1950s and 1960s, with relatively high growth rates and low inflation, undoubtedly provided a favourable environment in which theses changes in the industry could develop. Symeonidis shows that the suggested rationalization occurred, with the jute industry's largest five firms increasing their market share from 50 per cent in 1958 to 73 per cent by 1975.[12] However, the postwar era was to see a very different pattern of output and profitability within the industry than the Working Party believed would be the case. The scale of decline that was envisaged in 1946 was not to emerge until the 1970s. Before then the industry retained a level of employment and investment that was in contradiction to the expectations of the Working Party *Report*.

Employment

Employment within the industry, after initially falling to just under 16,000 in 1949, in fact rose above 19,000 by 1954 before a slow decline, such that it was not until 1972 that employment fell below 10,000, the level of employment estimated by the Working Party. Figure 4.1 demonstrates graphically that the picture of the 1950s does not correspond with that of the immediate post-war predictions of an industry rapidly declining.

A similar picture to that of employment can be seen in investment permitting a rise in number of establishments within the industry. Post-war conditions permitted the sustained expansion of the industry such that by 1958 a new post-war peak of eighty-nine establishments was operating.[13] The expansion of the industry came from an increasing level of specialization and diversification within the jute weaving aspects of the trade, thus specialist weaving firms rose from nineteen to thirty between 1954 and 1963. Weaving firms were emerging in response to new market opportunities with small-scale specialist production units rather than concentration and increases in scale. As can be seen from Figure 4.2, it was not until the 1960s that the number of establishments overall began to fall and when it did so it took place where the scale economies were to be expected. Thus between 1954 and 1963 while specialist weaving production units were expanding within the specialist spinning and combined weaving and spinning sections of the industry, contraction was taking place with spinning establishments falling from nineteen to eleven and combined spinning and weaving establishments falling from twenty-six to sixteen over the same period.[14] One final point to make about these changes was that due to merger and rationalization the number of firms within the industry fell much faster than that of establishments. Thus the picture we are left with during the 1950s is one in which, while concentration was taking place in terms of the number of firms in existence, the concentration in production and expected economies of scale were only emerging in the spinning sections of the trade and were not emerging within the weaving sections. Instead the industry was becoming more fractured as the industry became more specialized in its final products.

In order to understand these very different patterns of development within the industry it is crucial to understand the centrality of not simply the macro economic advantages provided by the 'Golden Age' but also the extent of activity within the industry to maintain or increase profitability. It is here that co-operation across the wider jute industry is of importance. Co-operation permitted the successful management of conflicting short-term interests between firms within each sector of the industry and conflicting long-term interests between differing sectors of the industry.

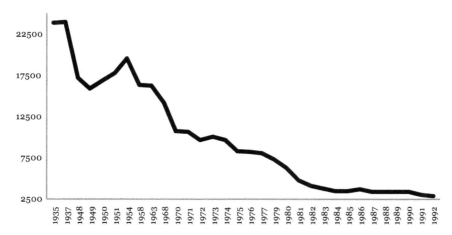

Figure 4.1: Jute employment 1935–92.

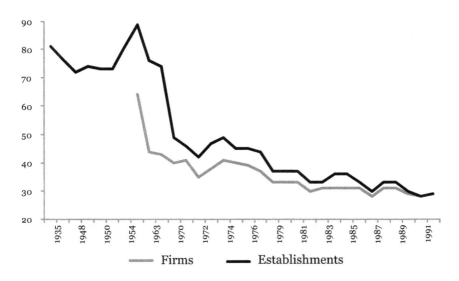

Figure 4.2: Jute firms and establishments 1935–92.

Competition and Co-operation

Competition within markets is expected to ensure that individual firms could gain market share by using price competition for what was in the main standardized intermediate industrial products. Such competition could also help resist attempts at cartelization, ensuring that price cartels proved to be transitory and ineffective, as the Indian Jute Manufacturers Association had found in the interwar era.[15] Further, if the industry acted competitively then the lower cost producers would continue to limit the extent to which substitute goods would reduce the market size for jute products, and for the same reasons also reduce the impact of low cost international producers on domestic producers' market share. A move towards a more competitive market approach was the goal being sought by government as it developed competition policy by the mid-1940s. Price competition was also being viewed, within government, as a means of promoting efficiency and investment within industry, so aiding domestic growth. This development in economic thinking towards competition policy itself originated in the recognition that the interwar years had seen a marked rise in concentration levels across industrial sectors, leading to firms gaining new levels of market power.[16] As Robinson noted in 1941 'In the wider sphere of general industry combination has advanced rather than receded... the growth of the scale of productive units has in recent years been such as to bring almost the majority of industries into a condition where they are dominated by a few large firms'.[17] Cairncross also notes that within the Economic Section a consensus existed over the introduction of competition policy as early as 1944 and any disagreements lay only with the extent to which government could be pro-active in promoting competition and preventing monopoly.[18]

This approach arguably reached its clearest enunciation in the publication of the National Plan in 1965. As it stated '[n]ew legislation in the field of monopolies... should help to ensure a more dynamic and efficient economy. In some industries this should help to ensure that industry remains in the van of technological progress and is able to compete effectively at home and abroad. In others the need is for structural change to take advantage of technological developments'.[19] The extent to which government was successful in shifting towards a competitive market and whether or not limitations on these changes hindered subsequent economic growth lie at the heart of much of the debates over relative economic decline.[20]

The difficulty with this approach to market competition for the jute industry was the recognition, shared both by government and the trade, that it could never compete with the low cost international producers, hence the assumption that protection was required in the *Report*. In particular, Indian production, which had before the Second World War captured some 60 per cent of the world market in manufactured jute goods, was understood to have a cost base that Dundee could never emulate.[21] The Board of Trade explicitly recognized this in 1952, setting out its view that;

> 'It is the general view that, without some form of assistance, this [return to open competition] can only result in a fairly rapid decline in Dundee production, in part because Indian supplies would, on price, capture an increasing share of the available remaining market, here and overseas, and in part because of confidence in Dundee in the inevitable result that there would be further loss of workers to other developing industries in the Dundee area and that no real efforts would be made to continue or to improve efficiency'.[22]

Competitive market strategies were also limited in their appeal due to the inability of firms to generate significant economies of scale to warrant the large scale investment required to support price competitive strategies. The *Report* highlighted that in the spinning section of the trade the modal firm size was a firm with 3,000–4,000 spindles and in the weaving section 200–50 looms. The *Census of Production* reported that in 1951 the modal firm size across the whole trade was only 100–199 employees. It was these small and medium sized firms that achieved the highest levels of net output per person employed. Large firms with over 500 employees only achieved 77 per cent of the net output of these smaller firms.[23] As late as 1992 government data from the *Business Monitor* series, the replacement for the *Census,* continued to demonstrate the advantages of small scale production processes, with the modal firm size falling to below 100.[24] Thus the evidence suggests small and medium sized firms continued to generate the most efficient forms of production for the industry. Efficiencies were derived from the specialization that was emerging in production processes and in addition from common geographically focused externalities within Dundee. The development of collective interests in Dundee's industry can be considered to have been an example of the clustering identified by Michael Porter giving rise to geographically based competitive advantages.[25] In Chapter 3 we saw how, within the labour supply, segmentation developed not simply between male and female workers but between spinners and weavers. A segmented labour market had emerged within Dundee which provided employers a high level of existing skill within which it could recruit its workforce. In other areas of human capital formation jute employers were also able to ensure jute interests were represented. Jute interests could stretch to the development of curricula through the Dundee Chamber of Commerce's appointed representatives to the governing bodies of the main public school Dundee High, where many managers were educated, and to the Dundee Technical College where technical training in engineering for skilled mechanics and factory supervisors within the jute industry was taught.

Externalities also emerged in the provision of shared functions such as overhead capital formation in port facilities and the creation of local capital markets for investment. Here, as with the labour market, the role of the Dundee Chamber of Commerce and the jute interests domination of its operations was important.

The running of the Dundee Port Authority and the freight rates charged were a key area of concern for the collective interests of Dundee's jute employers. Given the importance of Dundee's docks in the prosperity of the city it is not surprising that the running of the harbour, its improvement and the prices charged for importing and exporting through the docks, were of central importance to jute employers. Prior to the development of extensive road links in the late 1960s and 1970s only the railways provided any reasonable alternative for domestic goods traffic. With Dundee's wealth so tied to the international trade in raw jute and its manufactured output the docks played a crucial role in the city's industry. A collective approach to minimizing transport and distribution costs was beneficial to all, although not necessarily in equal measure. In order to influence the development of collective goods for the jute industry the Chamber of Commerce played a crucial co-ordinating role. The Chamber of Commerce emerged, as Boyce has noted of the nineteenth century international shipping trade, as an institutional solution to the high cost of attaining reliable information on market making opportunities.[26] The Chamber elected three of its members onto the Harbour Board Trustees and continually monitored and discussed any changes in the freight rates into and out of the docks. Similar importance was given to consideration of rail and postal costs by the Chamber of Commerce with regular discussions over the costs and regularity of international postal deliveries.[27] Here the interests of the largest employers met with those of other sections of Dundee's employers and the Chamber could be present itself as speaking on behalf of a wider set of employers.

For over 130 years after the Dundee Chamber of Commerce's formation in 1835 the Chamber of Commerce provided the jute industry with a reliable voice presenting the jute industry's interests as those of the wider business community.[28] Formed initially by seventy-three initial subscribers drawn almost exclusively from the jute trades the Chamber's membership was constituted largely by jute firms of all types from weaving and spinning firms through to merchanting and manufacturing firms until the Second World War. The 1937 membership list shows that, jute and related trades apart, the only large firms who were members were J.J. Cunningham Ltd and Scottish Oils & Shell Mex Ltd in oil manufacturing, Turnbull & Yeaman Ltd and Willison & Scott Fithie in oil merchanting and the ball bearing manufacturer Skefko Ball Bearing Co. were members.[29]

After the Second World War this dominance continued. Correlating the 1948 Inspector of Factories listing with membership lists of firms from the Chamber of Commerce shows that whilst only three of sixty-nine listed large firms, accounting for just 4 per cent of the jute workforce, were not members of the Chamber of Commerce in 1937, in general engineering the number was forty-nine out of sixty-one plants, accounting for 47 per cent of employment in the sector. Indeed, of the twelve firms in general engineering who were members ten were engaged in jute machinery production or older industries such as boiler making and in the case of Dundee's single largest individual workplace a ship-building firm, the Caledon Shipbuilding and Engineering Co. Ltd, employing 3,000 workers.[30] The Director Chairman of the Caledon, it should be noted, also acted as one of the government appointed 'independent members' on the Jute Working Party.

The jute industry's control of the Chamber was institutionalized through the appointment of its Directors.[31] By 1960 the Directors of the Chamber of Commerce were appointed from the Association of Jute Spinners & Manufacturers, the Engineering and Allied Employers Dundee & District Association, the Dundee Jute and Linen Goods Merchants Association, the Dundee Ship Owners & Ship Brokers Association, the Dundee Importers' Association, the Dundee Produce Association, the Flaxspinners and Manufacturers Association, the United Kingdom Jute Goods Assoc (Dundee Branch) and the Jute Carpet Manufacturers Association.[32] Thus all but one of the associations appointing members as Directors of the Chamber of Commerce were either directly involved in the jute trades or, in the case of the Engineering & Allied Employers Association and the Ship Owners and Brokers, important related trades providing logistics and distribution facilities or capital plant and equipment required in the industry.[33]

The significance of this dominance can be seen from the President's statement, Mr T. D. Bruce, himself a jute manufacturer to the Annual General Meeting in March 1960;

> 'Dundee's foreseeable future is very much tied up with jute industry and I speak now, not as a jute manufacturer, but as President of the body on which the local industry, commerce and trade in the District is represented... any action which affects the [jute] industry should only be taken in consultation with those who represent the City and its industrial and commercial life'.

That Bruce could so closely tie the city and its wider industries interests to those of the jute industry is indicative of the close relationship between the Chamber of Commerce and the jute industry.

Given its composition it is not surprising that the Chamber of Commerce readily adopted viewpoints that aligned itself closely with the jute industry. While its role as a coffee house and exchange for information may have been superseded in the twentieth century, its role as a voice of business within Dundee to government at Westminster or to the Scottish Office and to the local authority became of greater importance. For example, it played an important role in limiting the growth of new industries in the city in 1950 in order to protect the supply of labour into the jute industry.[34]

Importantly, this relationship between the Chamber of Commerce and the jute industry was a subordinate one. The Chamber's views on the jute industry's co-operative organization and pricing agreements were never subject of discussion by the Chamber and the outcome of the Restrictive Trade Practices Court case in 1963 (see below) was not referred to in the Director's minutes. The jute industry's associations were careful to ensure jute discussions remained firmly within the confines of the industry bodies themselves. Instead the Chamber became either a means of asserting the jute industry's rights within political circles or a vehicle whereby the jute employers responsibilities could be transferred when necessary. Thus, while the Chamber would in the 1950s support limitations on new industries due to shortages of jute employees, in 1964, following the announcement that price competition would be introduced into the jute market, the Director's minute would state that the Chamber now believed other employers within the city had new obligations.

> [T]here is little doubt that it [price competition] will bring about in the future a reduction in the number of employees in the [jute] industry. The possibility of this has been hanging over the industry for so long that some aware inclined to minimize the risk. Now that it is a fact it be hoves all concerned to take such steps as will ensure alternative employment for those who may become redundant.[35]

The relationship between the Chamber of Commerce and the jute industry only began to breakdown once the dominance of the jute industry wained and the Chamber of Commerce began to expand its membership base beyond that of Dundee. In 1965 the Chamber saw an increase in membership of almost 40 per cent due to the decision to form District Committees and permit membership from outwith Dundee, including Forfar, Montrose, Fife, Arbroath and Brechin.[36]

The lack of evidence for the advantages of a competitive market approach in the post-war era ensured that nowhere within the industry could support be found for proposals focused upon competitive markets. Two alternative approaches were however evident for the industry; either co-operative strategies within each sector of the trade or a co-operative strategy encompassing the whole trade. Within each sector of the trade limited co-operative strategies could emerge.

In the spinning sector the smaller number of larger firms that existed could utilize their market power to extract economic rent from the more atomized weaving sector. The extent of market power depended however on the degree to which competing spinning firms maintained similar prices and the degree to which new entrants could be prevented from gaining access to raw jute to compete this oligopolistic market power away. Similarly, for the more atomized weaving sector their profitability was dependent upon findings ways to limit the degree to which their profit margins would be squeezed by both a concentrated spinning sector, for their inputs of spun yarn, and a more concentrated manufacturing sector, for their outputs of woven cloth. Also manufacturing firms themselves could again forego individual potential growth in market share using price competition in product markets such as industrial bagging, webbing for the electrical and construction industries or jute used of carpet backing if they could extract higher margins from either the weaving section of the trade or by enforcing prices to end users through the distribution channel. Finally, and perhaps most problematically, merchanting firms, engaged in distribution and marketing of jute final products, could choose to maintain prices for domestically produced finished products to end users if they believed potential competition through the development of merchants making available low cost imports or substitute goods such as paper bags and synthetic fibres could be restricted. The limitations of these co-operative strategies within these differing sectors of the industry is given as an explanation by Masrani for the failure of moves towards price fixing in the interwar years.[37]

The development of integrated firms in the industry introduced a still higher level of complexity to these co-operative strategies. Firms with a vertical structure were capable of boosting profitability internally without the negative impact of higher costs generated by inter-firm co-operative arrangements. By engaging in a wide range of activities across the trade a firm could insulate itself from the effect of higher prices within any specific sector of the trade. So Jute Industries, a highly vertically integrated firm, could establish a merchanting division within the United States to effectively benefit from low import prices of Indian finished goods, despite the fact that its own Dundee produced goods were losing out to Indian competition. As Jute Industries maintained they were able to ensure profits derived from 'J.I. know-how in the market place'.[38]

The alternative to these sector specific co-operative strategies was a more encompassing co-operative approach extending across the whole of the trade.[39] For such as strategy to emerge individual firms had to be convinced of the attractiveness of foregoing short-term interests in gaining market share from competitor firms through price competition, or potentially long-term profits through loss of markets from substitute goods or increased import penetration, in favour of long-term profitability derived from price fixing and cartelization across the industry. Such co-operation also had to manage the differing levels of monopoly power that existed within each sector of the trade, and balance the conflicting interests that existed in what was a dynamic relationship whereby prices and costs changed over time. Co-operation therefore had to overcome conflicting economic interests originating from differing sections of the trade which had their origin either in the threat of market competition from other industries or from within the trade itself. In doing so, however, firms were aided by the fact that co-operative strategies acted as an alternative to large-scale investment in an environment where scale economies were not self evident.

A further aspect of co-operative strategies requiring understanding is the consideration we give to the motivation of firms. While it is a useful starting point to infer rationality from narrow economic perspective it is an insufficiently nuanced approach to do so. Firms, as with individuals, may be considered to have differing rationalities and while profit maximization or sales maximization may be a helpful economic starting point wider questions of motivation require consideration. Certainly philanthropy played an important role in the physical construction of the city, its parks and its universities. The long tradition of family ownership can thus be identified as being a factor here and of those, such as Jute Industries Ltd, which were publicly owned, a strong family connection remained. Thus individual business leaders' social and political viewpoints also need to be considered in understanding the resolution of potential areas for conflict within the industry. Thus co-operation required a further prerequisite for its success; employers capable of creating and maintaining a commonality of viewpoint in the perceived interests of the trade, a viewpoint which could in specific instances lead individuals, or firms, to move away from a narrow view of profit maximization, whether in a competitive or co-operative strategy, in favour of a broader sense of economic wellbeing for the industry as a whole A common shared ideology had to emerge in the context of the trade's interests which encapsulated all sectors of the trade, was sufficiently flexible in recognition of the subtleties deriving from disparities across the trade, and yet was sufficiently hegemonic to deter dissent from developing and breaking apart the ideological consensus that existed.

The 'Three Wise Men'

It is here we can identify the role played by William Walker, Herbert Bonar and Lewis Robertson, who collectively became referred to in government and the industry as the 'Three Wise Men' These three leading employers played a central role in the organization of the co-ordination of the Dundee jute industry and undertook to negotiate with government on all issues linked to jute. Their social background was similar, in all cases originating from long established family run firms and educated in Scotland's public school system, and all being knighted for their services to the jute industry during their careers. Lewis Robertson and Herbert Bonar were second generation owners of their family's firms J. F. Robertson & Sons Ltd and Low & Bonar Ltd respectively while William Walker was third generation from the founder of Jute Industries Ltd.[40] Bonar and Walker had become established as authorities within the industry in the interwar years, with Bonar being described as the 'most able businessman in Scotland' and becoming Jute Controller during the Second World War while Walker headed the jute manufacturers employers association the AJSM.[41] Yet it was perhaps Lewis Robertson who may be identified as playing the most active role in the post-war era, as it was he who undertook the detailed work of co-ordinating the industry.

Lewis Robertson, the younger of the Three Wise Men, a trained accountant joined the family firm, J F. Robertson & Co., in 1946 upon his return to Dundee after the Second World War. He quickly gained a detailed knowledge of the industry's financial situation, in part from the knowledge gained as accountant to Low & Bonar.[42] In a comment on Robertson's abilities Dr. Stout, Director of the Jute Industry Research Association described Lewis Robertson to D. N. Charlish of the Board of Trade as 'by far the most able of the younger men in Dundee, and seemed cut out for the role of Dundee's leading spokesman when the older generation e.g. Sir William Walker and Mr. Bonar, retired from the scene 'Lewis Robertson's attributes were identified as his 'academic abilities' and Charlish noted his oratory ability to make 'a well-turned speech without saying anything of substance' during his speech to the Annual Dinner of the UK Jute Goods Assoc Dinner in May 1961.

These attributes ensured Robertson became the leading spokesperson for the industry. As author of the AJSM's precognition statement to the Restrictive Trade Practices Court case his intellectual abilities were essential to the success of the AJSM. Similarly it ensured Robertson's authority within the wider jute industry. Thus when it came to co-ordinating responses to the Restrictive Trade Practices case it was Robertson who wrote to the London Jute Association (LJA), and others, to warn them of the dangers caused by detailed documentation of their collusive views. Thus, the Chairman of the LJA noted the letter received by Robertson highlighting 'difficulties which had arisen in the Restrictive Trade Practices case due to the comprehensive nature of minutes. It had been found that these were often too long and were inclined to record opinions expressed during the debate by particular individuals, giving their names.'[43]

Such attributes while advantageous in the development and control of co-operative inter-firm strategies, and particularly in negotiation between government and business, were however not entirely accepted within the Dundee jute community. In a hint of the tensions that lay beneath the surface of these co-operative strategies Stout suggested that Robertson was 'regarded with some suspicion in Dundee', his 'academic' and 'sarcastic' approach generated a 'feeling that he is not only too clever, but rather too anxious to show he is'. These suspicions went further, with Stout suggesting his financial history led him not to be trusted within the tightly knit Dundee community. His family firm had been made bankrupt twice to no apparent harm to the family yet 'there are a good many who have suffered' and the decision to establish a paper sack factory 'in Hull', perhaps unsurprisingly, made him 'even more unpopular than it would otherwise have been'.[44]

Lewis Robertson's personal history was so tied up with the history of the jute industry that even his exit from the industry is of interest. His participation in the industry continued until 1970 when he was ousted as Chairman and Managing Director from Scott & Robertson, the firm Robertson Industrial Textiles had merged with in 1965, by the family members of the partner firm.[45] In doing so Robertson then moved from poacher to game keeper becoming a member of the Monopolies and Mergers Commission throughout the 1970s and the first Chief Executive of the Scottish Development Agency.[46]

The history of leading figures within the industry further indicates that while the co-operative strategies existing within the jute industry retained a degree of longevity the pressures pulling them apart were never far beneath the surface. Resilient figures such as Lewis Robertson, Herbert Bonar and William Walker were necessary to maintain firms' unity but equally the band of warring brothers that made up Dundee's jute community could only be cajoled into retaining a unity of purpose when faced with more significant external threats.

Entry Barriers

Both international and domestic restrictions existed which severely curtailed the opportunities for new entrants into the industry. Entry of new spinning firms into the UK jute industry was restricted due to limited supply of raw jute by the banning of exports of raw jute from India from 1950.[47] Political instability following partition between India and Pakistan in 1947 created instability within the world's jute industry.[48] As described in Chapter 1, above, the concentration of jute processing and manufacturing within the India ensured that Indian economic policy moved towards protecting the supply of raw jute inputs into its industry through the banning of exports of unprocessed jute. As a result world exports of raw jute were satisfied almost exclusively by exports from the newly formed state of Pakistan.

The impact of these political constraints, from the fall-out of Indian independence, for the UK jute manufacturing firms was that those spinning firms that had survived into the post-war period retained a high degree of control over the supplies of UK produced yarn into the weaving section of the trade. This control was further reinforced by domestic restrictions which originated with the British government. Weaving firms were unable to gain direct imports of jute yarn, from India prior to partition, or through Pakistan exports after partition, without access to the quotas provided by the British government's centralized buying and distribution mechanism operated through Jute Control. Jute Control's role was to directly import raw jute and processed cloth on government account and distribute these goods to producers and users of jute within

Britain. Thus Jute Control was a trading arm of the Board of Trade. The UK government's development of centralized buying, via Jute Control from 1939, prevented independent buying of either raw jute, processed jute yarn for weaving or jute cloth for production into finished jute products without quotas provided by the government's office.

Government control over imports of raw materials and finished goods was widespread during the war.[49] In 1954 these controls over the importation of raw materials and the distribution of goods across private industry were abandoned by the Board of Trade in favour of tariff protection. Exceptionally, however, in jute, controls were only modified and direct government trading continued. While the importation of raw jute was decontrolled in 1954, imports of manu-factured jute products in the form of spun yarn, woven cloth and finished goods continued to be controlled through Jute Control.[50] Indeed some imports, wider widths of cloth linked to demand from the carpet industry, continued to be banned altogether. Uniquely, then, Jute Control continued after the period of decontrol providing significant limitations on the development of the industry.

Jute Control's centralized buying was managed through the distribution of a series of quantity-based quotas to existing spinning, weaving, manufacturing and merchanting firms.[51] Thus all imported yarn and cloth flowed through Jute Control and only raw jute imports were in private hands, the private hands of the most concentrated sector of the trade. These quotas were based upon previous consumption and no new entrants were permitted access to the quota system without evidence that they had operated within the trade for the six months prior to the application for a quota. Since a firm could not readily establish without access to jute yarn, cloth or manufactured products, such a restriction acted as an effective barrier to entry either preventing entry altogether or permit-ting entry only through the support of one of the 110 existing quota holder.The Board of Trade noted 'at any one time the Control's sales were limited to this privileged group'.[52] Not surprisingly the growth of new jute factories outstripped the growth of new entrants into the industry, so that while the number of new establishments rose from seventy-three to eighty-nine between 1951 and 1958 the number of new firms rose from sixty to sixty-four respectively.[53]

While for the Board of Trade this arrangement provided the degree of protec-tion to employment in Dundee to which governments since the Second World War were committed, it also brought with it a recognition that the prices charged by Dundee's jute industry were excessive. The Board of Trade by 1956 were con-sistently contributing £2–3m to the exchequer as a result of its trading activities.[54] The Board of Trade official Mrs R. Esdale explained that the margins Jute Control was operating with were producing these large surpluses. Thus 'Control's purchases are made from the cheapest source of supply, Indian and Pakistan, while their sales into the various sectors of the trade are made at the prices equivalent to the "fair" Dundee price which is a good deal higher than the purchase price'.[55]

Such significant state trading by the Board of Trade was increasingly viewed with ideological hostility within government by the mid-1950s, as government moved towards favouring a more stringent competition environment within private industry. Thus Lewis Robertson, one of the 'three wise men' in the industry, commented unfavourably on the changing attitude of David Eccles MP, President of the Board of Trade, to jute control;[56]

'It has been obvious at meetings with Eccles [Board of Trade] that the fact that Jute Control's being a "control", rather quite apart from any other aspects of its activities, is rather an offence to him. This attitude ("Conservative freedom works") is bound to make them prefer, of two otherwise equal proposals, the one which would suppress the Jute Control and its also bound to cause Her Majesty's Government to oppose fairly strongly any proposal which could be classified as state trading'.[57]

With major limitations on the supply of raw jute opportunities for new entrants into the spinning sector were severely curtailed, while the quota system for domestic producers acted as an effective entry barrier to the weaving, manufacturing and merchanting sectors of the trade. As we go on to describe shortly, the Restrictive Trade Practices Court action in 1963 demonstrated that this institutional framework had a significant impact on potential entry into all sectors of the trade.

The extent of these restrictions upon entry were further facilitated by the co-operation between shipping interests and jute purchasers. The London Jute Association (LJA) acted as an importers association insuring and regulating the shipping of jute products. The LJA provided standardized contracts, stipulated the extent of rebates on damaged imports, provided arbitration between parties in cases of dispute and crucially co-ordinated with the Dundee manufacturers on any proposed changes to importation agreements. So, for example, when in 1961 the Pakistan government sought to change the contracts for exporting jute into European markets, it was the LJA that met with the Conference Lines shipping company, co-ordinated a response with the European Jute Association and crucially ensured to 'keep in close touch with Dundee interests'.[58]

Competition for the jute industry thus came therefore primarily from outwith the UK trade, either in the form of substitute goods including the development of paper bagging and synthetic fibres or in the form of international competition, particularly from the low cost producers in India.

It must be emphasized that neither Jute Control nor the quota allocations for imports automatically prevented the emergence of new firms. Instead what we saw was a rise in the degree of specialization within the industry. The rise in the number of weaving firms seems to derive from the development of specialist weaving firms focusing upon the production of woven cloth as jute goods for particular product markets. Jute found its way into a wider range of specialist products, especially for example the burgeoning carpet industry as a durable product for backing carpets and suitable for production in wider cloth sizes.[59] This expansion of the industry in the weaving sections provided an area where existing quota holders retained significant opportunities for diversification. One example of this expansion can be seen in the expansion of Jute Industries' Manhattan Works factory in 1949, where government sanction for steel and building materials was required for its development of new weaving facilities to permit circular looms to be employed.[60] More generally McDowall and Draper's study of the impact of protection for trade adjustment suggested that some 95 per cent of Dundee's production by 1963 was in areas where either Jute Control managed imports (40 per cent of Dundee's production) or were banned from imports entirely (55 per cent of Dundee's production).[61]

Jute Control then provided a powerful mechanism for encouraging co-operation within the industry. The supply of raw materials into the industry either as spun yarn and cloth or as finished products provided a powerful incentive to co-operate within the weaving, manufacturing and merchanting sectors of the trade. However, while entry restrictions limited the degree to which economic, or monopoly, profit could be competed away the potential for over capacity and price competition could still emerge from within the industry. Only by limiting the degree to which price competition was effective, particularly downstream in the area of jute cloth and finished products, would profits for all firms within the industry be protected. It was in this area where co-operation proved most apparent and most contentious both within the industry and between the industry and government.

Price Controls

Seven interlocking 'Gentleman's Agreements' in the industry established a wide range of restrictions upon competition among importing, spinning, weaving, manufacturing and wholesaling distributing firms. At the heart of the 'Gentleman's Agreements' were two agreements; the Gentleman's Agreement Yarn Prices and the Gentleman's Agreement Cloth Prices. These two agreements generated prices, publicized in the 'Brown Books', which acted as minimum prices for yarn and cloth in the industry. Based upon these two agreements five further, more detailed, agreements themselves generating fixed prices, covering domestically produced hessian cloth (the Dundee Hessian Piece Goods Recommended Prices agreement) and hessain cloth from imported hessian (the Imported Hessian Piece Goods Recommended Prices agreement), domestically produced bags (the Bags Made From Dundee Cloth Recommended Prices agreement) and bags made from imported cloth (the Imported Bags and Bags Made From Imported Cloth Recommended Prices agreement) and finally the agreement covering sewing tariffs (the Tariff of Recommended Charges for Sewing, Stamping and Bundling agreement).[62]

Together the agreements created prices at each and every stage of production and permitted firms to develop individual prices above a minimum pertaining across the industry. The need to charge higher prices at each and every stage of production for processing of jute, irrespective of actual costs was central to these agreements.

In one case Don Brothers Ltd, one of the larger manufacturing firms within the industry, used low cost oil in production and were able to charge lower prices for their output bringing them to the attention of the co-ordinator of these agreements, Lewis Robertson at the AJSM. In Robertson's note of the conversation with MacDonald at Don Brothers;

> 'I was greatly disconcerted to hear from Mr MacDonald this morning that Don Brothers were quoting identical prices for odour-diminished and normal cloths ... I pointed out to him very strongly the undesirable precedents that such a move could create and that first of all it was, in principle, essential to make an extra charge, however small, for any special services. Secondly co-ordination would become a dead letter if this principle were not adhered to. Third it was quite beside the point that there was a cheaper oil since, as I suggested, the introduction of a new cop machine might then mean that some firms would charge less for cops, manifestly an impossible situation.[63]

The outcome of Robertson's intervention was described in a note of the conversation with Don Brothers;

> '[they have] agreed, however, to suspend his quotations for this meantime... [They] later spoke to me to say the merchant in question was very much annoyed at having the offer suspended and had stated that he would obtain the material elsewhere' Don Brothers were therefore 'naturally anxious that all spinners should be in line'.[64]

In general the impact of these pricing agreements can be difficult to ascertain. What is beyond doubt however is that considerable effort was put into maintaining prices through the publication of pricing data, information exchange and monitoring of compliance by the trade associations within the industry.

The ability to maintain prices throughout the industry was not simply generated by the monitoring and enforcement powers of the trade associations. Free riding and opportunism was an inherent threat to the success of these agreements and where it was detected the firm involved readily defended themselves by reference to the actions of the rest of the industry. In the case of the spinning firm Thomson Shepherd, their defence against criticism of lowering prices on its prices for yarn was that as prices have fallen they;

'...frankly admit that they are no longer charging this particular extra and more or less say they are no longer considering themselves bound by the Brown Book because the rest of us have misbehaved about prices from time to time. [65]

Faced with potential collapse of the pricing agreements Robertson, one of the key individuals involved in monitoring compliance, made clear it was the personal relationships that existed throughout the industry that proved crucial to ensuring compliance with the prices determined in the Brown Books. In the case of Thomson Shepherd's refusal to abide by the Brown Book prices for yarn roves he wrote;

> It is precisely this type of petulant and impatient approach which has caused the generally unsatisfactory rove price position and continues to maintain it. ... I set forth my theory that ... If a state of affairs could be established in which Mr Ireland or Mr Hay of JI [Jute Industries ed.] knew by name whom to telephone at Thomson Shepherd in order to discuss in a frank and gentle manner prices which appeared to be of common interest... such a channel would bring about great improvements within six months or so.[66]

These interlocking relationships not only restricted horizontal competition between competing firms operating in the same stage of the production process, but also ensured collusion between firms vertically within the supply chain. Spinning and weaving firms were prepared to support and enforce collusive manufacturers' agreements on prices to ensure stability within the spinning section of the trade. Jute was unusual in that its geographical concentration was so high. While the close proximity permitted a high degree of monitoring to take place, its real value comes from the ability to gain willing rather than enforced compliance. The creation of a business culture in which inter-related businesses could develop co-operative strategies was perhaps the most significant achievement of the industry both before and after the Second World War.

The existence and importance of this business culture can be evidenced by the development of and inter-relationship between the jute industry and the Dundee Chamber of Commerce described above and secondly in the recruitment and creation of the managerial layer within the industry. Within the industry itself creating a culture of co-operation was understood as a major element of the managerial function. The companies had for a long time recruited army officers into senior manager posts within their Indian offices.[67] Jute Industries itself produced its own in-house magazine to develop its own company culture and at the highest level saw the inculcating of co-operative values as even more important. The importance of this industry, rather than firm, specific information should not be under-estimated. Jute Industries guarded the details of their co-operative arrangements with great secrecy, divulging them to only those whose discretion could be relied upon. As Walker stated to Robertson;

Mr Anderson was by way of being groomed to succeed Mr Hutton in a few years' time in responsibility for the selling activities ... though he was as yet not very fully informed of them.[68]

The significance of these cultural aspects of co-operation lies primarily in the understanding of how co-operative strategies evolved, were maintained and defended when under threat. While economic interest underpins these competitive strategies, their continuation and the longevity relied upon a complex set of social relationships which tied potentially conflicting parties together. The fact that the industry's spinning, weaving and manufacturing firms were all so concentrated within Dundee and its immediately surrounding area undoubtedly permitted a high degree of monitoring of the industry. But it was the social inter-relationships that facilitated the longevity of co-operation and helped to ensure the industry became unified in its defence of the restrictive agreements when faced by court action brought by the Office of the Board of Trade's Restrictive Trading Arrangements from the period December 1956 to March 1963.

Restrictive Trade Practices Court

The 1956 Restrictive Trade Practices Act required firms, and industry's collectively, to register agreements which restricted trade and for the first time established a legal mechanism, through the Restrictive Trade Practices Court, to investigate registered agreements and judge whether or not they could be deemed to be anti-competitive and against the public interest. Registered agreements were not automatically considered against the public interest agreements, some might be considered beneficial to the public interest due to the 'gateways' established by the Act, such as maintaining standards, health and safety or employment etc.[69] From the passing of the Act in November 1956 to 1959 over 2,000 agreements were registered, and the Court began the role of examining the extent to which collusive agreements within industry were in breach of the new competition framework.[70] The jute industry was one of the industries to receive a detailed examination and by 1961 the Restrictive Trade Practices Court declared its intention of holding an investigation into the jute industry's series of agreements.[71]

It was immediately obvious to officials of the Board of Trade after the passing of the Restrictive Trade Practices Act in November 1956 that the arrangements operating within Jute Control were both undesirable and indefensible. Through December 1956 and February 1957 Board of Trade officials were meeting with the Board of Trade solicitors and officials from the office of the Registrar of Restrictive Trade Practices to determine the degree to which the Board of Trade would be considered a party to the pricing agreements operating within the jute industry. While initially it was considered by the Board of Trade's solicitor,

Ryder, that the Board could claim to be a price leader in the industry and that firms were free to price either higher or lower than Jute Control's such arguments were recognized as 'torturous' and unlikely to convince the Restrictive Trade Practices Court. Initial discussions with Rogers, Assistant Registrar of Restrictive Trading Agreements, had indicated that Jute Control should immediately inform the trade that it was no longer party to any Gentleman's Agreements on pricing and that the Registrar would 'take the line' that these agreements were registerable, although not without a hearing of the court automatically declare the agreements illegal.[72]

The response of the industry itself was also immediate. The AJSM, British Jute Trade Federal Council (BJTFC), and three of the industry's key actors William Walker, Herbert Bonar and Lewis Robertson systematically set about the defence of the agreements and the frustration of attempts to undermine co-ordination of jute prices by the Registrar's Office for Restrictive Trading Agreements.[73] While an initial attempt to suggest that, due to the existence of Jute Control, and therefore government knowledge, the agreements were covered by Crown Immunity and not registerable under the 1956 Act was abandoned, the industry drew up arguments for their defence under the gateway of protecting employment.

The Board of Trade similarly recognized that simply moving away from government controls of supplies and prices would 'blow the bottom out of the industry' and the resultant unemployment it would create meant that such a move was not a straightforward decision.[74] As a result, by early 1957 the Board of Trade set about dismantling their involvement with the jute industry. To do so, however, was not as straightforward as they might have liked. Jute Control selling activities to the restricted list of quota-holders was at fixed, or 'equated', prices in line with those determined by Dundee's manufacturers. Prices were determined at six monthly intervals following investigations into the costs and profitability of the industry undertaken jointly by the industry's and the Board of Trade's accountants. Prices were then publicized throughout the trade via the Brown Books stipulating prices for each quantity, grade and finish throughout the industry'.[75] Jute Control's first problem then was how could it determine prices in the absence of co-ordination with Dundee's producers?

In July 1957, seven months after the enactment of the 1956 Restrictive Trade Practices Act, and on the recommendation of the Office of the Registrar for Restrictive Practices, Jute Control notified the industry that its prices would no longer be 'equated' with those of Dundee's manufacturers. From July 1957 until 1961, when the Board of Trade submitted written evidence to the Restrictive Trade Practices Court, the Board of Trade maintained that any similarities between Jute Control's prices and those of the Brown Book were a matter of coincidence rather than design and were a result of the trade itself choosing not to 'adjust their prices... in any way they wish'.[76]

The Board of Trade's Jute Control use of a fixed mark-up on imports as its mechanism for price setting provided the appearance of a movement towards de-control and a fixed tariff and thus a de-coupling of Jute Control from the Gentleman's Agreements. From July 1957, however, Jute Control could neither claim to be either free from price fixing nor removing import restrictions and introducing a tariff. For while a 'tariff' like mark-up was applied, the mark-up at 30 per cent, later reduced to 20 per cent in January 1960, was itself set on the same basis as the previously agreed 'equated' prices; based upon the negotiated costs and profit margins determined by the Board of Trade accountants in conjunction with the industry's own appointed accountants. Thus the marking up of prices replaced equating of prices rather than removing of price fixing per se. And the mechanism for determining the mark-up remained the same as had previously been used in fixing equated prices. Similarly, centralized state buying continued rather then the decentralized private importation of inputs affecting other industries.[77]

The trade itself recognized and accepted the decision to introduce a mark-up as an alternative mechanism for pricing, especially after the mark-up of 30 per cent was agreed following their 'vigorous pressure', as it permitted the industry to retain the ability to impose minimum prices.[78]

On the part of the industry the defence of the agreements was in two parts, first to frustrate the potential investigation and second to formulate a defence of the practices in terms of the gateway for protecting employment. As Robertson noted the discussions of the 'Three Wise Men';

> 'Mr Bonar has put one [fundamental argument] forward once or twice and it would be helpful to set it down on paper ... and let it be known to the Registrar or to the Board of Trade that we had such a thing up our sleeves so as to discourage them from pushing us up the queue for examination. ... The fact that the Registrar and the Board of Trade are quite aware how much of a nuisance we should be if we were examined is attributable to the preliminary memorandum which was sent to both of them'.[79]

However, once Jute Control had seemingly de-coupled their prices from the Gentleman's Agreements, frustrating the Restrictive Trade Practices Court was no longer a viable option. Indeed on 10 November 1959 the Board of Trade notifed the Registrar's Office for the Restrictive Trade Practices Court that the Board of Trade no longer had any opposition to bringing a case against the jute industry.[80] Subsequently, the Registrar for the Restrictive Trading Agreements issued notice of its proceedings and requested information on the jute industry's agreements from the Board of Trade and the industry in September 1960, and again in April 1962, before announcing its decision to set the Court hearing for January 1963.

The AJSM collectively produced on behalf of the jute industry a Precognition Statement to the Court, authored by Lewis Robertson in November 1962, in defence of the agreements. The industry's case relied on the support from government for the Gentleman's Agreements as a means to protect the industry as a strategic industry using Sections 21(1) (b) and (e) of the Restrictive Trade Practices Act permitting price fixing on the basis of the protecting consumers and protecting employment.

The precognition statement maintained that government's accounting processes sought to 'safeguard the United Kingdom jute manufacturing industry under conditions conducive to efficiency', and that the equated prices were maximum rather than minimum prices. So 'If firms over-charged for jute goods excess profits would accrue to the firms leading the BoT [Board of Trade] to subsequently lower jute prices. Equally if firms lowered prices to gain sales lower profits would lead the BoT to raise prices in order to maintain the industry'. Thus Jute Control acted as a market mechanism itself with an automatic correction mechanism similar to the price mechanism itself.[81]

Interestingly, the industry chose to avoid a partial defence of the agreements maintaining that the agreements were all interdependent upon one another and essential to the defence of the industry. '...the Seven Registered Agreements are inter-related and interdependent in that the need which they satisfy is the achievement of a uniform delivered price in the United Kingdom for all the classes of good covered'.[82] Similarly, although protection of employment was discussed, and one of the gateways permitted by the 1956 Act, it as not the main defence presented by the industry accounting for only five of the 120 pages of the Precognition Statement.[83]

Over one week the Court heard evidence from the British Jute Trade Federation Council (BJTFC), the six constituent associations of the BJTFC and the Association of Jute Spinners and Manufacturers, the United Kingdom Jute Goods Association, the Dundee Jute and Linen Goods Merchants Association and the London Jute Association. On 26th March 1963 the Restrictive Trade Practices Court published its 100 page report and ruled that all seven agreements were against the public interest and that the industry had 'fail[ed] to overcome the presumption that the restrictions are contrary to the public interest and we therefore declare in terms of Section 20 of the Act that all are contrary to the public interest'.[84] Further the court's view was that the government's Jute Control did indeed establish its prices in co-ordination with the industry as published in the Brown Book. While the court accepted that government support for employment in Dundee was justified, it rejected the assertion that price fixing was necessary for such support.[85]

The inability of the industry to successfully utilize the employment protection gateway as a defence is of interest for two specific reasons. First, the Court had rejected the arguments of the economist Professor Campbell of St. Andrews University who had collaborated with the industry in providing economic justifications for protection.[86] In so doing they were reaffirming the theoretical economic explanations of market competition for economic efficiency and growth that the legislation was founded upon. Second and most damagingly for the industry's case, was the limited degree to which a direct link between collusion and employment could be made. In preparation for the case the ASJM co-ordinated Sub-Committee on Protection Methods, which formalized the industry's position, recognized that a direct link had been 'destroyed' by Jute Control's decision first to abandon the Brown Book prices and second by its adoption of a fixed mark-up on imported goods. As the Sub-Committee explained;

> 'The Sub-Committee noted that the fundamental argument... which has been put before the Board of Trade and the Registrar, had been much disturbed if not indeed destroyed by the change in protection method. The kernel of the old argument had been that in order to avoid severe and continuing unemployment in Dundee it was necessary that 36/40/45" 10s imported must be sold in the UK at the *same* prices as 36/40/45" 10s Dundee'. [original emphasis][87]

Now the link between employment protection and collusion had to be less explicit. Thus;

> The Sub-Committee felt that it was possible to conceive of a new argument in substitution which would be, that in order to avoid severe and continuing unemployment in Dundee it was necessary that 36/40/45" 10s imported must not be sold in the UK, more than D lower in price than 36/40/45" 10s Dundee, on the basis that D should be the difference between the proper Dundee price and the imported price which became operative on 18th July 1957'.[88]

The response of the industry to the outcome of the ruling was immediate. It adopted the approach of other industries by moving towards voluntary information sharing agreements. On the same day as the Restrictive Trade Practices Court published its report the opening of the Jute Information Bureau (JIB) was announced. Operating from the Chamber of Commerce in Dundee with George Crombie from the AJSM appointed as Secretary, the JIB was to provide a 'channel for the exchange of information ... between producers and between merchants upon the prices and the terms and conditions of sale which they, as individuals are operating'.[89]

The 1963 Restrictive Practices Court case was to open up the extent of the jute industry's co-operative arrangements. For co-operative strategies to emerge individual firms are required to sacrifice their individual interests to those of the collective sector. The court case highlighted that the co-operative strategy adopted by the jute industry was one which Olson would recognize as an encompassing coalition in which not only did individual firms sacrifice their individual interests for collective interests but different sectors of the trade sacrificed their specific sectors interest to those of the whole trade.[90]

The jute industry's ability to maintain co-operative strategies did not however end with the Restrictive Trade Practices Court case. While information sharing and informal price matching provided an alternative to formal price fixing for the firms involved, government did not simply allow market forces to 'blow the bottom out of the industry'.[91]

By July 1963 the Cabinet was again discussing alternative proposals for protecting the industry submitted by Mr. Ord Johnstone, the civil servant and Registrar who had brought the case against the Jute industry. The Board of Trade proposed a system of tariff protection declining over a period and the eventual disappearance of state trading.[92] Crucially, Ord Johnstone argued that government delay would hinder change. He argued that 'The industry have ... been brought to the brink of change. It will be very much harder, if indeed possible at all, to start again at some future time if we retreat now'.[93]

On 13 August 1963 the government accepted industry proposals for the establishment of a new Working Group on the jute industry. From the outset the Board of Trade viewed the Working Group's role as shifting the industry to accepting a fixed mark up as a mechanism for controlling imported goods and challenging final objections from the industry. The chair of this new Working Group was to be the civil servant in the Registrar for Restrictive Trading Agreements Office who had brought the case against jute, Mr. Ord Johnstone. The Board of Trade also sought, unsuccessfully, to avoid the Scottish Office membership of the Working Group, as it was seen to be too close to the industry, and still further wished the enquiry to 'be dressed up to appear as nearly impartial as possible'.[94] Explicitly, the government made clear that its proposals for a fixed tariff on imported jute would only be postponed for one year to permit the enquiry to examine alternative proposals. Importantly, if the enquiry failed to come up with alternative proposals 'the Government's intention to introduce a fixed mark-up would be implemented'.[95] The Working Group met between November 1963 and August 1964 and produced a final report rejecting industry proposals for a permanent variable mark-up on jute imports but accepted an interim variable element of mark-up in addition to a fixed component of mark-up on imports. This variable element would be tapered protection 'to ease the transition from the present system' and reduced until 1967 when it would be further reassessed.[96]

The degree to which the Board of Trade considered the outcome of the Working Group report to be a success can be gauged by the discussions of their response to its publication. The chair of the Working Group, Ord-Johnstone, urged the Secretary of State 'to implement [the] new arrangements based on the alternative which has emerged, as soon after the Minister's have had the Report as we decently can. There must, of course, be a period of, say, at least two weeks before any announcement to give the impression that the report had had proper consideration.'[97]

While the Board of Trade had finally achieved its desire to move away from price controls and the implementation of an external fixed tariff, it did not succeed in fully removing itself from direct participation in the industry. Government decided, even after the Working Party, to retain Jute Control and the system of quota controls for importing firms. Jute Control, itself had not been declared against the public interest by the Restrictive Trade Practices Court in its 1963 ruling. The government's continued concerns over unemployment in Dundee weighed heavily on decision makers. Writing in 1969 the Board of Trade would write 'It is recognized that the new arrangements do not go so far in liberalizing imports of certain types of jute goods as some interests would have liked, but as the Minister of State's announcement in the House of Commons last November made clear, they go as far in liberalizing as is compatible with the need to maintain employment in Dundee and the nearby towns'.[98] It was not until the end of the 1969 when government abandoned price based mark-up restrictions in favour of quantity based import restrictions, following discussions over entry into the Common Market and the outcome of debates over protection for the much more economically significant cotton industry, that Jute Control was finally abandoned. The consequence of which is examined in the next chapter.

Between 1968 and 1971 the number of establishments fell from seventy-four to forty-six.[99] These changes correspond with the conclusions of Howe, who suggests that the decline in the industry set in during the mid-1960s and accelerated in the early 1970s.[100] Thus it was not until the end of the 1960s that market forces finally began to make their impact fully felt on the jute industry and it was then that the feared contraction of the industry did indeed develop, some two decades after the feared collapse highlighted by the original Working Party *Report* of 1948.

Co-operation undoubtedly played an important role in protecting the industry over this period. Co-operation within the jute industry benefited from the close proximity of the overwhelming majority of the industry within the city of Dundee, through the development over time of interdependence, and interpersonal relationships underpinned by a shared interest in the industry's economic prosperity. Crucially, these close relationships acted to limit the extent to which individual self-interest of specific employers could emerge so restricting free-riding undermining pricing agreements.

The success and longevity of co-ordination over two decades provided justification for employers to abandon narrow self-interest for collective prosperity. This success was itself a product of both efforts put into managing the industry by the jute employers' organizations, notably the Association of Jute Spinners & Manufacturers but also the existence of a small number of dominant producers in Jute industries and Low & Bonar. Both Jute Industries and Low & Bonar could enforce collective agreements through the recognition of its monopoly power as dominant firms in each sector of the trade.

The jute industry contained a range of differing interests, many but not all, linked to the specific activity of the individual firms. However, it would be far too crude to simply read from the specific economic interests of the particular sectors of the trade to their viewpoints on the management of the trade. Of course manufacturers favoured tariff protection while merchants and jute goods distributing sectors of the trade favoured freer trade, due to their ability to deliver lower cost products into the market. Yet all sectors had firms which combined manufacturing interests with distribution and sales. These firms were able to benefit from either or both proposals that emerged from specific sectors.

Similarly, all players with interests in the industry recognized a level of mutuality that encouraged the minimization of conflict and the maximization of co-operation across differing sectors. Wholesale goods and jute goods distributors wished to see their trade continue and therefore the primacy of their sector specific interests had to be reconciled with those of the manufacturers and producers of weaving and spinning firms.

It is in the development of a level of mutuality that the success of the jute industry's employers' co-ordination needs to be understood. The development of this mutuality contained a series of elements. Employers' recruitment policies created a managerial elite imbued with a culture of co-operation, while institutionally the industry developed an extensive layer of trade associations which were capable of codifying specific sectoral interests. Once codified at the sectoral level these could be collectively considered at an industry level by an overarching institutional set of organizations in the form of the Association of Jute Spinners and Manufacturers and the British Jute Trade Federation Council. These bodies were capable of relating to government bodies at the Scottish Office or Board of Trade level and importantly call upon wider support from non-jute bodies such as Dundee Chamber of Commerce and Dundee City Council when necessary. These institutional forms proved highly successful at defending the industry's interests throughout the period from the end of the interwar years through to the ending of co-operation by the end of the 1960s.

5 FIRMS' RESPONSES TO THE DECLINE OF THE INDUSTRY

As previously demonstrated, the decline of the Dundee jute industry had emerged by the first decades of the twentieth century. Only the introduction of Jute Control in 1939 succeeded in providing the industry with any measure of protection from international competition. At the end of the Second World War these competitive pressures re-emerged, resulting in the continuation of pre-war and wartime protection for the jute industry. Aided by the continuation of this protection, the post-war decades, until the 1970s, can be understood as ones of relative prosperity for the industry. Under Jute Control the industry underwent significant specialization into protected, higher-quality product markets. This was associated with changes in production processes in the form of increasing capital intensity, and an associated move away from a concentration on female labour. The main argument in this book is therefore that this decline was in many ways successfully managed in the period from the end of the Second World War until the final ending of Jute Control. The diminution of the industry thus took place simultaneously within the wider crisis in British manufacturing of that decade and, especially, the subsequent recession of 1980–1. In Scotland, and Dundee specifically, this was also reflected in the closure of newer manufacturing industry associated with the growth of foreign direct investment in the earlier decades.[1]

The response of the industry's firms to these pressures was multi-faceted. While production in the jute industry had been concentrated during the Second World War into sandbags and other 'vital products' for the war effort and returned to the 'same basic pattern of trading' in the immediate post-war years, it was clear that the jute bag was being replaced 'as the carrier of the world's goods'.[2] The jute bag became increasingly substituted by multi-wall paper, polythene and woven polypropylene sacks and eventually bulk handling and storage developed, resulting in a dramatic downturn in trade.[3] Many firms had continued to exist as small or medium sized family businesses, but faced with an inability to access significant capital or managerial and technical expertise, they either specialized into niche areas or sold out to the larger established firms. Among the manufacturing firms involved in the industry two dominant strategies can be highlighted. First, as described in Chapters 3 and 4, the firms engaged in investment strategies which sat alongside the negotiation and development of protection within the industry; specialization and changing production processes, being a common outcome of this strategy. This led to a concentration on markets where, initially at least, little international competition existed such as providing a wider product to act as a backing for the growing carpet industry. This specialization was already apparent by the early 1960s with, as Table 5.1 indicates, a movement of firms out of areas where international competition through imports occurred. Jute bags and sacking had been abandoned by the jute manufacturers as exports from Indian and Pakistan dominated world markets. For different reasons woven cloth was also an area in which little market competition existed, however this time it was due to the fact that the cloth produced was largely used in the further production of other goods within the vertically integrated industry. Thus as Chapter 4 demonstrated, by the mid-1960s, when price competition was developing, the industry was already largely specialized. A second common strategy adopted was for firms to engage in a variety of investment diversification strategies which permitted their transformation from jute manufacturers into, initially, manufacturers of artificial and other fibres and subsequently into more unrelated diversification, transforming themselves out of the jute industry entirely.

This chapter will explore these specialization and diversification strategies through an examination of Jute Industries and Low & Bonar. The experience of both of these companies can be utilized as examples of the development of responses to changes in competitive pressures within the British, and, most importantly, international market for jute goods. Strategies included altering and adapting the technologies used in order to specialize and improve the quality of jute goods produced, which in turn enabled each company to develop new markets and end users. In addition, each company diversified into the production of non-jute textiles, mainly but not exclusively polypropylene tapes and cloth. Finally, both companies, to varying extents, embarked upon a programme of investment in apparently entirely unrelated industries, taking advantage of the British government and Scottish Office's conscious development of Scotland's tertiary service economy as well as the focus on 'light industry' in the post-war years.

Table 5.1: Comparisons of imports with Dundee output in 1963.

Category	percentage of Jute Control's sales	percentage of Dundee cloth production
Heavy bags sacking, woolpacks	15	–
Hessian cloth	60	5
'Equated goods'	25	40
'Excluded goods'	–	55

Source: S. McDowall and P. Draper, *Trade Adjustment and the British Jute Industry: a Case Study*, (Glasgow: Traser of Allardyce Institute, 1978) p. 7, derived from *Board of Trade Journal*, 16 August 1963.

This chapter focuses upon on the period from the 1964 Working Group *Report*, in the aftermath of the Restrictive Trade Practices Court case to the 1980s. The chapter demonstrates how the firms engaged primarily, but not exclusively, in related diversification until the mid-1970s, and from then onwards unrelated diversification became increasingly important for their continued survival.

Post-War Diversification – 'The Name of the Game'

The threat of price competition within the jute industry, starting first with Jute Control's decision to abandon price setting in favour of a fixed mark-up on import prices in July 1957 and reaching its high point in January 1963 with the Restrictive Trade Practices Court case, was to provide a strong impulse to rationalization. Together these events may be considered to have acted as a catalyst to a process of rationalization within the industry. Between 1958 and 1963 the number of firms fell from sixty-four to forty-four, while the number of factories fell from eighty-nine to seventy-six.[4] While rationalization of production took place it was not the case that the industry was contracting. With the exception of production of jute yarn, *Census of Production* data indicates that other areas production were static or even rising. Hessian twill used in the carpet industry, linoleum quality hessian and other woven cloths together saw small increases in output from 1,331 to 1,478 cwt tons in weight between 1958 and 1963, and a large expansion, of 65 per cent in nominal values was also seen in more specialized areas of production in jute tow, pulled, dyed and carded jute products.[5]

This initial process of rationalization largely dissipated as threats of competition eased with the continuation of a form of Jute Control after 1964. Thus in the immediate aftermath of the Restrictive Trade Practices Court action until the ending of Jute Control in 1969, little further rationalization took place, so that by 1968 forty-three firms and seventy-four establishments remained in the industry. Despite this apparent stability, it was in these years that significant substitution effects can be detected within jute product markets. Thus the earlier growth of specialized jute product markets was now under threat with output of hessian twill for carpets, hessian for linoleum and other woven cloths falling 53 per cent by quantity from the 1963 levels. Smaller falls were also to be found in the most specialized areas of dyed, carded and jute tow. The impact of these pressures can be seen in the second, still more pronounced but more complex, wave of rationalization that took place between 1969 and 1972. In the initial phase of this second wave of rationalization between 1968 and 1971 the number of establishments was to fall to forty-six, just 38 per cent of the 1968 figure, yet the number of firms only reduced by two.[6] Thus firm's initial response was to close plants and concentrate production rather than merger or exit. However, as market conditions continued to deteriorate during the following twelve months the number of firms fell from forty-one to thirty-five with only a small reduction in the number of establishments from forty-six to forty-two.[7] Concentration of production gave way to amalgamation and merger, rationalization and exit from the industry. Direct comparison of official output data by quantity is not readily possible over this timeframe as the rapid changes in product mixes was underway and in addition the lack of a jute price index means price data also proves unreliable.[8] However, the major change with the development of polypropylene is nevertheless detectable in the official data. In 1968, whereas artificial fibres amounted to under 2.9 per cent of output by value, in 1972 output of polypropylene alone accounted for over 27 per cent of gross output by value and was the single largest commodity output of the industry, by quantity, accounting for almost as much as total yarn and cloth of all types combined.[9]

The rationalization that took place over these years appears to have been greatest for the medium sized firms. Thus, while the modal size of jute firm throughout the period remained small, with under 200 employees, the proportion of firms with less than 200 employees increased in the period from 1958 to 1971 from 47 per cent to 67 per cent.[10] At the other end of the spectrum only three firms existed with over 750 employees throughout the period. The two largest companies Jute Industries (later Sidlaw Industries PLC) and Low and Bonar could operate as two oligopolists due to their comparative size relative to the larger number of smaller companies operating in jute in the city, in terms of the physical size of their works and factories, the numbers employed, the production levels and profitability. Both companies had emerged as dominant firms in an earlier era of rationalization in the interwar years, as described in Chapter 1.[11]

Jute Industries and Low & Bonar may be taken as representative of the jute industry more broadly given the scope of their activities and the range of responses to changing markets in the post war years, which will become apparent in the following discussion. Admittedly it is problematic to omit the experiences of smaller jute concerns operating in Dundee in the post war years. However Jute Industries and Low & Bonar's response through rationalization and diversification, while perhaps not typical, is arguably most significant in the context of the management of decline. Low and Bonar Ltd, formed on 12 August 1912 out of the merger of the two constituent firms converted to a public company on 5 September 1947.[12] By 1950 its Dundee factories were had been supplemented by eight merchanting and distribution companies in South Africa and Canada servicing the African and North American markets in jute, flax and cotton goods.[13] Jute Industries Ltd, formed on 15 October 1920 as a holding company continued as a holding company throughout the interwar and early post-war era and it was not until the first wave of rationalization in 1966 that Jute Industries sought to centralize the production through a reorganization of production and creation of a single, and distinct, manufacturing division.[14]

By the mid-1960s competition within product markets was forcing a reassessment by the established jute firms. Although bags was a market largely abandoned by domestic producers in the early post-war era, the substitution effects for low cost bag producers was itself propelling international producers into more specialist markets. Thus competition from Indian, and by this time Pakistani, producers within jute was now moving into areas in which Dundee's specialist producers had retained some degree of monopoly power. Dundee's jute manufacturers were, as the *Census* data suggests, to find by the late 1960s that the threat in specialized product markets for carpet and linoleum backing was not only emerging in international markets by low cost producers but also substitution effects from cheaper alternative often domestically produced artificial fibres. Jute Industries and Low & Bonar anticipated such developments and began, in co-operation with the newly formed British Jute Trade Research Association (BJTRA), to improve and diversify its products in an attempt not only to increase sales but to retain markets. The firms' responses to both international competition in jute markets and domestic competition deriving from substitution effects can be understood as the beginning of each company's response in managing the inevitable decline of the market for jute products.

Specialized Jute Markets

The development of tufted carpet manufacture in the United States in the early 1950s was viewed as 'the biggest and most important development' within the industry.[15] The formation of the BJTRA, directed by the textile researcher H. Corteen after 1946, facilitated the search for new applications for jute textiles.[16] Research into developing improved fire retardant and water-proof properties were just two of the areas of research. One outcome of the application of this research was the recognition that jute cloth 'proved to be the ideal carrier base for tufted carpet'. As a result a new market was opened up to Jute Industries through its subsidiary, Jute Industries New York Ltd, which sold jute cloth into the American carpet industry market. Tufted carpet was more economical to produce than the woven equivalent due to the production processes involved. As a result it was cheaper for the consumer and became increasingly popular first in North American and increasingly in the British market as increased consumer disposable income ensured as Bartlett notes more people found themselves in the 'carpet-owning class'.[17] Jute Industries were able to exploit the expanding British and worldwide market for tufted carpet. In the UK Jute Industries supplied the standard backing in branded Axminster and Wilton carpets. However as tufted carpet replaced linoleum in British homes, the jute industry's gain in the carpet field was offset by the substitution effect of the reduction in consumption of linoleum manufacturers whose sales suffered.[18] Yet in spite of this in 1972 the management of Jute Industries argued that 'the floorcoverings industry rapidly became jute's major customer', largely as a result of the fact that in addition jute was also used as a base fibre in ancillary products such as underfelts and underlays.

Product market competition, again derived from Indian and Pakistani producers movement into more specialized, higher-quality products, ensured that Dundee jute companies first mover advantages were not maintained in carpet backing in world markets. Dundee's dominance in supplying the US market was, as with bags, challenged by Indian and Pakistani mills via price competition. The Indian academic Amiya Kumar Bagchi has demonstrated that indigenous Indian and Pakistani firms were more than capable of developing not simply lower manufacturing overheads based upon low cost labour but also manufacturing facilities with greater efficiency compared to that in Dundee.[19]

While competition in the area of manufacturing was difficult to restrict, a greater longevity in comparative advantage in the areas of wholesaling and distribution was recognized by the largest jute companies. Thus, foreign direct investment in the form of establishing branches, subsidiaries or associated companies was a strategy that was adopted by both Low & Bonar and Jute Industries. In the mid-1950s Low and Bonar stated in a promotional brochure that 'the merchanting scope of the parent company' had been extended with its 'Commonwealth interests', both manufacturing and merchanting activities, being built up through acquisitions and expansion. This included the establishment, through a subsidiary, Thomas Bonar & Company Limited, of a widespread merchanting and bag-making organization in Canada. Low & Bonar also formed 'a merchanting and making-up business in all of the main centres of both the Union of South Africa and Southern Rhodesia', with branches being established in Kenya, Uganda, Tanganyika, and other East African territories in 1950.[20] And while in manufacturing Jute Industries and Low & Bonar were unable to compete with international competitors, they retained first mover advantages in its established distribution channels. The origins of these sustainable competitive advantages often lie not in expertise in production technologies, which are readily imitable, but in the less easily codifiable and transferable relationships that emerge through relational contracting. Oliver Williamson has developed an understanding of the economic importance of transaction cost advantages, while Gordon Boyce has made a strong case for the importance of these forms of information based competitive advantages within a business history framework.[21] For example, Jute Industries, through its decision to use its US subsidiary Jute Industries New York Ltd, acted as an agent for the Far East manufacturers. It argued 'if you can't beat them, join them' and suggested that the Indian and Pakistani manufacturers whose products it sold 'benefited from J.I. know-how in the market place'.[22] It is exactly this 'know-how' that Tedlow argues was increasingly important in the development of markets and marketing in the US in this era.[23] The international and vertically integrated nature of the largest firms ensured they were capable of compensating for a loss of competitiveness in manufacturing through maximizing profitability in distribution channels. Profitability now derived from using international cost differentials, arising from within the manufacturing sector of the industry, even if these were at the expense of its own higher cost production facilities within Dundee. The levels of profitability ensured that Jute Industries was paying out a dividend averaging 18 per cent throughout the 1950s and 13 per cent in the 1960s with Low and Bonar's dividend payments averaging 20 per cent and 18 per cent respectively.[24]

Within international markets distribution channels could provide a competitive advantage for the continued dominance of the established firms as wholesalers, distributors and agents, yet within the British market no such competitive advantage existed. Here firms were not simply facing low cost international producers of jute products, but low cost domestic producers of substitute goods who themselves had access to substitute distribution channels. As demonstrated above by the *Census of Production* data, the late 1960s and early 1970s was a period of contraction for the Dundee jute industry in the face of competition from synthetic fabrics as well as imports from India and Pakistan. Despite the reality of the impact of this competition Jute Industries in its house magazine *J.I.L. News* in August 1973 attempted to claim that 'Jute is alive and well and living in Dundee', with management arguing that Jute Industries, now renamed Sidlaw Industries, had not 'relegated jute activities to a minor key'. They provided evidence to support this claim suggested that of the 5,000 people employed by Sidlaw, 2,000 worked in the 'jute end of the business'. The management also argued that 'capital investment hasn't exactly dried up either', with £100,000 being spent on Sulzer weaving machines to the cloth production facility at Camperdown works, Dundee.[25] Within three years, however, a much more pessimistic tone was evident, in 1976 Sidlaw estimated that the industry was 'well under half the size it was in 1966'.[26] The industry, it was recognized, had 'seen little recent investment' which had resulted in the closure of many mills in factories and a considerable reduction in employment. The company maintained that 'new agreements with India and Bangladesh' allowing for 'further substantial import liberalization' over the following four years were 'at the expense of Dundee production'.[27] Faced with further contraction Jute Industries, in recognition of its movement away from jute products, looked to a greater focus upon niche markets, specifically wallcoverings and decorative textiles. A reorganization plan involved 'reducing involvement in certain markets and rationalizing production units'.[28] It was envisaged that by doing so Jute Industries (Sidlaw) would be able to maintain its 'position in selected, more secure, traditional markets'. In considering its workers it suggested that 'job security must be offered rather than the prospect of a gradual erosion of employment'. However arguably Sidlaw was more concerned about gaining a 'strong profitable base' which it deemed 'essential to future to success', which was dependent on ensuring that 'customers must have better quality at prices reflecting improved efficiency in production processes and use of space'.[29]

Sidlaw's plan in 1976, which involved 'painful decisions' relating to rationalization, included withdrawing from 'markets of little or no return' in order to release capital for 'profitable investment' such as its focus on specialist wall-coverings for the U.S. market and related decorative fabrics. It also proposed concentrating its operations geographically to cut maintenance and transport costs, which would also bring revenue from the sale of buildings. Accompanying this would be the reduction of administrative and service resources. The result of this plan was the closure of several production units and the loss of a substantial number of jobs over the following fifteen month period. Major changes included the closure of its Caldrum West and Douglasfield works in late 1977 and the establishment of two new jute mills in Camperdown 'C' Range and high mill in order to concentrate production.[30] While Sidlaw's Den Burn works in Brechin were closed in early 1978, this resulted in weaving at Camperdown being modernized. It was planned to spend an estimated £2 million 'in a major modernization of weaving and improvements in spinning efficiency'.[31] The administration of Sidlaw Textiles was also moved from head office to Camperdown. Camperdown became the centre of Sidlaw's production of jute and flax based decorative fabrics and wallcoverings. When these plans were unveiled in 1976 it was estimated that 'taking into account the increased employment at Camperdown', 620 jobs would be lost in Dundee and 200 in Brechin, 650 were due to closures and 170 as a result of modernization of weaving.[32] Capital expenditure on weaving and spinning equipment became a feature of future rationalization programmes, with capital intensification replacing workers.

Further justification was provided by the recognition that the alternative to this rationalization programme 'to do nothing' would mean that Sidlaw's activity would 'steadily deteriorate and offer much poorer employment prospects'.[33] Thus, the rationalization programme was viewed by management as a last ditch effort to retain profitability 'the effective use of financial resources' as well as the 'long term prospect of secure employment'.[34] While the relevant trade unions were consulted, it is clear that Sidlaw completed its programme as envisaged. Notably Sidlaw applied for financial assistance with its modernization scheme under the Industry Act 1972 and discussions were held with the Scottish Economic Planning Department.[35]

The outcome of the 1976 rationalization saw Sidlaw Industries focus 'considerable effort at investigating new potential markets' for a narrow range of jute products. Sidlaw decided that 'major growth opportunities exist in decorative markets, particularly overseas, for a large integrated company such as Sidlaw'.[36] It was argued that expansion into these markets would 'offer an opportunity to offset the continued decline of certain traditional industrial markets'.[37] Following the establishment of 'an initial position in these markets', particularly in Europe, loom capacity was allocated for the production of fabrics for such specialist markets as wallcoverings and a subsidiary, 'Sidlaw of Scotland Inc' was set up in Atlanta, Georgia, to market and sell the finished decorative products in the U.S.[38] This was accompanied by a 'major programme of investment and rationalization' with the aim of 'establishing Sidlaw Textiles as the leading European producer of jute and flax-based decorative products'. The investment of £2 million spent on modernization of weaving and on improvements to spinning quality, as well as further 'substantial sums of working capital to finance its move forward into decorative and finished products'. In spite of the level of investment and the accompanying programme of rationalization Sidlaw of Scotland Inc proved to be unsuccessful, making particularly 'slow progress' in the early years.[39] The declining floorcovering industry remained the main consumer of jute and jute producers were increasingly reliant upon the market conditions facing carpet manufacturers in the British and overseas markets.

Low & Bonar was also rationalizing production in the late 1970s by making closures. As a result of 'the continuing decline in demand for textile bags' the company decided to close East Port Works in Dundee in September 1977.[40] Consultations were held with the relevant trade unions, and sixty female and thirty-two male employees were made redundant, despite the company's claimed 'strenuous efforts' made to 'find suitable alternative work within Low & Bonar's other operations'. Three months later the company also decided to close its Upper Dens Dundee works in March 1978, which specialized in large scale weaving of a heavier canvas products and flax mail bag cloth. This was attributed to the 'severe and continuing decline in the worldwide demand for heavy duty woven flax' and in particular the Post Office's decision to switch from its traditional flax mail bag to a polypropylene version.[41] A total of 180 employees were made redundant. The following year the Lower Dens mill, which produced flax yarn, was also closed with approximately 143 employees being made redundant.[42] These closures were also, as in the case of Sidlaw's, accompanied by investments in narrower, niche production of wallcoverings and decorative fabrics. So in 1977 Low & Bonar acquired Craiks Limited, a Forfar weaving company, this being the 'first stage of a textile development programme which will enable the Group to extend its activities into the domestic market'.[43] Low & Bonar also acquired Wemyss Textiles Limited, which produced a range of woven furnishing fabrics, a month later. The Chief Executive, Brian Gilbert, commented that this was 'a further step in the expansion and diversification' of the Low & Bonar's textile interests. Like Sidlaw, Low & Bonar were 'convinced that the market for woven furnishing fabrics and wallcoverings, both at home and overseas, was a growth area affording the opportunity for earning very acceptable profits'. Gilbert stated that Low

& Bonar was 'entering this market strongly and intend to employ considerable resources towards its exploitation'.[44] Thus, while Sidlaw established its own subsidiary, Low & Bonar entered the market for specialist, high-end domestic fabrics through acquisition and investment. Again, unlike Jute Industries' holding company approach prior to the 1970s, in this case acquisition was accompanied by investment and rationalization. Production was 'switched into the new areas of wallcoverings and furnishing fabrics' accompanied by 'a major re-equipment programme' which had the objective of 'improving efficiency and extending the product range'.[45] It would seem that Low & Bonar's move into decorative fabrics was more successful in the short term, perhaps as a result of the fact that it had acquired its interests in this area rather than establishing its own subsidiary, consequently there may have been less risk involved. However, despite the differences in approach to the new market segments the optimism for both companies was short-lived as performance failed to live up to expectations.

By the early 1980s both Sidlaw Industries and Low & Bonar began a sustained period of retrenchment and exit from the industry. Employment in the industry had fallen by a further 2,000 workers between 1973 and 1977 to 8,100 and was to fall to just 4,100 by 1982.[46] And, by 1982 the re-categorization of jute with polypropylene in the *Census of Production* signified the failing fortunes of the industry. This demise can be seen by the long and depressing history of closures instigated by out two companies.

In 1978 it became clear that Sidlaw's rationalization programme and accompanying investment in the production of decorative wallcoverings was not as profitable as had been envisaged. Arguing that 'what we now need is increased productivity to allow us to be competitive in the market place', Michael Walker, Group Chief Executive, stated that even although Sidlaw of Scotland represented 'only a small part of our total fabric production, the Textiles strategy of going forward in the market hinges to a large extent on the success of Sidlaw of Scotland'. Sales progress had been 'a lot slower than we had hoped for'.[47] Walker argued that this was exacerbated by the fact that textiles 'were changing into a market-orientated business' where 'the consumer is the undisputed boss', and that the traditional industrial textiles products, particularly yarns for the carpet trade, while important, were 'not enough on which to build a natural fibre based business for the future'.[48]

In December 1979 it was announced that Sidlaw Textiles had not made the 'anticipated recovery in trading performance'. While jute spinning had been busy for most of the year, export margins were tight. As a result jute spinning activity was reduced due to 'the contraction of both home and export markets'.[49] Spinning ceased in Camperdown High Mill in March 1980 and 215 weekly paid employees were made redundant, with employment in management and related staff also falling. Sidlaw in justifying its decision stated that 'certain fabric markets have become uneconomic and in others demand is low'.[50] The forecast became increasingly bleak with further concentration of spinning activity at Gill South Mills in 1980 as a result of further decline in demand for synthetic pile yarns for the tufted carpet industry.[51] This was accompanied by a lower demand for jute backing yarns from the woven carpet trade, with imports of tufted carpet and yarns from the USA exacerbating the situation.[52] Discussions of closures in Dundee commenced. In addition it was felt that capacity in the fabric section should also be reduced and cost savings efforts be effected. The combined economies involved resulted in approximately 700 redundancies or nearly 30 per cent of those employed in the Textiles Division in September 1979.[53] This dramatic decline in the numbers employed continued as it was expected that the 'Textiles Division will incur further losses as rationalization decisions are implemented'.

This prediction was realized. In October 1980 a further 113 redundancies (forty-one women and seventy-two men) were made. Employees at Lawside and Hawslaw works were issued with a memo which outlined 'the problems facing the Company'. These included the facts that 'demand for our products has fallen dramatically, and as always in such a situation, the price level at which we can obtain business has fallen below cost'. Consequently Sidlaw suggested that 'over the last twelve months we have made considerable losses'.[54] Thus in planning for the future and taking into account 'the fact that, in our view, the full depth of the recession has not yet been reached' the Board 'regrettably' came to the conclusion that it could only support one spinning location. It was decided that Lawside Works should be retained and Hawslaw closed. In addition, the dyehouse night shift was also be closed, and the female administrative staff of Lawside Works reduced by four. The memo stated that 'All of us are very aware that this is a frightful blow' with workers being assured that 'the Board could not let the present and projected position continue'. The workers were asked for their full co-operation and were assured that 'we will do all we can to deal with the problems as sympathetically as possible'.[55]

Less than three months later in January 1981 it was decided that all weaving and related spinning activities at Camperdown Works be closed due to the fact that markets for these products in the US and European markets had 'not developed as predicted'. The company reorganized its textile business into a single subsidiary company within four manufacturing locations. Even though it was argued that 'significant progress' had been made, sales and margins had 'fallen far short of forecasts'.[56] As a result of an assessment of relevant market and economic factors it was felt that there was 'no realistic prospect for this business'. It was estimated at the time that 340 jobs would be lost.[57] Sidlaw's remaining jute spinning mills at Manhattan Works, Dundee and Selbie Works and Gourdon, formed the basis of the newly structured 'Sidlaw Yarns', while 'Sidlaw Textiles' continued for the meantime to develop its 'fabric merchanting business'.[58] In recognition of the declining importance of textiles the company further changed its name to 'Sidlaw Group plc' in 1982.[59] It was argued that this reflected its role as a holding company rather than a textiles trading company. This was a deliberate move by the company to distance itself from its roots in the production of jute goods, and more recent history in textiles more generally. Yet in spite of the contraction in manufacturing production, in the interim report of May 1986 it is noted that textiles had 'a quite exceptionally strong first half in 1984–5' and had 'come through the dramatic fluctuations in raw material prices of that year and are trading at a stable and satisfactory level'.[60]

A year later it was reported that the textiles division had 'produced another steady performance' with profits of £1.8 million and in 1989 Sidlaw optimistically noted that it remained 'the world's largest producer of top-quality jute yarn for Axminster and Wilton carpet weavers in the UK and abroad'.[61] The traditional jute carpet market remained important with it being noted as late as 1990 that that jute spinning, which had 'a high export content and its quality and contract niches in the woven carpet trade'. However this was in reality the final gasp of the jute industry. The merchanting and pile yarn businesses, although remaining profitable, 'felt the effects on tufted carpet sales of the weakness in the UK economy' as the housing market fell into recession in 1990.[62] Six months later, and following 'a period of overhead reductions' accompanied by a reduction in output, the textiles division was still facing a 'tight trading environment' and a further fall in export markets especially, it was suggested, following German unification, prompting Jute Industries to begin its exit from jute manufacturing and the city of Dundee.[63]

In June 1991, it was decided that 'the cost base had to be reduced further through redundancies and changes to working practices' as a result of the continuing weaknesses in the UK economy and lower exports. There appeared to be 'no clear signs of a general recovery in the sector'. In November 1991, the outlook was as bleak, with the jute spinning business being 'particularly badly affected by the UK recession'.[64] Finally, in 1994 it was announced that Sidlaw was to sell its remaining textile division operations in Dundee, with its 560 employees. It is note worthy that the company had relocated its head office to Edinburgh only two weeks earlier.[65] The *Courier*, Dundee's leading daily paper, described this as 'the severing of the last of Sidlaw's connections with Dundee'. The Transport and General Workers' Union district secretary, Colin Coupar, expressed 'anger and disappointment' concerning the group's treatment of the textiles division in recent years. He argued that the division had 'been starved of investment' even though it had 'remained competitive and profitable in a very difficult market'. Coupar suggested that this was a 'tribute to the people in the division and shows its potential'. As was always the case the jute workers ultimately paid the price for the continuation of the firm. Coupar articulated the concerns of workers regarding the terms on conditions of employment under any new employer, with pension fund entitlements being a particular concern. In the company's statement Digby Morrow stated that Sidlaw could no longer pay enough attention to the textiles division. In addition, he suggested, the company had found 'much more substantial growth in packaging and oil and textiles has become an increasingly smaller part of the group's activities'

The case of Low and Bonar was not dissimilar. In 1980 the company was reducing its textile operations in order to 'combat the worst effects of the continuing recession in the UK textiles industry'.[66] This began with sixty-five of Craiks' employees being placed on short-term working. It was hoped that 'the severe drop in demand' for woven fabrics was a 'temporary problem related to the UK economy' and would be resolved.[67] This did not prove to be the case (see below) and the activities of Craiks Limited, Synthetic Fabrics (Scotland) Limited and Polytape were concentrated under a single organization, Low & Bonar Textiles Limited.[68] Each company reduced its output, a single weaving unit was based at Victoria Works, involving the transfer of their most modern equipment from Craiks. At the same time the work of Synthetic Fabrics and extrusion of synthetic tapes and yarns was located at Caldrum Works. A total of 130 jobs were lost.[69] A year later in 1981 Low & Bonar sold Wemyss Weavecraft Limited, though it was expected that the company would 'continue to trade as before' and 'no change in the level of employment' was expected.[70]

In assessing the strategies adopted by the dominant jute firms from the 1960s through to the 1990s it is worth disentangling different aspects of their competitive advantage. The strategies focused upon specialization in response to international competition had shown to be relatively successful in an era of rapid world economic growth, and expansion of international trade and protected home markets. These strategies continued to be based upon advantages from external economies of scale and small scale production. However, much of this success lay in the absence of competition and an early dominance over production technologies in specialized international markets. The very basis for the continued growth of Dundee's producers, a rapidly growing world economy and trade, also laid the basis for the emergence of the competitive threat Dundee producers were to face. Once international competition emerged Dundee's producers were rapidly under threat and their remaining competitive advantage derived from a continued dominance over distribution and marketing channels. Within the British market the continuation of protection restricting imports ensured their position, at least within the jute trade, and competition instead derived primarily from substitution effects. We may also conclude that when competitive pressures increasingly forced the companies to rationalize and concentrate production capacity, it did not lead to a reinvigorated competitive domestic industry and instead became the mechanism by which exit took place. As such the firms and their managers were justified in retaining a belief in the external economies of scale that had been the bedrock of the industry since its inception.

The advantages Jute Industries and Low and Bonar had retained were undermined as the world economy moved into an era of low economic growth combined with openness in global trade. Distribution channels which could utilize international cost differentials in production would only increase pressures within the vertically integrated firms for contraction at the production end, and lower world economic growth imposed greater limits to the degree of further specialization available. Under these circumstances the absolute decline of the industry seemed irreversible and certainly the companies managements' reflected and articulated an understanding of this inevitability.

In the jute industry's defence it can be said, however, that the macro economic pressures and fortunes it faced were not simply those of the jute industry. And, the jute industry fared no worse than many other British industries. As Booth notes 'almost every European economy witnessed similar developments' and the changes in British manufacturing were representative of 'a relatively intricate picture of the erosion of British economic power rather than a simple story of economic failure'. The 1980s saw deflationary policies lead to rising unemployment as governments imposed similar policies focused upon inflation rather than growth.[71] Booth goes further in making a similar point to that of much of the declinist literature by suggesting the only policy choice for government or firms themselves was to have moved out of these areas of industrial production much earlier. As Booth suggests '[In] retrospect, the pity is that the process did not begin in 1945'.[72] The implication is that the market signals were too weak to bring about change. Yet, while it may be justified to say that the major manufacturers in the jute industry were not attempting to move out of the industry in 1945, it is not the case that the companies were complacent. Manufacturers were keenly aware of the growing pressures facing the industry and actively attempting to find solutions. They clearly pursed investment strategies aimed at either specializing into higher value adding areas or moving out of jute altogether. Specialization was a dominant strategy adopted by all firms within the industry from the end of the Second World War. However, it was also a strategy available for adoption by international competitors and one Indian and Pakistani manufacturers increasingly adopted as similar competitive pressures developed threatening their profitability. The key problem facing the industry, whether in Dundee or in India and Pakistan, increasingly became the availability of substitute materials to jute. As we now show the need to develop strategies which facilitated the move into artificial and alternative fibres and, ultimately, out of jute altogether, was at the forefront of the major companies approach, perhaps not from 1945 but certainly by the 1960s.

Diversification out of Jute

According to the management of Jute Industries the United States was also responsible for providing the impetus for its diversification into man-made fibres. It was argued that as American industry was 'not keen on placing reliance on outside sources of raw materials', manufacturers of tufted carpets were keen to develop an alternative to jute, which could be produced and controlled within U.S. borders.[73] In order to combat the threat posed by this Jute Industries began research and development into the possibility of weaving polypropylene plastic tapes for use as a backing cloth in the tufted carpet industry. Low & Bonar shared this view and in 1966 the companies officially joined forces and formed two associate companies, Polytape Ltd which extruded polypropylene tapes and Synthetic Fabrics (Scotland) Ltd which produced and marketed woven polypropylene fabrics. The formation of these companies allowed both Jute Industries and Low & Bonar to retain a large share of the British market for primary tufted carpet backing as well as exports.

Diversification into non-jute fibres was not entirely a new development for Jute Industries nor Low and Bonar, or other jute manufacturers. From its formation Jute Industries had incorporated the activities of Stanley Mills, one of the oldest cotton mills in Europe, established in 1785. Stanley Mills continued to spin cotton yarns and weave cotton for machinery drives and cigarette filters until the late 1960s when its operations changed to produce synthetic fibres. Similarly, following the acquisition of Baxter Brothers & Co Ltd in 1924, Low & Bonar continued to spin, bleach, weave, finish and dye flax.[74] And by the mid-1950s Low and Bonar had established product areas with plastics for waterproofing tarpaulins and early cellulose production for film for packaging.[75]

Nevertheless, polypropylene was to become a related diversification of an entirely different magnitude. It was as Craig *et.al.*, suggest responsible for transforming Dundee's 'highly concentrated industry, based upon one product, into a part of a national textile industry'.[76] As the data from the *Census of Production* described above indicates the two companies, and other competitor jute companies, rapidly understood the significance of synthetic fibres for the textile market. Jute Industries began to introduce experimental weaving trials of extruded tapes in its newly formed 'Tape Department' within Stanley Mills from 1967, spending £143,000. Further focus upon synthetic fibres took place with the reorganization in 1971 of Jute Industries into a divisional structure with a specific General Textiles Division encompassed Sidlaw's interests in man-made fibres spinning.

Jute Industries also acquired Thomas Gill & Sons Ltd, a Yorkshire firm which produced man-made yarns for the tufted carpet industry. To keep its presence in the European and US markets Jute Industries also invested a fifty percent share in Cordova Spinners Inc, in Cordova, Alabama, which spun yarn for the tufted carpet industry and a 25 per cent share in N.V. Fibrilo of Zele, Belgium, which spins polypropylene for similar purposes. The end users of the Textile Division included carpet manufacture, carpet tile processing, dyeing and the weaving of industrial and domestic fabrics. Sidlaw Tile Services for example operated as 'one of Europe's major carpet tile commission manufacturing and printing services'. Along with Sidlaw of Scotland, management viewed Sidlaw Tile Services as prominent in its diversification programme in the early 1970s. This business developed throughout the 1970s with its original factory at Sanquar in Dumfriesshire being joined by a second in Kirkconnel. Sidlaw Industries' decision to reorganize operations into four divisions in 1971 based on distinct product groups: Jute Industries Division, General Textiles Division, International Division and Engineering Division, illustrated in Table 5.1, can be understood as a recognition that the company was now explicit in its attempt to diversify out of jute. While jute was still predominant in 1971, the management of Sidlaw Industries did not view this as a growth area. While, it was hoped that the research invested into the development of specialist end uses for jute such as textured wall coverings would succeed, the chairman, Sir John Carmichael, informed employees in Sidlaw News that 'diversification' was 'the name of the game'. While referring to the company's 'major role in jute' and their hope that it would 'make progress' he 'pointed out that things changed and that industry had to change with them.[77] Indeed by 1972 Sidlaw maintained that 'jute has not been the sole interest of the organization'.[78] In the same year it also acquired control of South Mills (Textiles) Ltd, which had flax, synthetic (mainly rayon) and jute textile interests.

In 1977 Sidlaw Tile Services also entered into an agreement with Tenneco Plastics N. V., Belgium, to manage the sales in the UK of the facilities for carpet tile coating and cutting.[79]

Polytape and Synthetic Fabrics would later also play a prominent role in the development of fibrillated yarns for Low and Bonar, which were marketed to both home and export markets. In 1977 the company launched Flotex, its synthetic carpet manufacturing subsidiary, a venture described as the company's 'new direction in textiles'. By 1979 Flotex Limited 'increased sales outlets for its carpets and successfully launched a new synthetic domestic product – Flotex 21'.[80] Flotex remained the 'one bright spot' in the textiles division in an otherwise bleak picture.[81] Therefore the late 1970s were a period of investment 'on new plant and equipment' and on the development of new products and processes'.[82] Low & Bonar were 'constantly looking for new opportunities' in areas which it had not previously operated. In spite of the fact that 'the world is a very competitive market place' this was the strategy that the company chose to adopt in the 1980s. Indeed Low & Bonar's chief executive of the textiles division suggested that some of their companies in the UK are 'still over-reliant' on the tufted carpet industry, instead what was needed was 'diversity into new prod-uct areas'.[83] By 1986 Bonar Textiles 'major activity' was the production of 'special polypropylene yarns' for the traditional woven carpet industry in the UK result-ing in a 23 per cent rise in employment to 163, which the company described as a 'step in the right direction in combating the unemployment in Dundee'.[84]

While the move into synthetic fibres seemed initially to provide a solution to the long run problems facing the jute industry it was to rapidly run into a different set of competitive pressures. The polypropylene sector of synthetic fibres was not simply emerging in an era of enormous competitive turmoil of the early 1970s, as the 'Golden Age' of economic growth gave way to a period of economic stagnation and inflation referred to as 'stagflation', but the petro-chemical industry, out of which the synthetic fibre industry derived, already had some very large dominant firms. The major oil company British Petroleum and the major chemical company ICI had since the 1920s discussed joint ventures in the areas of petrochemicals. While the BP and ICI joint venture was finally abandoned in 1947, and ICI focused upon its existing link up with the Ameri-can chemical company Du Pont, a joint venture between BP and the Distillers Co. saw the creation of the British Petro Chemicals Co. in the same year. The investment in a refinery in Grangemouth, Scotland saw the development of sup-plies of propylene, polyethylene and a range of other potential inputs into the synthetic fibre industry. Subsequently British Petro Chemicals, renamed British Hydrocarbons Chemicals in 1957, formed a series of joint ventures, all of which were with major internationalized companies, to exploit a range of significant markets for the outputs of the petrochemicals industry, with for example Forth Chemicals formed with the US firm Monsanto, Distrene Co. with the Dow Chemicals and Bakelite Xylonite Co. with Union Carbide.[85] From the opposite end of the supply chain similarly large textile manufacturers were also capable of entering into the synthetic fibres market, with the British firm Courtaulds being the dominant company in cotton and rayon before the war. These new com-petitors could emerge to threaten existing firms' first mover advantages with for example Courtaulds entry into Dundee in 1946, the establishment in Dundee in 1972 of Whittaker Textile International by the US textile multinational Whit-taker Corporation, or towards the end of our period in 1986 Shell's take over of polypropylene producer Don and Low.[86] These entrants could also use their scale to transfer, or sell, production out with Dundee. So in July 1981 Whit-taker's closed its Dundee factory while in 1995 Don and Low's polypropylene production was sold to Union Carbide.[87]

In contrast to jute, Dundee had little or no locational advantages in the pro-duction of synthetic fibres. The raw material inputs did not require expertise in the establishment of relationships with buying and shipping agents in order to provide supply chains to the myriad of small scale raw material wholesalers and producers. The capital intensity of wide loom weaving, for outputs destined for industries such as the carpet industry, reduced the necessity for a workforce with uniquely locational skill sets, yet at the same time was not of such capital intensity that it was an imitable production technology. Thus Dundee's jute manufacturers had little or no informational advantages in these new markets and neither could they develop alternative forms of physical barriers to entry. Without the ability to create low unit costs out of high fixed costs they were, as Lazonick suggests, unable to either develop oligopolistic market power or significant barriers to entry.[88]

By the mid-1970s these pressures were already being felt and Sidlaw Industries were again reassessing their focus. Following the 1976 reorganizing plan Sidlaw's chose to move away not simply from jute but also other textiles. In June 1977 Jute Industries (Sidlaw) released a statement to the Stock Exchange which outlined the sale of its interests, in Polytape Ltd, Synthetic Fabrics (Scotland) Ltd and N.V. Fibrilo S.A. to Low & Bonar.[89] Jute Industries received £915,000 in cash. While these companies had been struggling to maintain profit levels, Low & Bonar anticipated a 'better outcome' for the following year. The accompanying press release stated that 'for some time' Low & Bonar and Jute Industries (Sidlaw) had 'considered it desirable and indeed necessary for the future development of Polytape and Synthetic Fabrics that one partner should be in control of the companies'.[90] While it was suggested that both companies had 'separately been planning the development course of their respective textiles divisions' with this being 'an appropriate time to make the move now announced', it may be telling that Jute Industries (Sidlaw) intended to use the money received to 'reduce its borrowings'.[91] Mr Gilbert, Chief Executive of Low & Bonar stated that no redundancies would be made and added that the company intended to 'make substantial investments in both companies in the future and are sure that these companies will continue to be a significant force in their market areas'.[92]

The decision to sell Sidlaw's synthetic fibre interests marks a divergence in approach between Sidlaw's and Low & Bonar at this point in time. Sidlaw's was seeking to find diversification routes out of the textile industry as a result of the declining profitability, while Low & Bonar was seeking to achieve a competitive advantage within the market for synthetic textiles.[93] Further retrenchment out of textiles came in 1985 when Sidlaw Tile Services was sold and Sidlaw industries focus in textiles became almost entirely limited to merchanting and marketing as part of its International Division.[94]

In contrast, Low & Bonar continued to invest in the field of synthetic fibres. In 1980 it invested $1 million, through its Canadian subsidiary Bonar & Beamis Limited, in two low density polyethylene extruders, which had the capacity to produce three million pounds of film a year.[95] However in the same year, and as a result of the 'serious recession in the UK woven carpet industry', Low & Bonar decided to reduce the output of Polytape as demand had declined. The company was also to be rationalized with production being concentrated to one site, Caldrum Works, with the closure of Bow Bridge Works and the loss of forty jobs.[96]

If the major companies can be demonstrated to have recognized the necessity of related diversification strategies it only leaves the criticisms that perhaps they were either slow to do so or, alternatively, on too small a scale to be successful when they undertook their diversification. Both criticisms may have some validity, yet it would need to be recognized that if either alternatives had occurred it could only have increased competitive pressures on the firms involved. As noted by Howe in his quantitative study of the 1970s, 'None of the results of the tests give conclusive positive evidence [for increased profitability]'.[97] Thus the major limitation of the diversification strategies was that the diversification that took place did not lead the firms involved into less competitive markets but rather the reverse, the markets they entered were already, or rapidly became as competitive as the jute industry had become.[98] This problem not only affected related diversification but also unrelated diversification as we now demonstrate.

Diversification Outside Textiles

The major jute companies Jute Industries and Low and Bonar had began investing in unrelated industries as early as the 1950s and 1960s with acquisitions of companies involved in engineering. Jute industries subsidiaries included design as well as 'overhead handling equipment' such as specialist cranes while Low & Bonar obtained controlling interests in companies operating within the electrical power transformers and other ancillary equipment industries.[99] These forms of diversification were to be of growing significance from the 1970s as competition within jute intensified and related diversification strategies in synthetic fibres also failed to provide a sustainable competitive advantage.

In Low and Bonar's case, the recognition of the importance of unrelated diversification can be gauged from the company's public statements by the second half of the 1970s. Low and Bonar's acquisition of Bonar, Long & Company Limited enabled Low & Bonar to further diversify into overseas markets, with products being 'shipped to all parts of the world' with export trade representing nearly forty percent of the total production output.[100] Low and Bonar recognized that 'these very substantial Commonwealth interests have proved important factors in the expansion and well-being of our company'.[101] By 1977 49 per cent of Low & Bonar's profit came from its African operations, with 24.2 percent from the UK/EEC and 26.6 percent from Canada.[102]

Low and Bonar were sensitive to future growth prospects. Thus in September 1979 the company reduced its shareholding in Nigeria as a result of 'the economic situation prevailing in other parts of Africa' while shortly afterwards, in 1980, expanded their international investment via the acquisition of Stranger

& Company Limited in Melbourne, Australia, a company producing high and medium voltage electrical equipment.[103] The company stated that this would provide 'a direct base in Australia and access to the important markets of southeast Asia and the Pacific basin'.[104] A year later Low & Bonar purchased a 15 per cent holding in Electrical Equipment Limited in Sydney, creating 'a valuable trade and technological link welcomed by both organizations'.[105]

The degree to which genuine competitive advantage of these unrelated diversifications was derived from the geographically specific market based information, in turn derived from the extensive networks and distribution networks, is questionable. However, more clearly related to the companies core competences in textile production, marketing and distribution was the movement into other forms of unrelated diversification. For although Low and Bonar were moving out of woven fabrics with their diversification strategies they were not, entirely, moving out of the textile industry altogether. Instead Low and Bonar recognized that a number of applications for non-woven textiles existed. It was therefore able to develop its interests in non-woven textiles, described as 'a fast growing area', by acquiring a 51 percent share of Carolina Formed Fabrics Corporation.[106] The intention was to open a plant in Dundee which would utilize the same technologies as the plant in Carolina. Growth in this industry was estimated at ten per cent per annum in the USA and twenty per cent in the UK by the mid-1980s. This was due to the demand for such textiles and their 'increasing application and use'.[107] Low & Bonar divided non-woven textiles into two categories, disposable and durable. Disposable described products that were discarded after one use such as nappies, sanitary napkins, hospital masks and hats. Durable products included wall-coverings, blankets, handiwipes and inner linings for clothing. Thus a diversity of products could be manufactured in the field of non-woven textiles. Arguably Low & Bonar showed a great deal of insight and business acumen in exploiting this opportunity. Bonar Carelle was established in Spring 1987, and 'made good progress in developing major customers' and 'achieved consistent sales growth'.

Such investment complemented the earlier success of its polypropylene based diversification such as the Flotex floorcoverings and high specification polyethylene yarns produced by Bonar Textiles for carpeting. Another 'major opportunity' found while diversifying the company's product range was artificial grass surfaces for sports and display areas. Notably 'the grass-blade-like fibres' made in Dundee are 'now being specified by all major UK producers of sports surfaces which can be found as artificial tennis court, football and hockey pitch surfaces'.[108] In addition the company was 'starting to interest' overseas customers. These fibres could be mixed with the weaving capabilities of the company into 'carpets' to surround swimming pools, for the decks of yachts, for the entrance to hotels and as imitation grass for display purposes, exhibitions or public functions. Newlyn

Jones, new Chief Executive of the Textiles Division, described such expansion and investment as 'the image of a Textile Industry geared to the 'modern living of the 80s'. This theme of 'modern textiles for modern living' was supported by investment in research programmes with Institutes and UK universities. Essentially such investment and diversification proved to be profitable for the Textiles Division with sales increasing thirty-nine per cent and sales nearly doubling.[109]

Low & Bonar was arguably more successful in its diversification in the mid-1980s into the more closely related specialism of non-woven textiles. By the end of the century only four small manufacturers of polypropylene products remained in Dundee, employing a few hundred people. Of the major old Dundee jute firms, only Low and Bonar sustained a presence in polypropylene, but with only one of their plants in the City, the rest in Belgium, Hungary and China.[110]

The unrelated diversification strategy adopted by Sidlaw Industries in the 1980s provides an example of the way in which firms are capable of developing new core competences and moving into entirely new industries. Although, as we see below, the experience of the petro chemical industry may have provided Sidlaw Industries with sufficient managerial knowledge to recognize the importance of the industry it was to find itself moving into.

Diversified investment became a larger feature of the Jute Industries' operations from 1971 when the Board decided to change its name in favour of one that would 'not tie it so closely to one single fibre'. After consultation the Board decided upon 'Sidlaw Industries Ltd', with 'Sidlaw' being taken from the range of hills which overlook the company's Dundee headquarters.[111]

The company's operations were arranged into four divisions in 1971 based on distinct product groups: Jute Industries Division, General Textiles Division, International Division and Engineering Division. As described above, while jute was still predominant in 1971, the management of Sidlaw Industries did not view this as a growth area, however it was still hoped that the research invested into and the development of specialist end uses such as textured wall coverings would 'make progress'. Thus the chairman, Sir John Carmichael, informed employees in *Sidlaw News* that 'diversification' was 'the name of the game'. While referring to the company's 'major role in jute' he 'pointed out that things changed and that industry had to change with them.[112] The main activity of the International Division was the merchanting and marketing of both Sidlaw and other products.

Sidlaw's Engineering Division experienced the greatest level of investment and expansion and provided the background to their developments within the emergent oil industry. Sidlaw Industries' investment in North Sea Oil, marked a major departure in its investment and diversification strategy. In March 1972 Sidlaw acquired the Aberdeen Service Company, a private partnership exploiting the early opportunities in providing services for the exploration and drilling companies operating in the North Sea. At this time the management had informed its employees in *Sidlaw News* that it intended 'to get closely involved with the exciting world of North Sea Oil'.[113] This is exactly what the company did. A year later it also invested twenty percent of the equity for Seaforth Maritime Ltd, a company which built and rented workboats for the industry. In 1974 when the Scottish Secretary of State, William Ross, opened Aberdeen Service Company's Peterhead Base, it was suggested that 'there was no need to emphasize the fact that this joint government/private enterprise project was already a success' as 'the bows of moored rig supply boats towered over the VIP platform, cranes swung drill pipe and casing from quay to deck and forklift trucks scurried about like demented beetles'.[114] Sidlaw also provided twenty per cent of the equity of Grampian Developments Ltd, a company which was originally formed to develop land near Dyce Airport, Aberdeen, and whose first project was to build a hotel. The company later became Skean Dhu Ltd and built a number of hotels and office buildings in Aberdeen. Sidlaw increased its interest in Skean Dhu Ltd to 31.4 percent in 1980, with a third hotel opening in Aberdeen. Sidlaw later sold its shares in this company for £4,638,509.[115] Therefore Sidlaw's interests in the North-east of Scotland were substantial and Sidlaw, under the leadership of Sir John Carmichael, became an early investor in the development of services for the North Sea oil industry.

In the 1980s Sidlaw invested further in the North East of Scotland. In February 1980 Sidlaw acquired Supply Ship Services (UK) Ltd, a private company which supplied bonded goods to the North Sea oil industry through Aberdeen and Peterhead.[116] While Sidlaw's Textiles Division produced losses in March 1980, the profits gained by the Oil Services Division resulted in a 'policy of expansion in oil-related activities in the North-East of Scotland'.[117] It was argued that the prospects of the division would continue to improve 'as North Sea exploration and development activity revives'. In 1981 Sidlaw continued with its policy of expansion by acquiring Eastern Marine Services (& Supplies) Ltd, which operated as a general oilfield stockist and supplier to the oil industry of tools, chemicals, lubricants, ropes, pipe fittings, safety clothing, laundry equipment and galley equipment.[118] However the most significant acquisition in the long-run would prove to be Sidlaw's purchase, through its subsidiary Aberdeen Service Company Ltd, of the freehold of the quay forming the South Bay Marine Base at Peterhead for £2.4 million from the Secretary of State for Scotland in 1981.[119] As a result Sidlaw was establishing itself as a major player in North Sea Oil and related fields in the 1970s and early 1980s.

In April 1984 the Sidlaw Group acquired a fifty per cent share in Drexel Oilfield Services (HK) Ltd, a multinational group of oilfield equipment manufacturing and service companies based in Hong Kong, with subsidiaries operating in the Far East, Europe, North America and the Middle East.[120] This investment, paid in cash, was worth £4,982,854. It was felt that Drexel's activities were complementary to those of Aberdeen Service Company and would help Sidlaw to establish itself in international markets for oil servicing. Ten days later Sidlaw acquired United Sterling (Far East) Ltd. This was a small trading company based in Hong Kong which significantly had become involved in the provision of services for the emerging offshore oil industry in China, and also supplied specialist products such as industrial diamonds to the countries of the Far East. It was suggested that this investment represented 'a further consolidation of Sidlaw Group interests in economic prospects of the Pacific basin', which had already 'proved a useful link for those profit centres in the Group which have a direct interest in that area'.[121] These investments were followed in 1987 by a joint venture with SMIT International of Rotterdam, in which Sidlaw owned fifty-one per cent, to provide installation, inspection, repair and maintenance services, principally to the oil and gas industries on the UK Continental shelf.[122]

It is possible that such investments in international markets were an attempt to combat the downturn in exploration activity in the mid 1980s.[123] In December 1988 it is noted that the 'continuing recovery in the oil services sector' are reflected in that year's profits.[124] However by 1990 Sidlaw was rationalizing and concentrating its activities in the North East of Scotland, with Aberdeen Service Company (ASCo) selling its 'investment properities' in Aberdeen, which raised funds of approximately £1.85 million.[125] Simultaneously, in order to 'respond to competitive pressures' it was decided to reduce 'headcount' by twenty per cent, reduce 'take home pay' and adopt 'changes in working practices'. Fortunes in the oil industry were again to recover with a growth of activity in the Northern sector of the North Sea at the end of 1990. ASCo offered 'high quality management, workforce and facilities' and it was therefore felt that it was 'well placed to compete successfully for market share and thus benefit from this upturn in activity'.[126] This proved to be the case and in January 1991 ASCo was awarded a two year contract, worth £1.5 million, to 'assume total responsibility' and provide the onshore supply base facilities and services for the 'hook-up and commissioning works' for BP's Miller Platform in the Northern sector of the North Sea.[127] The deal involved ASCo providing BP with office accommodation and quayside facilities of berths, cartage, fuel and water as well as six acres of open storage and 40,000 square feet of covered storage at Peterhead. However, all of BP's Northern and Central North Sea supply operations were consolidated at Peterhead, to improve efficiency and save approximately £5 million a year. This resulted in BP's supply base in Dundee, which provided support for the Forties and Buchan Fields, to be progressively scaled down over the next year.[128] That a Dundee based company operating in Peterhead was responsible for the loss of jobs in its home city repeated the experience of the Dundee jute manufacturing industry when Jute Industries merchanted Indian produced carpet backing into the US market. ASCo gained another two major 'hook up contracts' for the Miller and Bruce fields in 1991. Sidlaw's management argued that this involvement in offshore construction support work compensated for a downturn in exploration drilling.[129]

In the mid-1980s, preceding the period of contraction of opportunities related to the oil industry in the North East of Scotland, Sidlaw also began to invest in another developing industry, namely electronics and computing, with a view to establishing itself in international markets. In February 1984 it acquired Gate Microsystems Ltd with a view to incorporating this company into Sidlaw's already established microcomputing service business, Unicorn.[130] It was noted in 1986 that 'microsystems continued to expand their geographical coverage' and would benefit from investment in increased resources.[131] However, Sidlaw's interest in this field was short-lived, perhaps as a result of the vast international competition in such markets.

In the late 1980s Sidlaw began to focus on developing its role in the packaging industry, which was far more successful. Sidlaw's move into packaging also involved acquiring and investing in a range of established companies, often based in England. In 1989 Sidlaw Group, now describing itself as 'the Dundee-based textiles and oil services group' agreed a merger with HPC, a plastics packaging company which operated in Brentford, Byfleet and Birmingham. HPC manufactured and sold polythene and polypropylene products such as bags, gloves and aprons for medical use.[132] Digby Morrow, the chief executive, highlighted the 'significant growth potential' in flexible packaging, which he described as an 'attractively rated sector'. He also felt that there was 'good opportunities for synergy with our existing textile business'.[133] In the same year Sidlaw also bought Derbyshire plastics packaging group Transrap for £9 million. This company designed, manufactured and printed 'high value-added' flexible packaging and it was 'one of the main manufacturers of biodegradable cellulose bags in the UK'.[134] On this occasion Morrow stated that the acquisition of Transrap was 'another major step for us towards creating a significant packaging business'. He stated that he was 'very pleased with the progress made so far' after the acquisition of HPC' and 'Transrap is another quality company with a strong management team which complements what we already have'. Morrow expected both financial and commercial benefits from the combination of the two businesses, 'with prospects for sales growth enhanced by the addition of Transrap's strong marketing and sales force and by opportunities for cross referral of business'.[135]

This was followed by the acquisition of MGS (Plastics) Ltd in January 1990 for £1,516,000. This company extruded, converted and printed polythene film into products for banks and security firms. It was stated that MGS would complement the range of existing flexible packaging products and would have the added bonus of bringing qualification to 'both BS 5750 and Ministry of Defence standards'.[136] Morrow explained that the acquisition of MGS completed 'phase one' of Sidlaw's development plan with the company 'moving quickly to rationalize' its packaging interests to 'improve operating efficiency, increase capacity and reduce overheads'. He suggested that 'in the space of a year' Sidlaw had 'established a packaging division with an annual turnover of around £20m, a good management team in place and scope for attractive organic growth'.[137]

Also in 1990, a year in which the packaging division 'near doubled in size', Sidlaw further expanded, by acquiring MCG Venus Packaging for £3.7 million in cash. Morrow suggested that this would 'further strengthen our presence in this sector'.[138] Notably, this acquisition expanded Sidlaw's packaging division by fifty per cent to more than £30m turnover. MCG Venus employed 246 people and was located in Ilkeston, Derby, close to Transrap's operations. This investment again represented a move away from Sidlaw's Dundee origins. MCG Venus extruded, printed, and converted polythene, polypropylene and co-extruded films.[139] Around £2 million was then invested in 'an intense, but fairly lengthy, period of integration and rationalisation' which saw 'immense change internally' including external appointments from the packaging sector. Sidlaw's 'broad customer base' within the packaging division included serving medical, health, pharmaceutical and food-related businesses. It was this flexibility that the management suggested was 'a major strength' in coping with the economic situation in the UK and polymer price increases.[140] In spite of this Sidlaw's management argued that 'caution' was required until there was a 'return of consumer confidence' accompanied by economic recovery. By 1990 Sidlaw described itself as 'the Scottish-based packaging, textiles and oil services group'. The order in which it placed its divisions was significant. Packaging was now the major growth sector of the business.[141]

The experiences of Jute Industries and Low and Bonar are by no means typical, most jute firms merged or exited the industry, but did represent the experience of the dominant section of the industry and are instructive because of their ability to demonstrate the range of strategies adopted in response to industrial decline. While both companies followed similar strategies in their initial phase of diversification, into a related field of synthetic fibres, once this industrial sector faced similar problems to the earlier jute industry the companies took divergent paths. Low and Bonar continued with specialization and a focus on the development of niche markets, developing woven and non-woven market sectors. In contrast, Jute Industries took advantage of the emergent North Sea oil industry to diversify out of textiles. It should be said that while this is an example of unrelated diversification, we should recognize that the company had some experience of the petrochemical industry. Interestingly, once the company moved into profitability it utilized the retained profits in order to move back into a related field to synthetic fibres it had exited, this time packaging.

The social cost of the restructuring and ultimate exit from the industry of these and other jute companies was of course borne by the thousands of low paid, and by this time predominately male, workers in the city of Dundee. As a result worklessness in Dundee in the 1980s and 90s reached levels not seen since the 1930s and whose impact was only mitigated by the availability of unemployment benefits. Nevertheless, it is no surprise therefore that labour disputes in the city, especially those such as against the closure of Timex watchmaker, reflected a polarization and bitterness that was at the heart of the industrial landscape of the city.

6 INFLUENCING GOVERNMENT

The Second World War brought a major watershed for the jute industry and for Dundee. For Britain generally the war created a new economic and social settlement, characterized above all by a state commitment to a much more active role in securing economic welfare, and especially 'high and stable' employment.[1] More narrowly, the imposition of Jute Control in 1939 gave protection to the Dundee industry for the first time. As a result of these two factors, in the decades following the war, jute's position would be negotiated with the government in a context in which protectionism was an established fact, and the removal of that protection fundamentally constrained by the political impact of any consequential unemployment in Dundee.

A New World

The new social settlement derived from the character of 'total war', and its impact in generating both full employment and a shift in the balance of political forces which underpinned commitments to a much greater role for government in securing popular economic and social well being.[2] Integral to this settlement was expanded welfare provision, especially major social security expansion based on the Beveridge social insurance model, coupled with the foundation of the NHS, and the provision of free secondary education to all. Alongside that provision was a recognition that full employment was central to popular welfare, leading to the 1944 *Employment Policy* White Paper and policies designed to fulfil its promises.[3] However, while there was a great deal of emphasis on preparations to deal with an expected general slump in demand, it was also recognized that unemployment in the 1930s, and potentially in the future, had a large local and regional component, and that policies needed to be implemented to address this problem. From such considerations came the Distribution of Industry Act of 1945.[4] This built on, but much extended, the Special Areas powers of the 1930s, allowing the state to offer substantial subsidies to encourage investment in areas deemed particularly prone to unemployment. For jute and Dundee the effects of all this were both general and specific. At a general level it meant that sensitivity to unemployment became embedded in governmental attitudes in a manner inconceivable in the 1930s. More specifically, it meant that the fate of jute would be decided within a framework that took for granted the need to attract alternative employment to the city to offset losses in that industry.

Jute Control was set up to regulate imports of both raw jute and jute products, in the context of desires to sustain supplies of a strategically important good.[5] The industry was also subject to a process of wartime concentration to minimize its call on resources used for non-strategic purposes, especially resources of labour. In the event, the industry contracted more than intended by policy-makers, and by the war's end was struggling to attract more labour-especially the women who at this time dominated its workforce.[6]

Concern about the efficiency and long-run trajectory of the jute industry led to it being subject to investigation by a government-created Working Party, part of a general pattern of much greater state scrutiny of industry characteristic of the 1940s. The *Report* of this Working Party offered a detailed examination of the industry's condition, and recommendations for its future. The central recommendation was a 'deal', whereby the industry would pursue a policy of grouping and re-organization to enhance efficiency, in exchange for the government protecting the industry from foreign competition.

On protection, the *Report* argued that there was: 'no prospect of the jute spinning and weaving industry in this country achieving stability, unless it is afforded protection in the home market when it is again subjected to the competition which existed before the war from low priced imports of jute goods from India...we have satisfied ourselves that no amount of re-organization and re-equipment on the part of the home industry will bridge the gap between costs of production in the two countries'.[7] What the Working Party wanted was an interwar style 'deal' of protection in exchange for increased efficiency. Thus they argued that there was great scope for modernization of the industry through voluntary amalgamation, rationalization and re-equipment, but:

> 'To enable the industry to develop on these lines, however, it is essential that it should be assured now that, when necessary, it will be afforded protection against low-priced Indian imports. At the same time, we are strongly of the opinion that the industry should not be granted protection unless it is prepared to carry out reorganization and re-equipment on the lines indicated'.[8]

But as the President of the Board of Trade, Harold Wilson, immediately made brutally clear, such a deal was not possible. Long-term protection could not be offered to the industry because of 'our commitment under the trade agreement with India to afford free entry of Indian jute goods into this country' and he referred to the 'possible reactions in India to an assurance now of protection in the future'. He went on: 'in any event it would be contrary to normal tariff policy to give assurance of protection at some future date under conditions which could not now be foreseen'.[9]

British government concerns about protecting jute were twofold. In the short term; 'an announcement of our intention to protect the UK jute industry might bring to a head current resentments of a more general and political nature and lead to retaliatory action'. In the longer-term the fear was of having to pay an unacceptably high price to protect jute in any negotiations, given its importance to India, a price in the form of loss of trade preferences, demands for new preferences, or increased tariffs on British goods.[10] In public this was the sole reason given for refusing the Working Party's request, though the Board of Trade also objected to protection on the grounds that it believed such a policy would reduce competitive pressure on the industry, and thereby slow the necessary reorganization.[11] Importantly, there is little evidence in the records concerning jute of any concerted pressure on the industry from post-war governments to pursue such 'rationalization', though the process of amalgamation did reduce the number of small firms substantially.[12] Thus, there was no formal 'deal' done between the industry and the government, though there is evidence of an *ad hoc* relationship between debates around protection and the industry's emphasis on its modernizing efforts.

The rejection of protection for jute needs to be put in the context of the Attlee government's general approach to trade policy. This may be characterized as 'make us good Lord, but not yet'. On the one hand, Labour committed itself to the liberal, non-discriminatory approach to post-war trade evident in the (abortive) negotiations for an International Trade Organization, and shown practically in its support for the General Agreement on Tariffs and Trade (GATT). On the other hand, the parlous state of the balance of payments, and especially the shortage of dollars, immediately after the war meant that any rapid transition to such a regime was ruled out.[13] Nevertheless, the long-term trend was clear, and under the Conservatives after 1951 both the improvement in the payments situation and ideological pre-disposition led to a clear if cautious move to freer trade, alongside an explicit rejection of long-standing Conservative support for extending Imperial Preference.[14]

Though the Attlee government rejected the Working Party *Report*, it was not suggesting an immediate reversion to free trade in jute goods. There was an acceptance that for the time being the Jute Control should continue, for strategic, but above all, employment, reasons. On the former, a Board of Trade brief spelt out the risks of becoming 'more and more dependent upon India for bags for the movement of food and other essential commodities. Supplies might be cut off either by war or by civil disturbances or economic difficulties in India'.[15] Thus Wilson had consoled the industry with the statement that 'it would not be allowed to fall to a level that would imperil the state'.[16]

Concern with the employment position of Dundee pre-dated the war's end. In the City, limited pre-war efforts to address the problem were rejuvenated and expanded from 1943, when the City Council created an Economic Development Committee.[17] Locally and nationally, wartime discussions were predicated on the unlikelihood of jute regaining its former size. A Board of Trade official in 1943 estimated that post-war long-term unemployment in the city might amount to 27 per cent.[18] After pressure from the city, such pessimism led to the early use of the 1945 Distribution of Industry Act to provide subsidies to attract new industries to the area, and in particular the provision of advance factories for rent and an industrial estate.[19] These efforts proved successful in the short run, to the extent that by 1949 the jute employers persuaded the Board of Trade to suspend attempts to attract new industry to the area, given the current shortage of labour in jute.[20]

This post-war labour shortage was short-lived, and after 1954 numbers employed in the industry slowly fell again. Concern with the unemployment consequences of the decline, which had been strong around the end of the war, abated only briefly. The story of the period from the 1950s to the 1970s was going to be one of the government reducing protection of the industry step-by-step, whilst being constantly concerned with the employment effects in Dundee and the surrounding areas.

The decisions on balancing these two concerns were made in London, albeit with sensitivity to Scottish opinion, largely articulated through the Secretary of State for Scotland, who became, in Iain Levitt's words 'more of a Minister of Employment than anything else'.[21] The Scottish archives show that there was much debate on the issues surrounding jute in Edinburgh,[22] but little evidence of London conceding a decisive voice in policy. Partly this was because the question of jute was bound up with foreign affairs. But it was also because London was insistent that Scottish economic issues should always be placed in a UK context. A contemporary example of this was the response to the 1961 Toothill Report, where London's lack of enthusiasm for some of the report's proposals derived from a belief that it was too focused on Scottish as opposed to UK wide issues.[23]

While the Working Party's proposals on protection had been rejected, there was no rapid move to change the Jute Control. Indeed, in 1951 the government gave an unofficial assurance that they would sustain an industry of 100,000 tons per annum in order to keep employment at close to its existing level.[24] The new Conservative government, with its election slogan of 'set the people free', found the complex apparatus of the Jute Control ideologically distasteful, with its flavour of Labour's *dirigiste* policies, but as the new Prime Minister was told 'We are precluded from imposing a quota by GATT. So the only way we can protect your one-time constituents is by a cumbrous control system, under which the Ministry of Materials imports jute goods and sells them at an artificial price related to the cost of manufacture in Dundee. But for this I would have abolished all jute control long ago'.[25]

The Erosion of Support

Conservative concerns led to the creation of another in the line of post-war working parties on the industry.[26] This one was chaired by the Ministry of Materials because of the drive to end the wartime control of raw materials, which by 1953 embraced jute and little else.[27] In the discussions that followed the problem was seen as reconciling the desire for de-control and belief in the efficacy of competition with the fears of unemployment in Dundee. Initially the idea of a subsidy to the industry found favour, but was eventually ruled out as impossible to reconcile with sustaining competitive pressure on the industry, and also setting an unacceptable precedent for other industries.[28] The *Economist* argued that jute was a test case of the government's free market resolve, and advocated a limited tariff to give Dundee protection only 'at the margins'.[29] But a tariff would have been in overt contradiction with the trade agreements with India, so in the short run the government contented itself with abolishing state trading in raw jute, but continued to protect Dundee by keeping the Jute Control to regulate the price of manufactured products. This decision came only after the production of official papers which made clear the political sensitivity of the unemployment issue.[30] Official sensibilities are indicted by the words of a senior civil servant who at this time wrote: 'If it were an English town, we could probably ignore the problem...But Dundee is not in England, and I frankly do not think it is practical politics to say that Dundee must have no protection'.[31]

In the medium term the government looked for a way to change this protective system, which was deemed especially objectionable because by setting the price of imports equal to Dundee prices, it gave no incentive for the home industry to increase efficiency. In fact, the Jute Control system was underpinned by price agreements in Dundee which set the base from which the Control calculated the price to be paid for Calcutta goods. One way of addressing this issue was for the Control to sell imports at a declining mark-up on Dundee prices, and this idea came to the centre of discussion in the next round of policy-makers debate on the industry's future, beginning in 1956.

This round was instigated by pressure from India, pressure which while always in the minds of officials as a possibility, had not previously manifested itself in serious form. But in 1956 a senior official from the Indian Ministry of Commerce (H. Iengar) suggested that the price charged for Indian imported goods be reduced to halfway between Dundee and Calcutta prices, with the revenue from the remaining protection being used as a 'deficiency payment' to help Dundee producers.[32] This idea was taken very seriously in London, but eventually rejected as setting an unacceptable precedent of protectionism. Instead, the government resolved to focus attention on 'squeezing' Dundee by reducing the mark-up levied by the Jute Control on imported goods – mark-up which had tended to move upwards in the mid-1950s.[33]

The 1956 and 1957 discussions made clear the diverse pressures on the government to reduce protection – from domestic users of the product, and from the Indian producers and government, counteracted by representations from the City about the employment consequences.[34] Within two years the same pressures for easier entry for imports led to warnings that further reductions in protection were on the agenda, driven by the Board of Trade's concerns about 'the loss of business to paper sacks, the export interests of large users, the European Free Trade Association (EFTA) and its problems, and the Restrictive Trade Practices Act'.[35] While the meaning of the first two of these is self-evident, it is worth noting that the later two points added further complexities to the story. The EFTA aspect was part of the broader British debate about relationships with Europe. While EFTA would involve free entry of goods from Portugal, any customs union embracing EEC members would necessitate reductions on restrictions on imports of Belgium jute goods.[36] A reduction in Britain's protectionism on European jute goods was in turn likely to strengthen the Indian government's case for cuts in the barriers to admission of Indian goods. As we have seen in Chapter 4, the Restrictive Trade Practices aspect was eventually to have a major impact on the industry. The industry's price agreements were intimately related to the protection issue, because of the way that the Jute Control based its level of protection on 'Dundee prices' which had a uniformity grounded precisely in those agreements.[37]

Further cuts in mark-up in 1960 proved only a temporary resolution.[38] By 1963 the issue was firmly back on the government's agenda, and the discussions that followed led to the broadest debate yet on the stance of government on the industry, and the dispute eventually went as far as Cabinet. Three pressures revived the debate. First, 'it would be right, particularly just before the Kennedy Round and the UN Conference, to meet the Indian's urgent request for some move towards restoring their rights n the UK market' Second, 'the current level of protection was working against the interests of merchants and users of jute as an industrial material' and third, 'that the Government should cut the link (inherent in the arrangements) with the industry's pricing system which was condemned by the Restrictive Practices Court'.[39]

In the light of such considerations, the Board of Trade proposed a reduction in the mark-up on the prices of key jute imports progressively over the next four years.[40] The Secretary of State for Scotland argued that as they stood the unemployment effects of the proposals would 'lead to major political and economic difficulties for the Government in Scotland'. He proposed much smaller changes in protection, leading to an industry more concentrated on fewer lines than currently.[41] This was the outcome agreed by the Cabinet, but with the proviso that the majority of the changes proposed would only come into operation after allowing a year for the industry to itself come up with better ideas.[42] To follow this through, another working party was set up, and this carried out the most exhaustive examination of the industry since the 1948 Report.[43]

In its initial response to the Board of Trade's proposals, the AJSM argued that the issue of substitution of paper was not related to protection, as paper's advantage was too great for head to head competition, and that in any event bags were only 20 per cent of Dundee's output. Second, the Association emphasized that Britain provided a market for only a small proportion, around 5 per cent, of the export market for Indian jute manufactures. Third, they argued that the Restrictive Practices Court decision had not been against protection *per se*, but only against the mechanism used because it was implicated in price-collusion in the industry.[44] Alongside these points, the Association defended protection both because of Pakistan's export duty on raw jute and minimum export prices and India's ban on raw jute exports, and in addition because they argued the industry was pursuing higher efficiency very seriously. In support of the latter, both the work of the British Jute Trade Research Association and the academic analysis of Carter and Williams were stressed. The picture of an industry taking advantage of the profits accruing from protection (and price-fixing) to move up-market is discussed in Chapter 4.[45]

The Board of Trade pressed for 'a normal protective duty and a reversion to private trade in Commonwealth jute goods'.[46] They saw the timing as opportune with the possible coming to the City of Pergamon and Du Pont's 'of solving once and for all the problem of Dundee's excessive dependence on an industry which stands no chance of being competitive in the long run with Asiatic Commonwealth producers'.[47] However, the Board did not get all its own way, as the reduction in protection was phased in because of Prime Ministerial worries about the forthcoming general election.[48] The timing of the reduction was defended on the basis that in relation to India and Pakistan it would be 'presentationally important vis-à-vis UNCTAD'. It was politically opportune because the industry was currently 'healthy' and struggling to get all the labour required. Unemployment in Dundee was at its lowest since 1956, and a number of new jobs were in the pipeline.[49] Another element in discussions in the early 1960s was the Tay road bridge, because this (along with the Forth Bridge) was seen as 'opening-up' Dundee's communications, and thus reducing one perceived obstacle to more rapid economic development.[50]

In the 1964 Working Party report the Dundee employers (the AJSM), while protesting about the employment consequences for Dundee of any reduction in protection, argued specifically for a continuing variable element in the mark-up on Calcutta goods to take into account fluctuations in the margin between raw jute prices and the price of the finished product. They also argued for more differentiation in the protection levels between areas where Dundee had little chance of competing (and where protection should be ended), and areas where effective competition was more realistic, and high protection should be sustained.[51]

The proposal for moving to fixed mark-ups was implemented, but still left the form of protection accorded jute anomalous, as a Board of Trade review in 1968 emphasized: 'virtually every aspect of our present regime is open to criticism: monopoly state trading, the mark-up system against Commonwealth countries, the exorbitant levels of the mark-ups levied; the quantitative restriction on EFTA goods; and the protection of yarn by selective buying by the Jute Control. Such a system should not be retained if more normal arrangements would do the same job or a better one'.[52] In 1969 the jute control was wound up, and all imports returned to private trade. In its place would be a system of quotas. Discussions in the early 1960s, at the time of proposed EEC entry, had focused on a tariff regime, but, still outside the EEC in 1968, Britain went for quotas, both because of the contractual obligations to Commonwealth members, and because of the difficulty of knowing where to pitch a tariff: 'it is difficult to identify the point at which a tariff will be protective while at the same time allowing a measure of imports to come in'.[53]

The review process leading up to this decision included an undertaking to the Indian and Pakistan governments that these quotas would be reviewed annually and would be expected to increase over time. But the commitment was hedged around with the words that increases in imports would have to be 'commensurate with the growth of the UK market for the types of jute goods in question, and does not endanger the employment position in the Dundee area'.[54] But the quota deal of 1969 had coincided with a faster than expected rise in imports, and a faster than expected fall in jute employment in Dundee. The Board of Trade view was that the problem in Dundee was not mainly due to increased imports: 'the present situation in Dundee is primarily due to the effect of the economic squeeze on jute's main outlet, the carpet industry, and greatly increased use of synthetic substitutes. By comparison the impact of imports has been minimal and quota levels are therefore much less crucial than Dundee will believe or accept'. This position led them to disclaim the commitment given by the previous government about only increasing quotas if the aggregate market was increasing; if total demand was falling this would have meant no cuts in quotas, ever.[55]

The Beginning of the End

Dundee suffered badly on the unemployment front at the turn of the decade. Employment in jute fell by 4,500 between 1967 and 1970, while at the same time there were significant job losses at National Cash Registers (NCR), one of the flagship multinational 'new industries' attracted to the City at the end of the Second World War. By September 1970 the official unemployment rate had reached 4.7 per cent.[56] In recognition of the unemployment problem, the quotas were extended unchanged in 1972 in the lead up to Britain's accession to the EEC in January 1973.[57]

After that date in 1973, other EEC countries had free access to the UK market, while quotas and any other trading arrangements with those outside had to be negotiated largely at EEC level. EEC negotiators agreed a deal with India that the common external tariff on jute goods would be cut substantially, with quantitative restrictions on cloth and yarn removed, in exchange for Voluntary Export Restraints (VERs) by India. Though negotiated at Community level, these VERs included national quotas. Similar arrangements were subsequently made with Bangladesh, the initial agreement for both countries covering the years 1976–9.[58]

The industry was hit by the first serious post-war recession in 1974–5, then saw a few years of relative stability in the late 1970s, before being hit very hard by the 'Thatcher slump' at the beginning of the 1980s.[59] Even before the latter, the question of protection for jute was back on the political agenda because of the need to negotiate a successor arrangement with India and Bangladesh, to replace the one which ended in 1979. In deciding what line Britain would take in the EEC group negotiating the new deal, the perennial concern with unemployment in Dundee was once again in play, a point made especially by the Scottish Office; by January 1980 they were stressing in correspondence with the Department of Industry that 'local unemployment is very high and the economic outlook for the area remains bleak'.[60] The AJSM had already made its case against lower quotas in the starkest possible terms: 'The level of activity has now declined to the point where any further erosion would make the remaining mills non viable and would almost certainly result in the total extinction of the industry'. By 1979, as they pointed out, employment in the industry was down to 4,650 and the unemployment rate in Dundee had reached 8 per cent.[61]

But in Whitehall, opinion was firmly against protectionism, and the only issue was how quickly to phase out the agreements with India and Bangladesh. For example, rather than seeing the slump as a reason for going slowly on changing the agreements, Cecil Parkinson argued that 'it would be disastrous if the present recession were to cause a worldwide retreat into protectionism of the kind which added so much to the difficulties of the 1930s'.[62] Support for rapid liberalization also came from the Overseas Development Administration, whose position combined 'Thatcherite' ideology with more pragmatic considerations. The first was embodied in the argument that 'While I do not underestimate the problems of unemployment in Dundee, I do not think it would be consistent with our policies in other spheres to postpone the adjustment that is needed, and is sooner or later inevitable, by continued protection at the taxpayer's or, as in this instance, the consumer's expense'. The second point was that the Thatcher government had reduced overseas aid to India and Bangladesh, and cutting jute quotas would help restore relations with those countries.[63]

There was little significant disagreement in Whitehall, apart from the Scottish Office. As in 1963, it became a matter of isolating that Office in order to prevent any effective opposition to the liberalization policy.[64] This was done, and the agreement came to an end in four years.

The 1980s and 1990s saw periodic attempts to revive the protection issue. After 1981 the AJSM was reduced to a tiny organization, but it occasionally sought to make its voice heard on the plight of the industry.[65] In late 1982 the chairman of the Association made a 'last ditch appeal to safeguard the jute industry' at a UN Food and Agricultural Association meeting. The terms of this appeal are worth quoting to indicate the inevitably rather forlorn tone such pleas had now take on:

'I still believe it is in the best interests of the future of the world jute manufacturing industry that a relatively small UK industry should be permitted to survive. There is still a small but highly-experienced reserve of advanced technical skills and expertise in the processing of natural fibre in the Dundee area and a breakthrough into new fields, such as Dundee has led in the past, is, I believe, now more than just a possibility'.[66]

Support for the industry was also voiced by Tayside Regional Council (which took over many local government functions from the City authorities in 1974). Its convenor argued in 1986 that 'if the Government does not introduce quotas on certain Dundee-based products over the next twelve months, the industry may simply disappear, resulting in the loss of a significant number of jobs'. He was supported by a local MP, Gordon Wilson, who noted that jute had already disappeared from Germany, Holland and France.[67] The *Courier* saw these activities as part of a 'life-saving concerted effort to find a rescue package for the 1,200 jobs remaining in the once-thriving jute industry in Tayside. A meeting with Ian Lang, the Scottish Industry Minister, was eventually arranged, but he refused any protection for the industry.[68] This seems to have been the last whisper of protectionist urgings.[69]

The Political Economy of Protection

This narrative of a declining industry battling to sustain protection against foreign imports can be analyzed in the framework of the 'political economy of protection' literature, as has been done by Mary Rose for cotton.[70] This literature is based on standard neo-classical assumptions, in which protection is treated as an economic good, with patterns of supply (from the government) and demand (from the industry) which can be analyzed in terms of cost and benefits for the two sides, in a world of costly and imperfect information.[71] This framework yields useful heuristic devices for thinking about the prevalence of protection, rather than hard and fast 'predictions'.

This approach suggests that protective forces are likely to be most effective where the industry is characterized by a small number of large firms who are able to effectively organize lobbying activity by presenting a unified front to government.[72] This was increasingly the character of jute. The AJSM consisted of a significant but shrinking number of mainly quite small firms, combined with a few large, dominant players.[73] This structure helped it to maintain a unified bargaining position when dealing with government. In the crucial years of the 1950s and 1960s, as indicated above, the 'three wise men' seemed able to sustain a powerful position in those dealings. On the other hand, there were significant domestic counter-lobbies from the bag manufacturers and users who, of course, lost out from protection. Because jute products were an intermediate good (cloth for bag producers or carpet-makers), rather than selling directly to consumers, these counter pressures may have been the more united and more effective.

It was employers who governments negotiated with, not unions. As shown in Chapter 3, the post-war years of decline were notable for quiescent industrial relations, with workers and unions unable to play a significant role in the bargaining over the fate of their industry. While unions and the City authorities were involved in the public debate on protection and employment in the City, the business of negotiation was largely done by the AJSM. However, despite employer dominance, the post-war political environment did mean that, unlike in the interwar period, wage reductions were never a realistic prospect as a way of responding to competitive pressures, and this in turn may have pushed the employers to focus more attention on protectionist lobbying in the absence of that cost-cutting alternative.[74]

The 'supply' of protection may be influenced in part by the electoral significance of the industry. While Rose's story is about the ineffectiveness of Lancashire's lobbying compared with the story of US cotton, the fact that cotton production in Britain was spread across a swathe of marginal Lancashire seats raised its political profile.[75] By contrast, jute was highly concentrated in Dundee with two non-marginal (Labour) seats after 1945, and even if the neighbouring seats are taken into account, the total number of constituencies involved was no more than six.[76]

In comparison with cotton, protection in jute was much more significant through most of the 'Golden Age' of the 1950s and 1960s. Cotton had no protection from Commonwealth imports between 1932 and 1958, and even after that date much less than jute had under the Jute Control of 1939–69.[77] One obvious reason for this difference was 'path-dependency'. Jute obtained protection in 1940 for strategic reasons, and this meant that where, in cotton, the industry was pressing for the *imposition* of protection, in the jute case it was the politically much less difficult matter of slowing the erosion of an established fact.[78]

In both cotton and jute the pressure for protection of the domestic industry had to contend with the fact that the major competitors were poor Commonwealth countries. British governments faced significant pressure from India against protectionism, and they listened both because of fears about the potential retaliatory loss of tariff preferences for British goods in India, and because of a increasing focus on facilitating development in poor countries, and Britain's belief that this meant especially aiding the development of poor Commonwealth countries.[79]

The narrative so far has emphasized an ultimately losing battle to sustain protection in jute, embedded in a context where government had strong commitments to trade liberalization, especially in regard to imports from poor Commonwealth countries. On the other hand, in accordance with the predictions of the political economy of protection literature, both cotton (after 1958) and jute did have some protection, the latter down to the 1980s, attracting sympathetic attention as low-wage, labour-intensive industries suffering unusually acute competitive pressures. The 'big picture' of the post-war textile trade is the sustaining of trade restrictions in that sector longer than most other parts of manufacturing.[80]

The reason these restrictions were so long-lived was primarily because of the employment issue.[81] As the Dundee jute story illustrates, post-war governments down to 1979 were extremely sensitive to the employment consequences of decline, and sought to balance the pace of contraction against the creation of other employment opportunities. Concern was not just rhetorical. As stressed above, all discussions of protection of jute were framed in part by the likely employment effects. More particularly, the delay of the review due in 1967, and the freezing of quotas from 1969 to 1973 is in large part explained by the surge in unemployment in Dundee in those years. In a longer perspective, governments in this period did have some success in attracting alternative employment to the area, so while unemployment throughout the period was higher than in the rest of the UK, on trend it was comparable with the rest of Scotland until the late 1960s. After 1979, as in so many other industrial areas, unemployment shot up, as long-run sectoral decline was accompanied by a general collapse of demand for industrial workers.

Government support for trade liberalization was not just about international obligations, but also reflected the belief that competition would encourage efficiency and innovation. The industry argued in 1948 that protection was a pre-condition of investment and greater efficiency, but had been rebuffed in that argument, whilst actually obtaining a continuation of protection, albeit on a diminishing basis, for the next thirty years. The industry, while campaigning for protection, also moved substantially up market, as shown in Chapter 4.[82]

Protection and its Consequences

In 1948 the Working Party argued that 'the object of policy should be to strengthen the industry by preventing encroachment by Indian imports and thus to provide a basis for expansion of output. This we are convinced can only be realized by affording protection to the industry when it is again subject to competition from low priced imports from a country with much lower wage standards than those obtaining in this country'.[83] The low wage argument for protection was not accepted by the government, and protection against the bulk of Indian imports was progressively eroded, while retained much longer for products at the top end of the market. Writing in 1960 Carstairs and Cole made a compelling argument that the industry had adjusted well to post-war circumstances, especially the erosion of protection at the bottom end of the market: 'the industry has turned steadily away from common Hessians which are least able to compete with Indian imports, and more in the direction of higher-quality products in which Dundee equipment and skilled labour have an advantage. It is, moreover, in these high-quality products that the extensive investment in the Dundee industry since the war has overwhelmingly been concentrated'.[84] It is also the case that protection of this part of the product range remained substantial. In the short run this protection encouraged investment in the industry and thus facilitated adjustment by changing the product mix. The investment was also helped by money from regional assistance.[85] But, as always in economic history, what worked quite well as response in one period, roughly from 1948 to the mid-1960s, faced new difficulties in the next period, as the very fact of protection encouraged market substitution, into polypropylene. Again, firms in the industry proved responsive, many of them moving fast into this new product. As a result, unlike in the USA, it was initially the jute firms who led the way to polypropylene, not the petro-chemical producers of the raw material.[86]

In a capitalist economy what firms produce is unconstrained by anything other than their own calculations of profitability. Allocation of firms to particular sectors of output is always contingent. In the case of Dundee jute, the firms survived-at least for a time- while jute production didn't.[87] But even where firms survived, their employment levels collapsed. One of the characteristics of polypropylene is that it is much less labour intensive than jute, requiring only around one-sixth of the labour per yard needed in jute.[88] But in the longer run the rise of polypropylene was accompanied by the domination of the sector by the raw material producers, giant petro-chemical firms who organized the industry on a global scale.[89] Thus, for example, Don and Low were taken over by Shell in 1986, who in turn sold their polypropylene interests to Union Carbide in 1995. By the end of the century only four small manufacturers of polypropylene products remained in Dundee, employing a few hundred people. Of the major old

Dundee jute firms, only Low and Bonar sustained a presence in polypropylene, but with only one of their plants in the City, the rest in Belgium, Hungary and China.[90] Don and Low continue to produce polypropylene products at their factory in Forfar.[91]

As the above narrative has indicated, the post-1945 story of jute is of an industry which for almost twenty-five years was able to stave-off decline with the help of government protection. As Table 2.1 shows, employment in the industry actually rose in the early 1950s, before falling back later that decade and then stabilizing for the next ten years. Decline after 1969 was however relentless, and the industry withered away over the next thirty years. This pattern of stability and decline cannot solely be accounted for by government policy; it also reflected substantial success in the industry in finding new markets for jute, especially in carpet and linoleum backing, as discussed in Chapter 5. However, this repositioning was eventually undercut by the declining use of jute for these purposes.

But undoubtedly the pattern of stability followed by decline from the end of the 1960s owed a great deal to changing policy on protection. In the first decades after the war the industry gained from the creation of Jute Control, its existence creating a form of 'path dependency' whereby it was much harder for the government to abolish this protectionist device than it would have been to establish such protection anew. This constraint on government was greatly reinforced by sensitivity on the employment issue, whereby, at least down to the 1970s, Dundee's employment level was always a consideration in deciding the scale of protection.

The general sensitivity of post-war governments to employment levels is well-known, though how closely woven it was into decision-making on the fate of a specific industry has never been made so clear as here in the case of jute. There is also no evidence in Dundee of any discounting of the significance of unemployment in jute because it included a significant number of women.

In 1946 a Board of Trade official stressed that 'They were all well aware many of the firms coming to the city wanted women labour and they were out to see no woman in the district would be out of work'. Targets for women's employment continually formed part of the discussion of employment in the late 1940s.[92] A decade later a civil servant summarized what seems to have been the predominant view when she noted that 'whatever the rights and wrongs of it, large numbers of Dundee households have been reliant on the earnings of women in the jute industry-many of them be it remembered, married to men also employed in the industry. The loss of these earnings will create just as serious a social problem as the loss of men's wages'.[93] While sometimes separate male/female unemployment rates are quoted in policy discussions, by and large the key issue is the overall rate.[94] While the shrinking of jute employment in 1959–73 hit women disproportionately, the employment of women overall in the City grew rapidly, partly because of a large female presence in the new industries in electronics and light manufacturing.[95]

Protection of jute was continuously on the defensive in post-1945 Britain. It offended the commitment to trade liberalization, as embodied especially in the GATT. It offended both Commonwealth and development sentiment, as it hit mainly poor producers in India. It also contradicted the belief that enhanced efficiency requires the cool winds of competition. Such beliefs usually found at least one active champion – the economic Ministries, the Treasury and Board of Trade, were generally keen to pursue free trade. The Ministries responsible for foreign affairs and aid tended to stress the damaging effects of protection on India – sometimes assisted by Indians themselves. The Board of Trade tended to favour competition as a route to efficiency – though, perhaps especially in the 1940s, it also tended to see amalgamations and increased scale as routes to lower costs as evidenced in the 1948 Working Party *Report*. Also important as an anti-protectionist force were the jute importers and users, especially the UK Jute Goods Association.[96]

Against these pressures Dundee could directly mobilize only limited political armies – but effective ones as long as the primacy of full employment was accepted across the political spectrum, and no other policy goals supervened. But by the late 1960s the concern with adjusting to pressures for freer trade, alongside a belief in the need for economic 'modernization' left jute increasingly vulnerable. The abolition of Jute Control in 1969 was a key turning point, as the employment figures tell us. Later, after 1979, with unemployment unambiguously downgraded as an objective, the writing was clearly on the wall.

Protection was important to the Jute industry and its decline in the post-war years, but its precise impact is contentious, and this issue is returned to in the Conclusions, below.

7 THE DECLINE OF JUTE AND THE
ECONOMIC HEALTH OF DUNDEE

This chapter assesses how well Dundee coped with the decline of jute. As Chapter 2 has made clear, that decline was by no means uniform over the post-war period. The industry actually expanded into the early 1950s, and thereafter down to the end of the 1960s the decline was gradual. In this period jute was still the single largest industry in the city, and making a substantial contribution to the local economy. (Table 7.1 summarizes the employment structure in 1951). But from the beginning of the 1970s the decline accelerated, slumped again in the early 1980s, and by the beginning of the 1990s the industry had shrunk to insignificance, disappearing entirely at the end of that decade. However, while the local economy in many ways shared the relative prosperity of the industry in the 1950s and 60s, and its miseries in the 1970s and 80s, from the low point in the recession in the early 1990s around 1992 some degree of local recovery was evident *despite* jute approaching its final demise.

Table 7.1: Employment in Dundee by sector in 1951.

TEXTILES	19,698
(jute)	(15,684)
DISTRIBUTIVE TRADES	12,188
ENGINEERING, SHIPBUILDING AND ELECTRICAL; GOODS	9,409
(textile machinery and accessories)	(2,778)
(shipbuilding and repairing)	(2,102)
PROFESSIONAL SERVICES	6,627
(medical)	(2,664)
(education)	(2,435)
TRANSPORT AND COMMUNICATIONS	6,447
(railways)	(1,726)
(trams and buses)	(1.334)

Source: *Census 1951, Scotland vol IV Occupations and Industries*, p.xxxvii.

The discussion of this chapter is therefore broken down roughly into these three sub-periods. It should be noted that these largely mirror phases in the performance of the British economy as a whole. The first was the period of the long boom, or 'golden age', with low unemployment and inflation, and high growth by historic standards.[1] The second was the period of the first OPEC crisis, followed by 'stagflation' in the mid-1970s, and then followed by two major recessions at the beginning of the 1980s and 1990s, separated by the unsustainable boom of the mid and late 1980s.[2] Finally, following the exit from the ERM in 1992, Britain experienced a second 'long boom' which lasted until 2007. It is unsurprising that Dundee's economic state substantially, although not wholly, mirrored that of the national economy.[3] The local economy in this period was much less reliant on global forces than before 1939, as the importance of the highly globalized jute sector shrank, and even within jute the switch to end-uses such as carpet-backing, and away from bagging, reduced dependence on international markets. For a while, as discussed below, Dundee became more subject to some 'global' forces (notably investment by multinational companies), but by and large the welfare of its citizens after 1945 became much more dependent on the national (rather than international) economy, and national policy decision-making, than in the past.[4]

In assessing the economic health of Dundee through these changing circumstances, a primary focus will be on employment. For the great bulk of Dundonians who were wage and salary earners, and with limited financial assets, the availability of work, and the terms on which it is available, were crucial to their prosperity. Much research reinforces the intuitive sense that work and wages are not only crucial to income levels, but affect many other aspects of well-being.[5] Hence while we need to look especially at (un)employment and wage levels, we would expect levels and variations in these to have a major impact on poverty and on health, and also, though less straightforwardly, on other measures of deprivation, such as family breakdown, drug usage or likelihood of criminality. (In the final part of this chapter, for the recent period, we can make use of the newly-derived Scottish Index of Multiple Deprivation, which gives a significant weight to employment, but incorporates a range of other measures of deprivation). Of course, employment isn't the key to all matters of economic welfare. In particular, demographic change, especially an ageing population, has helped to generate much higher levels of dependence on non-wage incomes, especially state-funded benefits, so major changes in the scale and form of these, which have been important for the well-being of many Dundonians, must be noted.

The Long Boom in Dundee

Jute mattered to the Dundee economy not only because of the numbers directly employed, but also because of the indirect effects. Most obviously, a large proportion of the wages paid in the industry were spent locally, and sustained local employment in shops, pubs, clubs, cinemas etc. Such employment was always significant in Dundee; even in the heyday of jute in 1911 the census measured 30 per cent of the employed population in such jobs. In the early post-1945 period these multiplier effects were increased by the rising wages in jute, partly brought about to counteract the attractions of other employment, and partly in line with national trends. This growth in incomes, in jute and other employments, was, of course, one of the drivers for the shift into service occupations, of 'de-industrial-ization' which is evident in the national data for the UK from the mid-1960s, as consumers spent a rising proportion of their incomes on services of all kinds.[6] By the end of the 1970s Scottish data showed food expenditure was down to 25 per cent, falling below 20 per cent at the beginning of the 1990s (Housing expenditure was around 10 per cent).[7]

The spending of other revenues from the industry is less clear. Distributed profits were always a small part of those total revenues, and we know nothing of their expenditure. On the one hand jute firms remained much more in local ownership than many Scottish companies, which were increasingly subject to takeover from companies outwith the country.[8] On the other hand, conspicu-ous public expenditures by jute capitalists, such as on Baxter Park or educational institutions in the nineteenth century, or Caird Hall in the early twentieth, do not seem apparent after 1945. In terms of undistributed profits, some went into the modernization of jute works and purchase of machinery, especially in late 1940s and early 1950s (see Chapter 4), and this stimulated a revival of the local textile machinery industry.[9] Investment in wholly new factories was confined to the Scottish Co-operative Wholesale Society, which re-built the Taybank Works in the late 1940s.

While ownership in jute remained predominantly local, the evidence suggests that the companies were increasingly diversifying, spreading their assets both sectorally and geographically (Chapter 5). Investing outside Dundee had always been an aspect of their activity, even in the industry's heyday, but in the post-war period became more significant as prospects for local profits seemed limited.

The import of raw jute involved labour intensive activities in the unload-ing of ships and movement of the material from harbour to factory. Exports more often went out through other ports, but this of course involved rail or road shipment from Dundee.[10] The effect of the contraction of the industry was registered in the decline of port employment from the 1950s, which reinforced the general trend for smaller ports to contract in the face of bulk-handling and containerization, and the related increase in ship size.[11] In Chapter 6 we have stressed that it was the combination of trade protection for jute and a newly emphasized national concern with unemployment which transformed rela-tions between the industry and the government from the Second World War. Acute local concern with unemployment was felt in the interwar period (see Introduction), and in the 1930s this showed itself with some small initiatives aimed at attracting industries into the area as the fragility of an economy based on jute was so evident. In 1931 the City Council published a pamphlet entitled 'Do It At Dundee: the Story of Opportunities offered by No Mean City' in an attempt to attract investors to the City.[12] There were also some movements on a pan-Scottish basis to seek to attract inward investment, but these seem to have mainly concerned industrialists from the West of Scotland.[13]

The key turning point in regard to significant intervention to stimulate local employment came with the shift in national policy. Whereas in the 1930s there had been only tentative and unambitious attempts by the National Government in London to help the 'Special Areas' (which did not include Dundee), the 1945 Distribution of Industry Act opened up a wholly new era of state-sponsored encouragement for investment in areas with high unemployment, beginning what came to be known as regional policy.[14]

Dundee was an early and significant beneficiary of such policies to subsidize inward investment (and simultaneously limit investment in prosperous areas by licensing building). The policy was concerned only with manufacturing, and the most precise data available is based on the jobs provided in new factory buildings. Between 1945 and 1951 space for 11,638 new jobs was licensed; this was equivalent to 13.6 per cent of Dundee's insured population in 1948, and involved a bigger percentage enhancement of manufacturing jobs than in any other area of Scotland.[15] By 1966 employment in these new factories had reached 11,407, and the new Industrial Estate had become a significant part of the economic landscape of Dundee.[16]

In the 1945–51 period a total of thirty new manufacturing enterprises were recorded in Dundee (some in new, some in old premises). Of these, ten were 'Non-Scottish firms', and this was evidence of the beginnings of a highly important factor in Dundee's prosperity in the 'long-boom' – the influx of foreign, especially American multinationals.[17] The coming of these multinationals was enormously important to Dundee's prosperity in the long boom. They not only came to employ large numbers directly, but by greatly increasing the local demand for labour (including a significant number of women) they levered up wages and conditions in other industries, not least in jute. Indeed, as we have seen, so worried were the jute companies by this pressure that for a while at the end of the 1940s they successfully persuaded government to hold back on attracting companies to Dundee lest they crowd out the demand from jute.[18]

After expansion in the 1950s and 1960s, by 1975 overseas multinationals employed almost 14,000 people in Tayside.[19] These jobs were overwhelmingly in manufacturing, and in high-technology sectors of electrical engineering in particular. So these companies were major agents of the transition of the Dundee (and Scottish) economy from its historic, striking reliance on the 'old staples', which in Dundee of course, meant especially jute. While these companies were attracted by the relatively low wages in the area, as well as subsidies and access to British and European markets, they offered jobs which in many ways were superior to those in jute. The work was cleaner and less damaging to health, and less subject to short-time working than had been common in jute. It is therefore unsurprising that, to the chagrin of jute employers, many of their workers 'voted with their feet' and chose to seek jobs working for 'the Yankee dollar'.[20]

However, many studies of these MNCs concluded that the designation 'branch plants' for these activities rightly suggested that they were not integral to the enterprise, that relatively little of the high-value activities such as Research and Development were carried out in such plants, and that linkages with the local economy were also very limited. So while the impact of these companies was certainly significant, and in many ways the key to local prosperity in the 1950s and 1960s, they had less impact on the long-run growth potential of the local economy than would have been the case if indigenous enterprises had been involved.[21]

The biggest of these American employers in Dundee were National Cash Registers (NCR) and Timex. NCR began local operations in 1946, producing cash registers and accounting machines.[22] At its peak in 1969–70 NCR employed 6,500 people in Dundee, spread over nine factories. It grew especially quickly in the late 1960s in anticipation of Britain's switch to decimal currency in 1971, and the boom in demand for decimal adding machines and cash registers this brought about. At this time 75 per cent of the workers were unionized, but there were no significant industrial disputes.[23] Timex was another major incoming multinational, initially establishing a plant in Dundee in 1946 to produce watches. By 1965 its workforce had reached 2,340, of whom 1,537 were women.[24]

The 1940s legislation which inaugurated significant aid for attracting employers to places like Dundee was straightforwardly aimed at reducing unemployment in 'depressed' regions. But from the beginning of the 1960s there was growing support for the argument that policy placed too much emphasis on unemployment, rather than focusing on positively encouraging expansion by concentrating on 'growth points', a view articulated in Scotland in the Toothill Report of 1961 and in the Scottish Plan in 1966.[25] Initially such ideas had relatively little practical import, and regional policy in the traditional sense, after becoming weaker in the 1950s, was revived in the early 1960s, and further strengthened by the Labour government in the mid 1960s, including the incorporation of a regional element in the Selective Employment Tax and the Regional Employment Premium.

Most studies found regional policy in the 1950s and especially in the 1960s effective in expanding the numbers of manufacturing jobs in the subsidized regions, a conclusion which applied in Scotland. Moore and Rhodes calculated that between 1960 and 1971 the total additional jobs amounted to between 70,000 to 80,000. But the impact of this expansion on unemployment was partly offset by the reduction in emigration and drawing into work of those otherwise inactive – so that the total was perhaps only a third of what was needed to sustain unemployment at average UK levels.[26] In Dundee regional policy was a major cause of the influx of multinationals noted above. This helped offset job losses not only in jute, but also in shipbuilding, where over 2,500 had been employed in 1951.[27]

Other public policies in the golden age brought benefits to Dundee. The national policy of full employment was probably limited in its *direct* effects on aggregate demand, but the general expansionary posture of macroeconomic policy partly accounts for the higher private investment and trade growth which were the key reasons for much higher demand for labour than in the pre-war period.[28]

Directly and hugely important was the growth of health and education provision, and the associated employment. In health those employed had risen to 2,120 by 1961, school teachers 1,500, though prior to its becoming an independent entity, the University College employed under 200 academic staff.[29] Expansion in these sectors was particularly beneficial to women, with over two-thirds of medical staff and school teachers being female in 1961, and this helped to offset the shift in gender composition towards men in jute, though of course the skill requirements of these 'new' sectors differed greatly from jute.

At a national level a paradoxical aspect of public policy was the use of nationalization as a mechanism of huge structural shifts in employment; for the humane 'management of decline' in many of the old staples.[30] This had only a small impact in Dundee, with the running down of railway employment, linked to the decline of jute and general motorization.[31] Private sector services continued to expand, with retail and distribution reflecting the growth of consumer affluence. By 1961 over 9,000 workers were categorized as 'sales workers', embracing everyone who worked in the retail sector.

As elsewhere in Britain, structural change in Dundee's economy was rapid in the long boom, a process much eased in 1950s and 1960s by general availability of jobs.[32] This was challenging for Dundee because it was unusually dependent on manufacturing in 1948, with 52 per cent of all insured workers in manufacturing, compared with a Scottish figure of 38 per cent, and manufacturing was subject to especially rapid changes.[33] The composition of manufacturing employment in the city showed this in the rise in engineering (especially electrical engineering), and the decline in textiles.[34] Though the picture is complex, it is likely that overall economic welfare in Dundee gained less from *increased* female participation in paid work evident across most of Britain, partly because it began from such a remarkably high, jute-driven, base. Across the war period (1931–51) there was indeed a substantial decline in female activity rates, though these were still twice as high as the Scottish average, but later an upward trend asserted itself.[35]

In 1950 Rowntree's last survey of York found a huge fall in poverty in the city since 1931, overwhelmingly due to full employment. While his precise estimates have been qualified, the general point stands and applies equally to Dundee; it was full employment, much more than the direct effects of the welfare state reforms of the Attlee government, that underpinned popular prosperity in the 1950s and 1960s.[36] This, of course, was an especially stark contrast with 1930s in Dundee, where unemployment in that decade had been so overwhelmingly high.

In Britain in the early 1960s there was a 're-discovery' of poverty, especially amongst those excluded from the labour market, most importantly the elderly.[37] The problems identified at the national level were also significant in Dundee, indeed were potentially a bigger problem in Dundee because of the demographics of a stable population.

Like many cities, Dundee in the 1960s was subject to comprehensive redevelopment of the city centre, with accompanying slum demolition. New city centre commercial development meant closing much of the docks, symbolizing the re-orientation of the local economy away from international trade connections, but also the loss of jobs in labour intensive port industries. In line with policy in many of Britain's cities, the focus in these years was improving housing by focusing on system-built multi-storey dwellings, compared with the inter-war and early post-war focus on peripheral estates of predominantly walk up and 'four in a block' flats.[38] This was coupled to the demolition of around 6,000 dwellings between 1968 and 1974.[39]

Commenting upon these radical redevelopments, in retrospect (on the occasion of the conviction of local politicians and developers for the corruption which accompanied it) the *Courier* noted that 'most councillors saw the period as a once-in-a-lifetime opportunity to act out their role as architects for the common good'. The result was 'Dundee has more council houses and fewer slums per head of the population than almost any city in Britain. And in the Wellgate it has a shopping centre admired throughout the world and which has been a roaring success from the day it first opened its doors'.[40]

This analysis (from a conservative newspaper), captures something of the 'modernizing' spirit of the 1960s, which in Dundee envisaged an escape from a world of 'Dark Satanic Mills' to one of planned advance, involving new buildings and infrastructure, new housing, and the whole area to be integrated by road travel, the latter seen as a source of both personal freedom, and efficient transport. In the early twenty first century this is a world view few sympathize with, but it was one which was widely shared across Britain at the time, though perhaps particularly strongly in Dundee, where the physical legacy of 'juteopolis' was so much disparaged.

The 1966 economic *Plan* for Scotland proclaimed that 'the general condition and prospects of the Dundee area, and particularly of the city itself, offer the most promising feature of the whole North-East'. It was recognized that the future of jute was likely to be further contraction, 'But despite this, Dundee itself has an impressive record of post-war successes in modern fast-growing industries and now has a substantial labour force skilled in the requirements of precision engineering'.[41] The *Plan* suggested the possibility and desirability of the city expanding to a population of a quarter of a million (from around 150,000), to create a substantial self-sustaining 'city-region'.[42] Some allowance must be made for the characteristic boosterism of such government plans, but this optimistic tone is also evident elsewhere; for example, in comments by academics. Thus Carstairs, in his contribution to the 1968 British Association volume on the city, endorsed the view that the local economy had proved 'resilient, flexible, capable and willing to expand'.[43] The President of the local Chamber of Commerce in 1970, who noted that: 'Over the last ten years, with the exception of one or two periods, there has been a general expansion in the area and if we may, without complacency, congratulate ourselves a little, it was a story of remarkable success'. But by the time this speech was made the President was contrasting this success with the warning that 'the situation today is less encouraging'.[44]

Years of Crisis

Optimism was sustained in the late 1960s by the opening of the Tay Bridge in 1966, and the establishment of the new University of Dundee with ambitious expansion plans in 1967.[45] But the rise of competition from polypropylene and the rundown of jute protection from the late 1960s detailed in previous chapters clearly fed into rising unemployment in the city evident from 1968. This was also the time when national unemployment rates started to push up, as the Labour governments sought to deflate demand to contain inflation following devaluation in 1967. Though not evident at the time, the national economy was now past its peak level of industrial employment, and de-industrialization was to become a national trend.

At the beginning of the 1970s concerns about the decline of jute were linked to a recognition that other sectors were also suffering. For example, when the AJSM participated in a protest on unemployment led by the Lord Provost in 1971, they noted that 'the jute industry has contracted over the years but the effect of this on the labour position in the area was greatly increased by reductions, redundancies and closures in other industries and companies within Dundee and District'.[46]

In late 1971 *The Times*, seemingly stimulated by the recent announcement of big job losses at NCR, published an article entitled 'Dundee: in the balance between boom and doom'.[47] This noted the reductions in jute employment as polypropylene grew, but noted that 'Until recently these changes were contained within a prosperous local economy, which successfully withstood the shocks'. It went on to quote a Dundee union leader as saying 'only two years ago we used to be a boom town. Now suddenly we are a doom town. It is the speed with which it has all happened that has shocked us'.

Three years later, *The Times* offered a surprisingly optimistic account of the city's economic position, even whilst noting 'Unemployment has never been far from Dundee's doorstep'.[48] But in the short run this optimism was misplaced as the given the impending macroeconomic policy shift in London, which in the wake of OPEC1 saw the Labour government in 1975 beginning to give priority to policies to reduce inflation, following which unemployment rose, albeit much less relative to output than in later recessions. National unemployment rose in 1975 and 1976, and it followed the same pattern in Dundee.[49]

Nationally, after the resolution of the IMF crisis in 1976, the government was soon reflating the economy. For all the excitements accompanying the inflation surge and fiscal deficits of the mid-1970s, in real economic terms the national economic outcomes of the decade were much less adverse than much over-heated contemporary commentary suggested. But in Dundee the picture was less happy, as jute's decline was combined with the retreat of the multinationals. As *The Times* reported in 1976, the loss of jobs at NCR in the early 1970s was now accompanied by worries (soon to prove justified) that the future of Timex in the city was threatened by the rise of digital watches. It reported a local study of employment which found a fall in overall employment in engineering and electrical goods. The peak employment by NCR in the city was in 1970, and decline was marked through the next decade, down to 1,000 by 1980. The pattern at Timex was different, with a peak in 1974 at 6,000 and decline more concentrated in the 1980s and 1990s.[50]

The next and much more serious blow to national employment came with the Thatcher slump after 1979. This slump was initially driven by an unprecedented appreciation of the exchange rate, which bore particularly hard on the traded, and hence manufacturing sector, an appreciation largely the product of monetary policy tightening. Unlike the recession of the mid-1970s, in the Thatcher slump the employment fall fully reflected the output fall, with unemployment continuing to rise until 1986, though output bottomed-out in 1981/2.[51]

The differential impact of the slump on internationally-traded manufactures was bad news for Dundee. As noted in Chapter 3, in jute, imports of carpets as well as jute products surged, and output and employment contracted fast – in many ways these were the decisive years pointing to the final demise of the industry. But there was also serious contraction in polypropylene production, equally hit by loss of competitiveness and the contraction of the home carpet industry. Other manufacturing activity also suffered. Shipbuilding contracted, and the Caledon yard closed in 1982, ending this activity in the city, though ship repair and work on oil rigs continued, a new firm, Kestrel Marine, growing to a 1,000 workers in 1983.[52]

There was also turbulence and contraction in the long-standing jam and marmalade industry, where the old-established firm of Keillers, having been previously bought by Nestle, was in 1984 purchased, with help from the government, by the Okhai brothers. They cut employment initially, but then expanded again before selling the company again to the English confectionery company Barker and Dobson.[53]

There were also further major contractions in the MNCs. As manufacturing companies they were affected by the generally unfavourable British macroeconomic environment of the 1970s and especially the early 1980s, but their reduced role also reflected changes in MNC's global strategies generally, decisions largely, of course, made in the USA. Timex shed almost 2,000 jobs between 1981 and 1983, when there was a bitter dispute over redundancies, (with final closure in 1993).[54]

The result of all this was that in Dundee by September 1979 the official rate of unemployment had reached 9 per cent, accelerated sharply in the early 1980s, fell a little in the last part of the decade, before rising again to reach 18 per cent by 1991, falling gradually thereafter.[55] But this figure became decreasingly reliable as a measure of real labour market slack because of changing definitions used in compiling the figures, but much more importantly the switch of unemployed people from claimants for benefit onto disability benefit.[56] Detailed estimates of the real unemployment rate in Dundee, taking this factor into account, are not available before the end of the 1990s, but these would suggest that this real rate is between two to three times the claimant count.[57]

The pattern of this employment decline clearly reflected 'de-industrialization', with the biggest falls in employment in manufacturing, where jobs in Food, Drink and Tobacco fell by 18 per cent, Engineering by 26 per cent, Textiles by 35 percent, but Professional and Scientific rose 17 per cent and Insurance and Banking 13 per cent.[58] As elsewhere in industrial Britain, the 'Thatcher slump' fell disproportionately hard on male manufacturing jobs; by this stage, as we have seen, even jute was a predominantly male industry.[59] Married women's participation continued to increase in 1970s – in Tayside the proportion of under-sixty married women economically active rose from 49.6 to 62.8 per cent, between 1971 and 1981.[60] Overall, the fall in employment levels in Dundee in the 1970s was larger than elsewhere in Scotland, but employment in services grew more rapidly than elsewhere due to the opening of Ninewells hospital, which was to grow to become one of the biggest employers in the city.[61]

As part of the declining enthusiasm for regional policy in 1970s, the Heath government switched to allowances rather than grants to save money, but at the same time there was an ideological switch towards 'urban policy'.[62] Important for Scotland was the creation of Scottish Development Agency in 1976, partly due to growing sentiment for a specifically Scottish body, but also similarities to the broad remit of the National Enterprise Board.[63]

The first Chief Executive of the SDA was Lewis Robertson, one of Dundee jute's 'three wise men'. In a valedictory article at the end of his five-year period of office, he emphasized the scale of the Agency's activity in Dundee, owning sixty-five factories by 1980, with twenty-four of these built since 1975. Also important was the conversion of big into smaller factory units, a crying need in Dundee as large mills became empty and small businesses needed to be encouraged. The SDA also supported the creation of an Enterprise Zone in Dundee, embracing six sites scattered around the city, but this initiative did not bear fruit until the after the Thatcher government came to power.[64]

The ideological suspicions of that government were bound to be aroused by the broad remit for a state-owned body such as the SDA, and its ownership of twenty-five million square feet of factory space, a significant role as venture capitalist, and responsibility for attracting new investment in Scotland. While Labour remained in power the Agency helped to fill the alleged 'finance gap', but its expenditure in this regard was trivial. It also became involved in major urban projects, which was in line with the general trend of policy in relation to social deprivation from the 1970s onwards.[65] But after 1979 the Agency had a much clearer remit, focused on attracting investment, and its aims in respect of maintaining employment were explicitly removed, and in 1981 this policy emphasis was reinforced by the creation of Locate In Scotland as the umbrella body for 'industrial policy' in Scotland. This encouragement to inward investment was deemed compatible with the sale into private ownership of most of the factories inherited by the SDA, and its investments in companies were also sold. Eventually the agency was abolished in 1991, for however far it became more commercial in its approach, it did not fit the ideological climate of the late 1980s.[66] The SDA was succeeded by Scottish Enterprise, with employer-dominated Local Employment Committees giving a more decentralized structure to the government's role in employment policy. This followed the trend under the SDA, where, in Dundee, the Agency led an elaborate Area Initiative (signed November 1982), which began with a focus on waterfront regeneration, but grew into 'a major attempt to revitalize the economic life of the city', but with a clear emphasis on training and skills rather than direct employment provision.[67] The focus was especially on high technology developments and tourism. One result was the Technology Park to the West of the city.[68]

The 1980s also saw a reduction in central government enthusiasm and funding for physical development as central to urban improvement. The focus was on improving the operation of the labour market, rather than the provision of employment, as the key to 'regeneration'.[69] There were some measures which sought to expand employment, but these tended to be very limited in scope, such as the Enterprise Zone, which was eventually established from 1982 to encourage investment by large tax breaks and freedom from planning controls.[70]

Dundee City Council has long been persuaded that the reputation as 'jute-opolis' harms the attractiveness of the city, and has pursued various strategies of 're-branding'. As noted above, the first example of this arose from the Dundee Project of 1982, and focused on high technology development, training, and major improvements to the city centre and waterfront to make it a much more desirable place to live and to visit.[71] By 1991 the Dundee Project had evolved into the Dundee Partnership which led to the launch of the 'City of Discovery', a name which related both to the specific initiative to bring Scott's ship to the City as a tourist attraction, and a more abstract reference to the idea of emphasizing the potential for scientific research, especially linked to the local universities.[72] Physically this strategy was linked to the idea of playing down the legacy of 'dark satanic mills' and seeking to focus attention on the waterfront, to take advantage of Dundee's striking, but in many ways neglected location close to the mouth of the Tay.

Given national trends and policies the city authorities were certainly facing an uphill struggle in trying to regenerate the city. The scale of the problems is evidenced by the substantial loss of population in the 1970s and 1980s. After stabilizing in the post-war years, that population fell from a peak of 182,000 in 1971 to 155,000 in 1991 (Table 7.2). The city had an ageing population, and was suffering a serious net loss of younger people to emigration (Table 7.3).

Table 7.2 Dundee Population 1951–2006.

1951	177,340
1961	182,978
1971	182,521
1981	177,545
1991	155,550
2001	145,560
2006	142,170

Source: *Census*; for 2006, General Register Office Estimates

Table 7.3: Population Changes in Dundee 1971–2001, as a percentage (post-1996 boundaries). Scottish figures in brackets.

Population Total	Working-age population	Persons in employment	Working-age/ Employment ratio
−21.31 (−3.07)	−17.91 (1.93)	−27.84 (1.75)	−8.54 (−0.12)

Source: census data, collated by I. Turok, 'Urban Policy in Scotland: New Conventional Wisdom, Old Problems?', in M. Keating (ed.), *Social Democracy in Scotland* (Brussels, 2007), p. 22.

Late twentieth century survey material gives us some idea of the impact of these patterns for social welfare. Analysis of the 1991 census using a twelve-element index of deprivation and looking at Enumeration Districts found Dundee to have 90 such districts or 16.8 % of the total in the City, making it comparable with Clydebank and Motherwell, but only approximately half the figure for Glasgow. This figure showed no clear trend since 1971.[73] An analysis from the mid-1990s of social security claimants found thirty-5 per cent of households in Dundee in receipt of benefit, compared with a Scottish national average of 33 per cent, and with Glasgow at 52, using the unitary authorities as the unit of analysis. Other data on poverty levels suggest a similar story of a city facing major problems of deprivation, albeit by most measures less severe than some areas of greater Glasgow.[74] Alongside these measures, parts of the city also suffered badly from the characteristic pathology of inner-city crime concentrations, in areas which were very similar to those where deprivation was most evident.[75]

Recovery of a Sort

While the recession of the early 1990s led to a further contraction in jute, and by that time it had become a minor part of the city's economy. For the national economy, the exit from the European Exchange Rate Mechanism in 1992 facilitated a long upswing in the economy which lasted until 2007, and provided a much more favourable national economic environment for Dundee than the previous two decades. However, some aspects of this period were double-edged in their local impact. In particular, in a fashion strikingly similar to that before World War One, the inhabitants of Dundee gained benefits from 'globalization' in the form of a flood of cheap imported manufactured goods, as they had gained from the flood of cheap food before 1913; but both periods also saw local employment hit by international competition. In the late twentieth century this competition continued the erosion of the number of jobs available in local manufacturing, which had been going-on since the 1960s, so that by the end of the century only just over 10 per cent of employment was in this sector (Table 7.4). Wage data suggests this employment was at the 'high end' of manufacturing, so that Dundee shared the national pattern of particularly severe loss of unskilled and semi-skilled jobs in manufacturing which has characterized these years. The influx of multinational investment in the post-war 'golden age' had been almost totally reversed by the end of the century, but NCR retained a small facility in the City, concentrating on development activity rather than manufacturing, and hence contributing to the upward movement of skill requirements in the labour market. The French multinational Michelin, which came to the city in the early 1970s and was the last major beneficiary of 'old-style' employment subsidies, and at the end of 2010 was the biggest local multinational manufacturing plant.[76]

The jobs which have replaced those lost in manufacturing have come from the service sector, but this category covers an extremely diverse set of activities. Nationally, as is well-known, the post-1992 boom was characterized by a huge expansion of financial services. In Dundee this was a very limited phenomenon. As shown in Table 7.4, less than 3 per cent of employees were in this sector, though the expansion of the Alliance Trust as a significant employer continued a long-standing Dundee tradition. Nationally the growth of financial services was one of the forces which underpinned the extraordinary redistribution of income to the wealthy, with both the top 1 and 5 per cent of the income distribution doubling their share of the national income in a generation, and returning Britain to inequality levels close to those before 1913.[77] But given the limited role of these services in Dundee, this has had little local direct impact on the local economy.

Employment in private sector retail and distribution services also expanded, though again in common with national trends, the retail sector became more concentrated, with the growth of Tescos in particular, which by the early 2000s grew to the largest private sector employer in the city.[78] Another major employer was DCThomsons, the most long-standing, stable source of private sector jobs, a company which on the face of it thrived on producing a resolutely old-fashioned set of products, newspapers and magazines, though it spread its investments widely, including into a range of newer media.[79]

The most striking shift in employment has been the growth of the public sector, with the expansion of the NHS and education, in both the school and college sector, and the universities. The categorization of employment does not use a private/public sector distinction, but the public sector component probably lies between 35 and 40 per cent (Table 7.4).[80]

Table 7.4: Employment in Dundee by sector in 2007 (per cent of workforce) (sectors with more that 5 per cent of the total).

Mainly Private Sector	
Wholesale and Retail Trade	15.8
Manufacturing	10.3
Real Estate, Renting and Business Activities	8.9
Transport, Storage and Communication	7.7
Hotels and Restaurants	6.3
Construction	5.3
Mainly Public Sector	
Health and Social Work	14.7
Public Administration and Defence; Social Security	13.2
Education	10.6

Derived from: Dundee City Council, *About Dundee 2008* (Dundee, 2008).

Initially the growth in health spending nationally was a continuation of the pattern established in the 1970s, noted in the previous section, for NHS spending to rise significantly despite all the ideological currents swirling around it. Under the Conservatives 1979 to 1997 the growth in this spending was below the long-term (1950–2004) trend of 3.7 per cent per annum, at 3.1 per cent, but still substantial; in what was to become the greatest boom in spending ever seen in the NHS, this figure rose to 8.1 per cent per annum between 2000/1 and 2004/5.[81] Locally, this was reflected in the Tayside NHS Trust becoming the largest employer, above all through the continued expansion of Ninewells, though other services also contributed. Total employment in Tayside NHS (which includes Dundee) grew by around 40 per cent during the boom after 1992 (from 10,301 FTEs in 1993, to 14,099 in September 2008). This growth was especially fast between 2001 and 2005.[82]

The story of education is somewhat different. Here, under the Conservatives, spending had grown very slowly, at 1.5 per cent per annum (the long-term trend was 4 per cent), but again in Labour's second term there was a striking surge, the annual rate of increase rising to 6.1 per cent.[83] As in health, this policy included a huge expansion of capital projects in these two sectors, alongside big increases in employment levels. In Dundee the rise in education spending was evident in both the school and college sector and in the two universities, though physically the impact on Universities was most apparent, with both the University of Dundee and Abertay putting tens of millions into new buildings on their campuses. More sustained was the expansion of employment (Table 7.4).

The expansion of the Universities has given them an economic weight in the City which is amongst the highest of any place in Britain. (Total student numbers for the two universities reached almost 23,000 in 2005/6.)[84] Their impact is magnified by the fact that academic salaries are high (the average full-time academic salary is in the top 10 per cent of the income distribution nationally), but universities also provide a significant number of other jobs ranging from higher professional to manual (though many of the professional as well as academic jobs go to 'immigrants' into the city). This expansion has been driven by a number of forces. Especially since the 1960s there has been a powerful 'science lobby' which has claimed that more expenditure on science and scientific research and development, and more trained scientists and technologists, is the route to faster economic growth, and university expansion has been an important consequence of that notion.[85] Such ideas helped the separation of Dundee University from St. Andrews in the 1960s, and its subsequent growth, which was uninterrupted though at variable pace except during the public spending cuts of the early 1980s.[86] Under New Labour expansion has been aided by a continuation of that lobby's effective activities, helping to secure Research and Development as one area of continued government 'industrial policy', alongside a target to expand higher education to reach a 50 per cent participation rate.

Other public sector employment expansion, especially by the City Council, reflects (as does that in health and education) the fact that the public sector now embraces some of the most labour intensive activities in the economy, where labour-saving productivity gains are very hard to achieve. The imperative to 'take labour out' which has been so powerful in driving up labour productivity (and diminishing employment) in manufacturing is simply not possible in most the public sector, where personal interaction with a medical or educational professional remains largely integral to the activity.

The outline of employment trends given so far suggests that Dundee's experience was broadly in line with those across the UK, but with the weight of public sector activity significantly greater because of the small scale of some private sector activities, such as finance. How does this pattern relate to the city's own strategies for renewal? These strategies have many roots, but in part they draw upon the same kind of thinking that has informed national approaches to the economy in post-devolution Scotland, such as *Smart, Successful Scotland* (2001), which focused attention on enhanced science and skills as the way to raise productivity and growth in Scotland. The human capital of individuals, and the social capital derived from effective communities were placed at the centre of future strategy. Neither of these was new (though the terminology was), skills and training having been emphasized in many government policies for faster growth since the late 1950s, and the emphasis on 'social capital' followed a period since the 1980s which had seen growing focus on community development.[87]

Initially, these broad approaches to policy issuing from Edinburgh placed little emphasis on cities as key sites of policy action, but later statements shifted the argument so that by 2004 it was claimed that 'Scotland's cities are vital to driving the overall economic health of Scotland'.[88] This rhetoric was backed by money, so in 2002 the document 'Building Better Cities' announced a £90 million growth fund over three years for infrastructure. To qualify cities had to produce a 'City Vision', which arguably helped to produce a strategic focus amongst local politicians.[89]

The 'Vision' produced by Dundee is one which continues the focus from the 1990s inauguration of the 'City of Discovery' the emphasis on the creation of high value jobs and top quality living environments, in order to attract highly skilled and resourceful people.[90] This strategy draws in part on Florida's account of the importance of the 'creative class', which in Dundee has been used to emphasize the potential local synergies between the universities and 'cultural industries' (for example, Art and Design at the Duncan of Jordanstone Art College, video-gaming at Abertay University), alongside a commitment to scientific creativity, especially in bio-medical fields, where links between the universities and spin-off research companies in this sector are emphasized.[91] The ambitious plan to redevelop the waterfront follows this same broad basis of thinking.[92]

But such a focus is problematic. As Turok has suggested: 'The focus on high value jobs and top quality living environments for highly skilled and resourceful people is a narrow basis for urban revitalization and growth. It will do little directly to improve the life chances of people outside the creative class, ie poor, low skilled and workless groups, and it may even cause harm through gentrification of inner-urban areas and displacement of low-income households'.[93]

How do developments in the recent history of Dundee relate to such criticism? It should be stressed that the high profile 're-branding' of the city and the production of 'Visions' may give a misleading sense of the City's role, much of which undoubtedly is focused on what has come to be called social inclusion, and reducing deprivation. Thus 'partnerships' to reduce social exclusion, and reduce deprivation are an important part of the city's policies.[94] Nevertheless, these grand plans, 're-brandings' and visions have shaped policy, and the spending of money.

The long upswing since 1992 undoubtedly reduced unemployment in Dundee; while the claimant count seriously understates the figure, it gives a broadly accurate picture of the trend. But for recent years we also have the benefit of careful estimates of the real level of unemployment based, as noted above, on calculations which add to the official data working-age people who are receiving incapacity benefit, but who in a fully-employed economy would find employment.[95] These calculations give estimates of 16.9 per cent for January 2002 (claimant count 7.6), falling to 11.4 per cent in January 2007 (claimant count 4.1). This data clearly suggests a continuing serious unemployment problem in the City even at the end of the 'NICE' period. However, it puts Dundee in a significantly better position than five other Scottish areas. This may reflect the fact that the worst areas across Britain tend to be areas of previous large scale concentrations of heavy male manual work (coalmining, shipbuilding, iron and steel), which was not Dundee's position. One other notable feature of this calculation is that it suggests that a significant proportion of this 'hidden unemployment' is female; while the official rate shows a ratio of 3.5:1 between men and women, the 'real' rate has a ratio of only 1.2:1. This may be a hidden legacy of jute, of older women who lost jobs in that sector and never regained employment.

Broader evidence on social conditions in Dundee comes from the 2006 Scottish Index of Multiple Deprivation (SIMD). This index adds together data about income, employment, health, education, accessibility , housing and crime to derive a summative figure, which is used to assess relative deprivation, The conceptual underpinning of this is the notion of relative poverty, expanded to embrace a range of activities of which the poor are deprived. It is also relative in the sense that it describes the position of each covered relative to the others, not the absolute level of deprivation. The SIMD uses 'data zones' of approximately 750 people, and ranks these from the most to the least deprived.[96] Dundee had 179 of these zones, and fifty-three of these ranked within the 15 per cent most deprived in Scotland. These covered 28.9 per cent of the City's population In a Scottish context this suggests Dundee is less seriously deprived than Glasgow and Inverclyde, but above all other areas.[97]

An issue which continued to be both hugely significant for the welfare of its inhabitants, but also the site of key tensions and battles, is housing. Having peaked at owning over 70 per cent of the local housing stock in the 1980s, in the last two decades of the century the local authority, urged on by central government, was seeking to shift much of that stock to housing associations, though tenants views on such matters were very mixed.[98] Also, given continuing problems with the rates (council tax) base, the City Council was keen to encourage the expansion of accommodation for the prosperous, rather than simply being the landlord of an increasingly residual housing stock. By 2000 a key notion of much twentieth century British politics, that local government would have a prime responsibility for housing provision, had suffered major retreat. In Dundee, as elsewhere in Britain, the two major recessions of the early 1980s and 1990s fell disproportionately on public sector housing tenants, emphasizing the close links between this tenure and labour market disadvantage.[99]

The strategy of regeneration involves attracting more middle-class residents, a policy reinforced by the loss of 17,000 largely better-off households when local government boundaries were re-organized in 1996, with the City Council regaining a full-range of powers. To try and raise its council tax base the city pursued a policy of 'increasing the number of new houses built in the higher council tax bands and demolishing the identified surplus housing to improve overall quality of the City's housing stock'.[100] Between 1999 and 2004 there was a drop of 3,000 properties in the lowest band (A) and a rise of 1,900 in the higher bands (D and above).[101]

There is a strong incentives for the council to demolish 'multis' because they get capital grants from the Scottish government to do so, and lose recurrent maintenance expenditure. This has led to a smaller scale repeat of the 1960s experience of demolition breaking-up communities, even though these 'multis' (though generally in better condition than the slums of the 1960s) don't conform to any contemporary ideal of housing. From the early part of the new century there were major private sector residential developments on the waterfront. This was clear evidence of the process of gentrification of the city housing stock, as council ownership became very much residualised.[102] Housing continues to be expensive, but housing benefit is paid from national not local public funds, and acts therefore as an 'inflowing' subsidy for private sector landlords.[103]

The Importance of the Public Sector

Almost as soon as the scale of competition to jute and the social problems of the city became widely recognized in the early twentieth century, radical plans for improvement of the city have been put forward.[104] The post-war years have seen a plethora of such plans, from the Tay Valley Plan of 1950, the Dobson Chapman Plan of 1952, through to the 'Vision' of 2003.[105] These plans have had little in common. Those of the 1950s and 1960s saw major physical redevelopment strongly guided by public authorities as the key to a prosperous future. By the beginning of the twenty first century there was much more reliance on the private sector, both in physical improvement and economic policy. Paradoxically, however, this fading of the social democratic dream of publicly-managed economic and social improvement has been accompanied by a striking trend towards much greater reliance on public sector employment.

Most of this expansion has come from national services (the NHS, Universities), or the increased national subventions to local services (especially education). The city's own revenue base has been hit hard by the loss of population (both through boundary changes and emigration), and the demographic shift towards a larger elderly population; but also the size of the on-working group amongst those of working age – the hidden as well as recorded unemployed. Paradoxically, also, the city now has lots of commuters who contribute little to its revenues, a major unintended consequence of improvement in the local transport infrastructure since the time of construction of Tay Road Bridge.[106] By 2001 18,000 people a day were commuting into the city, compared with 5,500 of a much larger working population in 1951.[107]

The national redistribution to the rich over the last generation has not helped Dundee. The redistributions from the generality of taxpayers to the poor have, underpinning some economic improvement for most Dundonians, even those without employment.[108] This shift was very much underpinned by national macroeconomic buoyancy, making enormously increased public spending politically possible, along with rising incomes. But the 'real unemployment' and SIMD data emphasize the limits to Dundee's capacity to overcome the end of juteopolis even before the banking crisis and recession unfolded after 2007. As the response to this crisis after the 2010 election became increasingly one of public spending cuts, the degree of vulnerability of Dundee to political decision-making in London and Edinburgh was likely to be exposed.

CONCLUSIONS

The decline of jute in Dundee has an air of inevitability. An unsophisticated product, with a large part of its costs of production comprising a foreign-grown raw material, it was unsurprisingly subject to devastating competition from producers in developing countries who could (with a little help from Dundonians) successfully enter the industry, using local raw materials. Yet, as we have sought to show, the story of jute's decline in Dundee is not a simple story of the undermining of 'juteopolis' by low-cost competitors. The industry responded pro-actively and in a range of ways to its problems. Even before the First World War it was moving its products away from the bags and sacking which dominated in the period of the extraordinary growth of world trade in primary products after 1870. At the same time it sought protection for the industry, a search which was only ultimately successful in 1939 because of the contingencies of war – always a powerful force in the industry's fortunes.

While the industry thereafter sought to make protection permanent, it could not and did not couple this defensive posture with neglect of the need for 'modernization' and diversification. Central to the story of post-war jute is the interaction of these two imperatives

At a meeting of the AJSM in May 1977 the jute employers sought to challenge the analysis of the industry's recent past put forward in a draft of the McDowall Report in dialogue with the authors of the Report.[1] This interchange between the Association and the academic authors represents the most focused analysis of the complexity of forces leading to the decline of jute evident from the 1960s. Central to the disagreement between the parties was the interaction in the decline between the erosion of protection and the rise of polypropylene. McDowall and Draper put the primary emphasis on the rise of polypropylene: 'the industry had been hit by technological change'. But they emphasized that this switch in fabric had been driven by a combination of the protection of jute (which increased the competitiveness of polypropylene) and the jute companies own actions in diversifying into the new fibre. This meant that by the late 1970s protection was no longer the key issue in the fortunes of the jute companies, though in the 1950s and 1960s it had enabled the industry to survive, make profits, and thus make it possible for diversification eventually to be pursued.[2]

By contrast, the AJSM argued for the continued centrality of protection for the future of the industry, and wanted to treat the advance of polypropylene as driven largely by forces external to the industry: 'The pace of polypropylene had been dictated not by Jute but by US Companies' they argued. The Association also strongly defended the continuation of protection: 'If protection was to go, the Industry would be seriously mangled'. They also disputed the view that protection had aided the expansion of polypropylene, claiming this was due to factors such as the high price of jute caused by the Indian-Pakistan war of the early 1970s. Finally, they claimed that profits under the Jute Control regime were not sufficient to enable the pre-existing jute companies to diversify.[3]

Despite the protestations of the AJSM, McDowall and Draper stuck to their view that to talk of a Dundee 'jute industry' was by this time a misnomer; so diversified was the industry that it could no longer be sensibly seen as a homogenous entity. Equally, they stressed that protection should be seen as having facilitated a successful 'trade adjustment' rather than as simply a mechanism for defending employment. Indeed, as they pointed out, while for the jute companies 'what they lost in jute they recouped in polypropylene, the losers in the short term were thousands of jute employees whose jobs disappeared (9,000 between 1966 and 1974)'.[4]

McDowall and Draper's narrative of the industry's development down to the mid-1970s is persuasive because of the nuanced account it provides. On the one hand, as they argued, it is clear that without protection from the 1940s, Dundee jute would have largely withered away. On the other hand, they couple this key point with a recognition that the protective regime was combined with major internal changes in the industry. They stressed the scale of investment in the early post-war period, the industry's good productivity record, and its movement up market. They further recognized that this outcome was in significant part due to the pressure maintained by the government on the industry despite its protective shell. Overall, they argue, 'with hindsight we can recognize in the Jute Control system a kind of trade adjustment policy which gradually made it easier for Indian, and subsequently, Bangladesh exporters to find markets for their goods in the UK while permitting the UK industry to transfer resources into lines in which it had smaller disadvantage vis-à-vis imports...In short, protection was undeniably necessary and it was effective in that jute companies survived to take the opportunities which technological change presented in the late 1960s'.[5]

It is important to emphasize the use of the word 'hindsight' here. There was no all-embracing master plan for jute in the post-war period. Control of imports was initially introduced for war-related strategic reasons; without the war, it is highly likely no such protection would have been forthcoming. But once established protection provided a means of defending the city's interests around which the major local interest groups – employers, unions, political bodies could unite. The slump of the 1930s had undermined both the traditional Liberal commitment to free trade (though this had been already weakened amongst employers before the First World War), and the hostility on the Left to trade controls borne out of a sense of international worker solidarity.[6]

Politically, it was not possible for the Attlee government to offend Indian sentiment by promising permanent protection, as urged by the 1948 Working Party. But the commitment to full employment, coupled with a recognition of Dundee's vulnerability to the return of the depressed conditions of the 1930s, led to a compromise in which protection was granted on a contingent basis. Two contingencies were involved. First, that any reduction in protection should not lead to a significant recurrence of unemployment. Second, that the industry should reform itself, 'modernizing' in the variety of ways spelt out by the 1948 *Report*.

On the first of these, as we have seen, defence of employment levels in the city proved an important element in all the debates about protection in the post-war years. However, this defence was eroded in effectiveness partly by the success in attracting non-jute activities to the city, which reduced its reliance on the industry and severed any straightforward assumption (of the kind still made in the 1940s) that without jute the city would be reduced to a desperate economic state. The attraction of such alternative employment had been recognized as necessary in the interwar period, symbolized by the City's publication of 1931, 'Do it at Dundee'.[7] But it was the Distribution of Industries Act of 1945, combined with American corporation's post-war desire to locate within Europe's protected markets which led to the influx. This inflow of investment underpinned the widespread perception at the end of the 1960s that Dundee's economy was a success-to the extent, ironically in the light of later developments, that it was expected to be the most attractive place for the location of the onshore activities of the North Sea Oil industry.[8] As we have seen, it was against this background that the problems of the beginning of the 1970s were seen so starkly as moving 'from boom to gloom'.[9]

This gloom, as shown in Chapter 7, proved justified, as the contraction of jute co-incided with the retreat of the multinationals from the 1970s. The full employment commitment, already politically-weakened by the 1970s, was no longer a strong card in discussions about jute. The careful 'management of decline' subject to the key criterion of the city's unemployment levels no longer operative.

The other contingency, trading protection against modernization of the industry, was never formalized, but its terms were clear in Harold Wilson's rejection of the 1948 Working Party's suggestion of 'unconditional' protection – though it should be stressed that their *Report* assumed modernization would be necessary to justify any protection granted. Wilson stressed that if in future he had to go to parliament to seek assistance for the industry to maintain a minimum size 'he would have to say that the industry has done its best to modernize'.[10] As analysed in Chapters 3, 4 and 5, the industry did indeed 'modernize' – significantly improving its productive efficiency while moving its products up market. However, this strategy could only sustain the industry for a period, and from the 1960s diversification, initially overwhelmingly into polypropylene, became the core strategy, with its disastrous consequences for employment.

On the government side the key player in the 'deal' with the industry was the Board of Trade. In the 1940s, under Stafford Cripps and Harold Wilson, the Board was central to the Attlee Government's policies aimed at improving industrial efficiency by a whole range of policy devices. This should be seen as a key aspect of the approach to jute, an approach which rejected the case for permanent protection in the 1948 Report, but embraced its 'modernization' agenda. The focus on 'supply-side socialism' led Labour towards a co-operative attitude towards much of the private sector: 'Labour would provide certain forms of support and subsidy, while industry must "put its own house in order"'.[11]

After the Conservative election victory in 1951 the *dirigistic* aspects of Labour's agenda were moved away from, and within this larger political context the Board of Trade 'was generally promoting liberal economic and commercial policies, in the form of greater competition and freer trade'.[12] This pursuit became more single-minded as the Board, and its successor Ministries, were able to point to the full employment enjoyed in Britain down until the 1970s as allowing greater scope for market forces. In Dundee, as we have seen, the generally buoyant economy in these decades facilitated the gradual reduction of support for the industry via protection.

From the 1970s this liberalizing policy direction was reinforced, first by EEC membership and then by the much more explicit pro-market ideology of the Thatcher government after 1979.

The most direct effect of these liberal trends on jute was, of course, the Restrictive Trade Practices case, which as noted in Chapter 5, the Board of Trade found complicated because it cut across the previous official support given to the industry's 'Gentlemen's Agreements'. While the jute case had unique features, it was symbolic of the general trend of the Board to move away from the kind of post-war policies which were deemed too supportive of restrictive action by industry. This trend was compatible with full employment, nationally and in Dundee, as long as the post-war boom of the 1950s and 1960s continued.

This liberal strand in state policy pressed by the Board of Trade was, of course, only part of the story of the state's role in the economy in these years. The Board of Trade itself was responsible for an aspect of government intervention which was hugely important to jute and Dundee – regional aid. Here there was also evidence of an ideological shift after 1951, as Conservative enthusiasm for state controls of the location of investment through Industrial Development Certificates, and for state subsidies to investment in the old 'depressed areas' waned. But this trend was reversed in the late 1950s as regional unemployment started to rise. After 1960 the focus of policy was less directly on addressing unemployment 'black spots' and more towards encouraging regional growth, but the general sense of a revived willingness for the state to provide resources for areas like Dundee was clear.[13] But such policies provided a necessary but not sufficient condition for the city to attract significant inward investment. They proved ineffectual in the much tougher macroeconomic times of the 1970s, which were also characterized by major restructurings in many multinational companies as the strategy based on investing in West European branch plants, so typical of American multinationals on the twenty-five years after the war, was seen as increasingly inappropriate.

Greatly expanded state support for research and development was a feature of post-war owing a great deal to the 'productionist' and scientific and technological enthusiasm of the Attlee government. In jute this led to the creation in 1946 of the British Jute Trade Research Association (BJTRA), where previously only the two largest companies in the industry had had research departments.[14] This was part funded by government and partly by the industry, and grew to have fifty employees in the early 1960s. It was involved in a very wide range of research activities, from concerns with the chemical characteristics of jute fibre through to the kinds of work study issues discussed in Chapter 3. It also from an early date became interested in synthetic fibres. Strikingly, its Director wrote an article on 'Rayon in the jute industry' as early as 1949.[15] By the mid-1960s it was doing extensive research on synthetics (encouraged by specific grants from the Ministry of Technology), especially polypropylene, and planning to change its name to reflect this new balance of activity, a re-naming to the Scottish Textile Research Association which took place in 1969.[16]

As noted in Chapter 6, the Scottish Office occasionally became involved in policy discussion about jute. There is no doubt that in the 1950s and 1960s there was a fair degree of sensitivity to Scottish unemployment rates in London, and insofar as the Office's pressure reinforced that sensitivity, it might be seen as effective on Dundee's behalf. Thus a senior official in 1953 criticized proposals for reducing protection for the Dundee industry in the following words: 'If it were an English town, we could probably ignore the problem and do as you suggest. But Dundee in not in England, and I frankly do not think it practical politics to say that Dundee must have no protection'.[17] However, the general picture seems to be one where the key decisions were made in London, with a clear desire to marginalize the Scottish Office when important decisions, such as on protection, were being made.

Parliamentary pressure for state support for Dundee's economy was exerted periodically, though perhaps unsurprisingly it was most in evidence in the 1970s and 1980s when things were going badly for the city.[18] However, Dundee was generally too small and politically insignificant to figure highly in parliamentary politics. Only in 1963 was the issue of the continued protection of jute considered important enough to go to Cabinet.[19]

Some counterbalance to that political insignificance was given by the well-organized and united front the jute industry and the city offered to government until the 1980s, when the combination of the Thatcher government in London and the recurrence of mass unemployment in Dundee divided the city's politics in ways which had not been seen since the 1930s. Until then a broad agreement between the employers in jute, the unions in the industry and the city authorities had been maintained, and the city largely 'spoke with one voice'.

This picture needs to be qualified by emphasizing that such unity was not maintained between the jute producers and the jute importers, the latter acting as supporters of trade liberalization in the disputes over protection discussed in Chapter 6. But their clout was reduced by the fact that they could not play the employment card; it was the Dundee spinners and manufacturers who could put themselves forward as defenders of the city's workers need for jobs.

Those spinners and manufacturers came together in the AJSM in 1918, and down to 1981 this provided an effective voice for the industry, with no evidence of significant policy differences amongst its members at any point in its history. No doubt this degree of unity was aided by the concentration of the industry in and around the city. There were occasionally some differences in wage bargaining strategy between the Dundee city jute employers and those in surrounding areas, but nothing that threatened the approach to major policy issues.[20]

The AJSM formally operated on a largely 'one-firm, one-vote' basis, except that Jute Industries, the largest company in the industry had three votes, but as Robertson noted in 1962: 'This equality is now, however, to some extent one of theory only since certain other firms within the industry have multiple votes by reason of having acquired, at one time or another, other members'.[21] Informally, for much of the time down to the 1970s the key decision-makers in the industry were the 'three wise men'.

Two of these came from the two biggest firms – Jute Industries and Low and Bonar, the third from a smaller but still significant firm.

The 'wise man' from Jute Industries (Sidlaws from 1971) was William Walker, a third generation jute employer. From Low and Bonar it was Hugh Bonar, the wartime Jute Controller and second generation jute employer. Third was Lewis Robertson, whose much smaller company merged in 1965 to form Scott and Robertson, though after internal disagreements he was ousted from the company and took no further formal part in the jute industry.[22] Robertson's role in this triumvirate seems to have been related to his exceptional political as well as technical grasp of jute's problems, qualities evident in discussions with government on protection, but especially in his role in the Restrictive Practices case, where he oversaw the strategy adopted by the industry.[23]

In 1948 the British Jute Trade Federal Council was created to give a single voice to the industry at a time when negotiations with government seemed especially to demand a single channel of communications. Despite its widely-based membership, the Federal Council was never a powerful body. It was small (with one full-time employee – a Public Relations Officer), and by definition federal in character. The division of interest between the AJSM as the over-arching body for the producers, and the UK Jute Goods Association, representing the importers, made the Council unable to speak for the industry as a whole.[24]

Unity of purpose amongst the producers was greatly aided by the price-fixing which from 1939 down to the Restrictive Practices Court judgement in 1962 found official support in the framework of Jute Control. But the Court's judgement did not effectively end these 'Gentlemen's Agreements', but rather replaced them with informal mechanisms to achieve the same end. These agreements, when lawful, were operated by a Prices Committee and two Co-ordination Committees, not by the AJSM.[25] But when it came to defending these arrangements in 1962, it was, as noted in Chapter 4, one of the AJSM's 'three wise men', Lewis Robertson, who largely formulated the industry's defence.

Until the mid-1960s the jute employers dominated the Dundee Chamber of Commerce. With few other major employers, the local 'voice of industry' was simultaneously the voice of jute. The influx of new, especially American companies, after 1945 shifted the balance of the DCC's membership, though initially without evidently changing its role. It is notable that when the industry sought to restrict competition for labour from these 'interloping' companies at the end of the 1940s it was able to get the Chamber to back this stance.[26] The Chamber's membership grew fast from 1964, drawing in not only the new large multinationals, but many other firms across a wide geographical area.[27] This trend undermined the role of the Chamber as spokesperson for 'juteopolis', and reinforced the role of the AJSM as the key political player in defending the industry.

The dissenting voice in jute's successful bid to limit competition from the multinationals for labour came from the trade unions, especially through the Trades Council. This may have reflected the strength of the CP in that organization, whereas in the jute union, where Communists were never significant, opposition to this policy is not evident.[28]

This disagreement aside, the post-war years were generally characterized by a 'united front' between employers and unions on the big issues facing jute. The DDUJFW was a a 'moderate' union that had no objections in principle either to protection, or to co-operating with the jute employers in defence of the industry. The Communist Party (which fielded parliamentary candidates in the city down to the 1980s) took a very different view about 'class collaboration' but was strongest in the Engineering Union, which only had a small membership in jute, drawing most of its strength from the shipbuilding and engineering industries.

Post-war party politics in Dundee down to the 1970s were dominated by 'moderate' Labour. From 1945 both Dundee MPs were Labour, and from the 1950s the Council was also predominantly from the same party.[29] This political complexion put no serious obstacles in the way of joint action between otherwise divergent groups in the city to defend jute. Often it was the City Provost, supported by both employers and unions, who spoke on behalf of the city's desire to sustain jute and the jobs it provided. Only after the election of a new, more radical Labour council in 1980 did the local political consensus fracture, but by then the fate of jute was already sealed.

The capacity of the Dundee jute industry to mobilize a united voice in its defence contrasts markedly with the situation before the First War when the predominantly protectionist employers faced a political left (Liberal and Labour) committed to free trade, albeit for diverse reasons. Between the wars, especially in the 1930s, enthusiasm for free trade waned across the political spectrum, but the city was unable to find a way to persuade national government of its case. As in so many aspects of British life, the Second World War greatly shifted the limits of the possible. Once established for strategic reasons, protectionism also provided one of the means for government, albeit with increasing reluctance, to deliver on the promise of full employment.

Dundee did enjoy a 'Golden Age' of full employment in the 1950s and 1960s. This, it should be stressed, was true for women as well as men. While, as we have seen, women formed a decreasing proportion of the jute workforce after 1945, the new industries which came in were also big employers of women.[30] Indeed, one of the attractions of the area to these companies was the ready supply of female labour, with its perceived greater manipulative skills adapted to the requirements of the new industries; and, of course, its lower wages than males. It is of note that national policy on employment in Dundee does not seem to have been much affected by the gender of the workforce. When one Board of Trade official argued for faster liberalization of the industry in the 1950s on the grounds that the jobs likely to be lost would be to a significant extent women's jobs, this view did not seem to gain support. As another (female) official noted: 'Whatever the rights and wrongs of it, large numbers of Dundee households have been reliant on the earnings of women in the jute industry – many of them be it remembered, married to men also employed in the industry. The loss of these earnings will create just as serious a social problem as the loss of men's wages. In the cases where the women are not married, I can only comment from personal experience that a girl must live.'[31]

This sense of economic welfare, both inclusive and focused upon employment as the key determinant, in many ways characterized this 'Golden Age'. It helped to underpin a successful process of 'managing decline', and a considerable degree of relative prosperity in the city. This management, by maintaining full (ish) employment facilitated the industrial diversification that was such an important part of the city's economic history after 1945. This diversification was directly encouraged by regional policy encouraging incoming firms, but as shown in Chapter 4, also involved the existing jute firms moving incrementally away from their old reliance on unsophisticated jute products.

This settlement which endured until torn apart by the forces that erupted in the 1970s. As shown in Chapter 7, in the 1980s and 90s, as far as Dundee was concerned there was largely *unmanaged* decline, with national government retreating in its commitment to the 'post-war consensus' in the face of the shock of OPEC 1 and the simultaneous re-ordering of the international economy. Only in the mid-1990s, with jute all but gone, did a degree of prosperity return. Now, however, a much larger role was played by direct state-funded employment, as public sector job growth in health, education and local public services played a crucial role in sustaining the city's economic fortunes. Alongside this, the state continued to play some role in encouraging investment in the region by Regional Selective Assistance, as well as measures more specifically aimed at aiding urban regeneration in Dundee. The growth of 'high-tech' private sector firms in such areas as biotechnology and computer games owed a lot to state funding, especially the funding provided to the universities from which much of this activity was spun-out.

Overall, post-war Dundee shows that, when there has been a willingness to deploy a range of policy instruments, the decline of jute has proved manageable; compatible with a reasonable degree of prosperity and economic security for the city's inhabitants.

NOTES

Introduction

1. M. Daunton, 'Britain and Globalization since 1850: I Creating a Global Order 1850–1914', *Transactions of the Royal Historical Society*, 16 (2006), pp. 1–38.
2. D. Aldcroft and H. Richardson, *The British Economy 1870–1939* (London: Macmillan, 1969), pp. 14–16, 190–214.
3. For the interwar period major works include D. Burn, *The Economic History of Steelmaking, 1867–1939* (Cambridge: Cambridge University Press, 1940); S. Tolliday, *Business, Banking and Politics: The Case of British Steel* (Cambridge, MA: Harvard University Press, 1987); B. Supple, *The History of the British Coal Industry, iv 1913–1946: The Political Economy of Decline* (Oxford: Oxford University Press, 1987); L. Johnman and H. Murphy, *British Shipbuilding and the State Since 1918* (Exeter: Exeter University Press, 2002), ch. 1 and 2; J. Singleton, *Lancashire on the Scrapheap* (Oxford: Oxford University Press, 1991). Surveys include L. Hannah, The *Rise of the Corporate Economy* 2nd edn (London: Methuen, 1976), ch. 3 and 4, and J. Greaves, *Industrial Reorganization in Interwar Britain* (Aldershot: Ashgate, 2005), conclusion.
4. Crucially, the industry has a large body of mainly unexploited archival sources, largely located in the Dundee University Archives (DUA).
5. 1891 Census data, cited in DUA KLoc/033 O. Graham, 'The Dundee Jute Industry 1828–1928' unpublished manuscript, Dundee, 1929; W. S. Howe, *The Dundee Textiles Industry, 1960–1977* (Aberdeen: Aberdeen University press, 1982), p. 149.
6. B. Lenman, C. Lythe, and E.Gauldie, *Dundee and its Textile Industry* (Dundee: Abertay Historical Society, 1969) Appendix II; Graham, 'Dundee jute', chapter 7.
7. B. Lenman, *Economic History of Modern Scotland 1660–1976* (London: Batsford, 1977), p. 212.
8. Board of Trade, Working Party: *Report* (1948) p. 7. 'The Most Highly-Localised Product in the UK'; S. McDowall and P. Draper, *Trade Adjustment and the British Jute Industry: A Case Study* (Glasgow: Fraser of Allander Research Institute, 1978), p. 9. The only scholarly business history of a jute firm is of one based outside Dundee, in Forfar: C. Whatley, *Onward from Osnaburgs: The Rise and Progress of a Scottish Textile Company, Don and Low of Forfar, 1792–1992* (Edinburgh: Mainstream, 1992).
9. Graham, 'Dundee Jute', figures 22–4. The peak in export volumes was 1906–7.
10. G. Stewart, *Jute and Empire* (Manchester: Manchester University Press, 1998) pp. 62, 3–4; on jute in India, see T. Sethia, 'The Rise of Jute Manufacturing in Colonial India: A Global Perspective' *Journal of World History*, 7 (1996), pp. 71–99.

11. J. Tomlinson, 'Thrice Denied: Declinism and the Narrative of British History in the Long Twentieth Century' *Twentieth Century British History* 20 (2009), pp. 227–51.

12. On this new social settlement, see especially T. Cutler, K. Williams and J. Williams, *Keynes, Beveridge and Beyond* (London: Routledge and Kegan Paul, 1986).

13. J. Tomlinson, *Employment Policy: The Crucial Years, 1939–1955* (Oxford: Oxford University Press, 1986); A. Booth, *British Economic Policy, 1931–1949: Was There a Keynesian Revolution?* (London: Harvester Wheatsheaf, 1989), ch. 7.

14. W. Parsons, *The Political Economy of British Regional Policy* (Beckenham: Croom Helm,1986), chs 3, 4.

15. M. Parker, *Thatcherism and the Fall of Coal* (Oxford: Oxford University Press, 2000).

16. D. Wass, *Decline to Fall, the Making of British Macro-Economic Policy and the 1976 IMF Crisis* (Oxford: Oxford University Press, 2008), chapter 3.

17. J. Tomlinson, 'Mrs. Thatcher's Macroeconomic Adventurism, 1979–1981, and its Political Consequences', *British Politics*, 2 (2007), pp. 3–19.

18. W. Beveridge, *Full Employment in a Free Society* (London: Allen and Unwin, 1944), pp. 51–2, 322. This high rate resulted from of a combination of job losses in the industry, and a low proportion of workers who sought employment elsewhere. This may well have reflected the extreme shortage of alternative local employment opportunities. The official figures, based on claimant data, also underestimate the number of women unemployed because of the working of the Anomalies Regulations Act, which debarred many married women from claiming.

1 The Story to 1939

1. On linen, see P. Ollerenshaw, 'Stagnation, War and Depression: The UK Linen Industry, 1900–1930', in B. Collins and P. Ollerenshaw (eds), *The European Linen Industry in Historical Perspective* (Oxford: Oxford University Press, 2003), pp. 285–307.

2. D. Chapman, 'The Establishment of the Jute Industry. A Problem in Location Theory', *Review of Economic Studies*, 6 (1938), pp. 33–55.

3. C. Whatley (ed.), *The Remaking of Juteopolis: Dundee circa 1891–1991* (Dundee: Abertay Historical Society, 1992). Comparative data on the industrial concentration of employment suggests Dundee was, for women, the most concentrated amongst substantial British cities in 1911, though for men the ranking is significantly lower. D. Reeder and R. Rodger, 'Industrialization and the City Economy', in M. Daunton (ed.), *The Cambridge Urban History of Britain vol 3 1840–1950* (Cambridge: Cambridge University Press, 2000), pp. 564–71.

4. British Association, *A Scientific Survey of Dundee and District* (London: British Association, 1939), p. 84.

5. Dundee's exports of piece goods to the USA fell from 28.1 million yards in the first four months of 1907 to 17.7 million in the same period of 1908 – a fall of almost 40 per cent: *Economist*, 66, 'Monthly Trade Supplement' May 1908, p. 13; for the major impact of this recession on one jute company's profits, see Whatley, *Onward from Osnaburgs*, p. 134.

6. B. Lenman, Lythe and Gauldie, *Dundee and its Textile Industry*, Appendix II; Graham, 'Dundee Jute Industry 1828–1928', ch. 7. DUA MS 15/1.

7. D. Wallace, *The Romance of Jute: A Short History of the Calcutta Jute Mill Industry 1855–1909* (Calcutta, 1909); A. Bagchi, 'The Jute Industry', in *Private Investment in India* (Cambridge: Cambridge University press, 1972), pp. 262–90; Stewart, *Jute and Empire*, pp. 38–92; G. Stewart, 'End Game for Jute: Dundee and Calcutta in the Twenti-

eth Century', in J. Tomlinson and C. Whatley (eds), *Jute No More: Transforming Dundee* (Dundee 2011), pp. 29–51.

8. B. R. Tomlinson, *The Economy of Modern India 1860–1970* (Cambridge: Cambridge University Press, 1993), pp. 118–22; Bagchi, *Private Investment in India*, pp. 262–90.

9. I. Menzies and D. Chapman, 'The Jute Industry' in H. Silverman (ed.), *Studies in Industrial Organization* (London: Methuen, 1946), p. 237.

10. Lenman, Lythe and Gauldie, *Dundee and its Textile Industry*; Graham, 'Dundee Jute', ch. 7.

11. Board of Trade *Hours and Earnings Enquiry* (London, HMSO,1906); Dundee Social Union, *Report on Housing and Industrial Conditions in Dundee* (Dundee: John Leng, 1905); D. Lennox, 'Working Class Life in Dundee for 25 Years 1878 to 1903' (unpublished manuscript, 1928), DUA MS 134.

12. We know far more about the early years of the century than later: E. Gordon, *Women and the Labour Movement in Scotland 1850–1914* (Oxford: Oxford University Press, 1991); W. Walker, *Juteopolis: Dundee and its Textile Workers 1885–1923* (Edinburgh: Scottish Academic Press, 1979).

13. Gordon, *Women and the Labour Movement*, p. 141.

14. D. Jones, J. Duncan and H. Conacher, *Rural Scotland during the War* (London: Oxford University Press, 1926), p. 268.

15. V. Wright, 'Juteopolis and After. Women and Work in Twentieth Century Dundee', in Tomlinson and Whatley (eds), *Jute No More*, pp. 132–62; N. Watson, 'Daughters of Dundee, Gender and Politics in Dundee: The Representation of Women 1870–1997' (Unpublished PhD Thesis, Open University, 2000).

16. Gordon, *Women and the Labour Movement*, ch. 5.

17. E. M. Wainwright, 'Constructing Gendered Workplace "Types": The Weaver-Mill-worker Distinction in Dundee's Jute Industry, *c.* 1880–1910', *Gender, Place & Culture*, 14 (2007), pp. 467–82; idem., 'Dundee's Jute Mills and Factories: Spaces of Production, Surveillance and Discipline', *Scottish Geographical Journal*, 121 (2005), pp. 121–40.

18. J. Tomlinson, 'The Deglobalization of Dundee, *c.* 1900–2000', *Journal of Scottish Historical Studies*, 29 (2009), pp. 123–40; Stewart, 'End Game for Jute', pp. 40–1.

19. A. Marrison, *British Business and Protection 1903–1932* (Oxford: Clarendon, 1996).

20. S. Masrani, 'International Competition and Strategic Response in the Dundee Jute Industry during the Interwar (1919–1939) and Post-War (1945–1960s) Period: The Case of Jute Industries, Buist Spinning, Craiks and Scott and Fyfe' (Unpublished PhD dissertation, St Andrews University, 2007); *Report of the Tariff Commission vol 2 The Textile Trades Part 7. Evidence on the Flax, Hemp and Jute Industries* (London: Tariff Commission, 1906). London School of Economics, Archives: Tariff Commission papers TC1 2/7. There was a crucial local debate in the Dundee Chamber of Commerce in January 1904, when a majority supported the idea of a 'bargaining' tariff: Dundee Chamber of Commerce minute book 15 January 1904 DCA GD/CC/4/8; *Advertiser*, 16 January 1904.

21. Dundee Chamber of Commerce Minute Book vol. 8 1895–1907 DC Thomson to Joseph Chamberlain 'The Jute Industry of Great Britain', 10 September 1903, DCA GD/CC/4/8 where the main emphasis is on an export duty on raw jute exported from India to non-Empire counties.

22. F. Trentmann, *Free Trade Nation* (Oxford: Oxford University Press, 2008), pp. 105–19; J. Tomlinson, 'Responding to Globalization? Churchill and Dundee in 1908', *Twentieth Century British History*, 21 (2010), pp. 257–80.

23. DCL: LHC, '1908 Election'. One Unionist leaflet distributed in the 1908 election item-
    ized the tariffs in European countries, and called for Britain to 'resume our power of
    fiscal negotiation with the view of trying to have such tariffs reduced'. Another called for
    Imperial Preference on jute goods in Canadian and Australian markets. The limited role
    of Britain as a market for German goods was emphasized in wartime enquiries: Board
    of Trade, *Departmental Committee on Textile Trades after the War* (London: HMSO,
    1919), pp. 91–2.

24. Dundee opinion was, unsurprisingly, hostile to a jute levy which did not discriminate in
    favour of exports to Britain, and was aimed solely at raising revenues in India: Dundee
    Chamber of Commerce, Minutes of Directors Meetings, 4 August 1905, DCA GD/
    CC/4/8; *Advertiser*, 28 December 1905.

25. B. Lenman and K. Donaldson, 'Partners' Incomes, Investment and Diversification in the
    Scottish Linen Area 1850–1921', *Business History*, 13 (1971), pp. 1–18; C. Schmit, 'The
    Nature and Dimensions of Scottish Foreign Investment, 1860–1914', *Business History*,
    39 (1997), pp. 42–68.

26. Lenman, Lythe, and Gauldie, *Dundee and its Textile Industry*, pp. 43–56; for a refutation
    of such declinism, S. Pollard, *Britain's Prime and Britain's Decline. The British Economy
    1879–1914* (1994).

27. S. Broadberry, *The Productivity Race* (Cambridge: Cambridge University Press, 1997), p.
    193; Lenman, Lythe, and Gauldie, *Dundee and its Textile Industry*, p. 54.

28. Board of Trade, *Hours and Earnings*; DSU, *Report*.

29. P. Ollerenshaw, 'Textile Business in Europe during the First World War: The Linen
    Industry, 1914–18', *Business History*, 41 (1999), p. 71; Jones *et al.*, *Rural Scotland*, p. 279.

30. Jones *et al. Rural Scotland*, pp. 283–5.

31. Ibid., pp. 287–8; on profits, see also Whatley, *Onward from Osnaburgs*, p. 134, who notes
    that Don and Low's profits went up tenfold between 1913 and 1914 and 1917 and 18,
    though as the author notes this increase needs to take into account rapid inflation.

32. Jones *et al.*, *Rural Scotland*, pp. 289–90, 297.

33. Discussion at Jute Trade Board 16–17 February 1921 on complaint of AJSM 'Many
    of the employers disliked the application of the Acts to the jute trade from the first;
    their dissatisfaction was intensified and steadily grew after the collapse of the trade last
    Autumn' TNA: PRO LAB/2/842/TBM11 4 April 1921; Walker, *Juteopolis*, pp. 419–
    25, 486–528.

34. AJSM *Annual Report, 1939* appendix H.

35. Jute Industries became Sidlaw Industries in 1971, the Sidlaw Group in 1981. Low and
    Bonar continues to exist today.

36. Working Party, *Report*, p. 10; Menzies and Chapman, 'Jute Industry', p. 257.

37. Working Party, *Report*, p. 11.

38. B. Gupta, 'Why Did Collusion Fail? The Indian Jute Industry in the Inter-War Years',
    Business History, 47 (2005), pp. 532–52; Menzies and Chapman, 'Jute Industry', p. 252.

39. Working Party, *Report*, pp. 9–10.

40. Marrison, *British Business*; F. Capie, *Depression and Protectionism: Britain between the
    Wars* (1983). During the war the industry used government enquiries into its future to
    press for an export duty on raw jute, but not for protection of the home market: Board
    of Trade, *Departmental Committee*, pp. 39, 93, 130.

41. G. Bonar, *The Industrial Outlook*, Lecture by George Bonar, 19 January 1929 (Dundee,
    1929).

42. There was a surge of German imports in the early 1920s, facilitated by the collapse of the Mark, but before protection was imposed in 1931 these had shrunk to almost nothing – from 35.7 million square yards in 1923, to 1.4 million in 1930: AJSM, *Annual Report 1939*, appendix J.

43. John Sime visited India in the 1920s with Tom Johnston, and focused much attention on Indian unions: T. Johnston, *Memories* (London: Collins, 1952), pp. 50–84; G. Doud, 'Tom Johnston in India', *Scottish Labour History Journal*, 19 (1984), pp. 6–21. This line of argument was put forward by the Labour spokesman (the MP for Dunfermline) in the House of Commons debate on jute in February 1938: Stewart, *Jute and Empire*, p. 134.

44. *Courier*, 3 February 1938.

45. Jute Industries AGM, *Courier*, 14 January 1936.

46. *Courier*, 15 July 1937 Sime's relationship with the Labour left/Communist focus of politics in Dundee seems to have been poor. The union rejected membership of the Red International of Labour Unions in 1922, and Communists were barred from office in 1928: Walker, *Juteopolis*, pp. 463, 530. It may also be significant that in the 1930s the leader of one of the other unions organizing jute workers (J. Reynolds, Secretary of the Dundee branch of the Dyers, Bleachers and Textile Workers) was de-selected by the Labour Party from standing in his council seat, and vociferously claimed this was due to 'Communist influence': *Courier*, 1 October 1937.

47. AJSM *Annual Reports 1932* to *1938*.

48. Stewart, *Jute and Empire*, pp. 125–37; idem., 'End Game for Jute' , pp. 43–5.

49. *Hansard* (Commons), vol. 314, 15 July 1936, cols 2168–9; vol. 331, 2 February 1938 cols, pp. 239–306; for examples of Dundee's arguments, Dundee Chamber of Commerce, *The Jute Industry and India* (Dundee, 1937); idem., *Critical Position of the Jute Industry* Address by the President 2 September 1937 (Dundee: Dundee Chamber of Commerce, 1937).

50. AJSM, *Annual Report 1933*, p. 13.

51. B. R. Tomlinson, *The Political Economy of the Raj, 1914–1947* (Basingstoke: Macmillan, 1979).

52. Stewart, *Jute and Empire*, p. 202.

53. *Courier*, 24 September 1937.

54. Walker, *Juteopolis*, p. 529.

55. M. Fogarty, *Prospects of the Industrial Areas of Great Britain* (London: Methuen, 1945), p. 11.

56. Working Party *Report*, pp. 55–61; Menzies and Chapman, 'Jute Industry', p. 259.

57. Walker, *Juteopolis*, p. 529.

58. Ibid., p. 513.

59. Menzies and Chapman, 'Jute Industry', p. 244; Fogarty, *Prospects*, p. 140.

60. Broadberry, *Productivity Race*, p. 253.

61. Menzies and Chapman, 'Jute Industry', p. 243.

62. Ibid., p. 245. Hannah, *Rise of the Corporate Economy*, pp. 60, 104; J. Jackson, 'Leading Industries' in J. Jackson (ed.), *The Third Statistical Account of Scotland: the City of Dundee* (Arbroath: Herald Press, 1979), pp. 118–24; Howe, *The Dundee Textiles Industry*, pp. 13, 73–9.

63. Jute Industries AGM 1922, in *Courier*, 20 February 1922.

64. Jute industries AGM 1934, in *Courier*, 16 January 1934.

65. Jute Industries AGM 1933, in *Courier*, 16 January 1933.

66. Working Party, *Report*, p. 36.

67. Fogarty, *Prospects*, p. 139. The problem was objections to conditions that Jute Industries wanted to impose for its commitment to this research initiative, but it is not clear what these conditions were: AJSM *Annual Report, 1922*, p. 19.

68. Ibid.

69. Working Party, *Report*, pp. 61–4.

70. Beveridge, *Full Employment in a Free Society*, pp. 51–2, 322. Beveridge points out that this high rate was the result of a combination of job losses in the industry, and a low proportion of workers who sought employment elsewhere. This may well have reflected the extreme shortage of alternative local employment opportunities.

71. Such discrimination predated the 1931 Act, with the 'genuinely seeking work' clause of unemployment benefit used against women: TNA: PRO LAB 2/1347/ED29473/6/1929 'Evidence to Morris Committee on Unemployment Insurance' in 1929, where Sime argues that married women find it harder to show they are 'genuinely seeking work'.

72. E. Wilkinson, *The Town that was Murdered; The Life-Story of Jarrow* (London: Left Book Club, 1939).

73. The financial burden of capital projects, especially housing, was a key issue in Dundee local politics in the 1930s: for example, *Courier*, 15 July 1937.

74. J. Phillips, 'The "Retreat" to Scotland: The Tay Road Bridge and Dundee's Post-1945 Development', in Tomlinson and Whatley (eds), *Jute No More*, pp. 246–65.

75. *Courier*, 15 March 1938, 23 March 1938.

76. Eastham, 'Scientific Study', p. 101.

2 De-Globalization and Decline 1939–99

1. The last raw jute imported arrived in Dundee docks from Chittagong on 20 October 1998. It was spun in the last operating jute works, Tay Spinners: *Courier*, 21 October 1998. This factory, the last jute mill to open in Dundee, in 1949, closed in 1999. Its machinery was later dismantled and taken to Calcutta: G. Stewart, 'Endgame for Jute: Dundee and Calcutta in the Twentieth Century', in Tomlinson and Whatley (eds), *Jute No More*, pp. 46–7.

2. Working Party *Report*, pp. 9–13.

3. Ibid., p. 13.

4. Ibid., pp. 13–16; Commonwealth Economic Committee, *Jute Manufactures* (London: HMSO, 1955), p. 2.

5. Government of Pakistan, *Report of Jute Enquiry Commission* (Karachi: Ministry of Commerce, 1961), p. 14; IJMA, *Annual Report 1947* (Calcutta: IJMA, 1948), p. vii.

6. IJMA, *Annual Report 1949*, p. v; *1950*, pp. v–ix. The industry was also disrupted by the Korean War in 1950–2: Government of India, *Report of the Jute Committee* (New Delhi: Ministry of International Trade, 1963), p. 1.

7. *Indian Jute News*, 29 October 1949.

8. *Jute Enquiry Commission*, pp. 142–3.

9. Government of Pakistan, *The Growth of Jute Industry in Pakistan* (Rawalpindi: Bureau of National Research and Reference, 1968), table 14. A small proportion of this capacity was in West Pakistan, rather than in East Pakistan (previously East Bengal), the old home of jute.

10. *Report of the Jute Committee*, p. 1.

11. International Bank for Reconstruction and Development, *Indian Exports of Jute Manufactures: Problems and Prospects* (Washington DC: IBRD, 1969), p. 10.
12. Until the end of the 1950s trends in the USA looked highly unfavourable to the industry's future: Economist Intelligence Unit, *World Jute Study* (London: EIU, 1956), p. 2.
13. Ibid., pp. 10–11.
14. Ibid., p. 1; *Report of the Jute Committee*, p. 2.
15. M. Thigpen, P. Marongiu and S. Lasker, *World Demand Prospects for Jute* (Washington DC: World Bank, 1982), p. 7.
16. Ibid., p. 7; M. Levinson, *The Box. How the Shipping Container Made the World Smaller and the World Economy Bigger* (Princeton, NJ: Princeton University Press, 2006).
17. The rise of polypropylene in Dundee is discussed in Chapter 6.
18. H. Frank, *Polypropylene* (London: Macdonald, 1969), pp. 1–9, 119–20. Production began on a small scale in the UK in 1959: D.Coleman, *Courtaulds. An Economic and Social History vol. III Crisis and Change 1940–1965* (Oxford: Clarendon, 1980), p. 175.
19. Of course, environmentally, the displacement of jute by polypropylene was a disaster, with social costs of the pollution problems of the latter's production and disposal not reflected in its selling price: J. Boyce, *The Globalization of Market Failure? International Trade and Sustainable Agriculture* (Amherst, MA: Political Economy Research Institute, 1999).
20. FAO, *Impact of Synthetics on Jute and Allied Fibres* (Rome: FAO, 1969).
21. Thigpen et al., *World Demand*, pp. 9, 21–2.
22. Ibid., pp. 25–7.
23. UNCTAD, *International Agreement on Jute and Jute Products, 1989* (New York: UNCTAD, 1996), paras.1–15.
24. FAO, *Impact of Changing Technological and Economic Factors on Markets for Natural Industrial Fibres* (Rome: FAO, 1989), pp. 16–17.
25. M. Thigpen and T. Akiyama, *Prospects for the World Jute Industry* (Washington DC: World Bank, 1986), pp. 26, 55.
26. FAO, *Impact*, pp. 18, 19.
27. In the early 1980s India produced 41 per cent of world output, Bangladesh eighteen per cent, China 17 per cent and Thailand 6 per cent: Thigpen and Akiyama, *Prospects*, p. 18.
28. Data from Annuaire statistique de l'industrie europeenne de jute compiled by B. van der Steen 'The Jute Industry: A Statistical Overview' www.iisg.nl/reserach/jute-industry. pdf, accessed 19 October 2010. On the Belgian industry, see Krediet Bank, *The Belgian Textile Industry. Part I Cotton, Wool, Flax, Jute* (Brussels: Krediet Bank, 1966), pp. 52–7.
29. Thigpen and Akiyama, *Prospects*, p. 18.
30. Ibid., pp. 20–1.
31. Thigpen et al., *World Demand*, pp. 22–4.
32. 'A SWOT Analysis of Indian Jute Industry' at www.indiantextilejournal.com/articles/ FAdetials.asp?id+1929 accessed 12 October 2010.
33. FAO, 'The Competitive Position of Jute Manufacture in Western Europe and the Far East' *Monthly Bulletin of Agricultural Economics and Statistics*, 11 (1962), pp. 3–4.
34. A. Carstairs and A. Cole, 'Recent Developments in the Jute Industry', *Scottish Journal of Political Economy*, 7 (1960), p. 121.
35. Working Party *Report*, p. 93.
36. Ibid., pp103–4.
37. IBRD, *Indian Exports*, pp. 17–18.
38. Whatley, *Onwards from Osnaburgs*, p. 194.

39. Working Party *Report*, p. 108; Commonwealth Economic Committee, *Jute manufactures*, pp. 3–4.
40. Whatley, *Onwards from Osnaburgs*, p. 195.
41. This was a long-term issue; before 1914 the British had unsuccessfully looked for alternatives to Bengal: Board of Trade, *Report of Departmental Committee to Consider the Position of the Textile Trades after the War* CD. 9070 (London: HMSO 1918), p. 34.
42. 'The British Guiana Fibre Research Co. Ltd', 21 October 1957, TNA: PRO BT 64/5122.
43. Whatley, *Onwards from Osnaburgs*, p. 243.
44. FAO, *Impact of Synthetics on Jute and Allied Fibres*, pp. 10–11.
45. Howe, *The Dundee Textiles Industry*, pp. 29–30; Whatley, *Onwards from Osnaburgs*, p. 195.
46. Boyce, *Globalization?*, pp. 3–4; van der Steen, 'Jute Industry', pp. 4–7.
47. E. Hargreaves and M. Gowing, *Civil Industry and Trade*. History of the Second World War. (London: HMSO, 1952), pp. 225, 214.
48. Ibid., p. 197; Working Party, *Report*, p. 14.
49. Ibid., *Report*, p. 14.
50. *Report of the Jute Committee*, p. 28.
51. Working Party, *Report*, p. 16.
52. Ibid., pp. 17–19.
53. Menzies and Chapman, 'The Jute Industry', pp. 260–1; Working Party *Report*, pp. 95–7.
54. Howe, *The Dundee Textiles Industry*, pp. 28–9.
55. Ibid., p. 26.
56. Carstairs and Cole, 'Recent Developments', pp. 130, 133.
57. From 51,000 tons in 1964, to 23,000 in 1976: Howe, *The Dundee Textiles Industry*, p. 61.
58. S. McDowall, P. Draper and T. McGuinness, 'Protection, Technological Change and Trade Adjustment: The Case of Jute in Britain' (St Andrews University: Department of Economics Reprint series no 14, 1976), p. 48. Also, McDowall and Draper, *Trade Adjustment and the British Jute Industry*, pp. 1–9.
59. McDowall *et al.*, 'Protection', pp. 47–8.
60. Howe, *The Dundee Textiles Industry*, pp. 60–1.
61. Stewart, *Jute and Empire*; B. Tomlinson, 'British Business in India, 1860–1970', in G. Jones and R. Davenport-Hines (eds), *British Business in Asia since 1860* (Cambridge: Cambridge University Press, 1989), pp. 92–116.
62. M. Kidron, *Foreign Investment in India* (London: Oxford University Press, 1965), pp. 10, 40, suggests that by 1950 this trend meant three-quarters of the shareholdings in jute mills run by managing agencies were in Indian hands, but the proportion of Indian directors was only 51 per cent in that year (up from 5 per cent in 1920).
63. B. R. Tomlinson, 'Colonial Firms and the Decline of Colonialism in Eastern India 1914–1947', *Modern Asian Studies*, 15 (1981), pp. 468–9.
64. Ibid., pp. 484–5. See also A. Bagchi, *Private Investment in India* (Cambridge: Cambridge University Press, 1972) pp. 262–90; O. Goswami, 'Co-operation and Conflict. European and Indian Capitalists and the Jute Economy of Bengal, 1919–1939' *Indian Economic and Social History Review*, 19 (1982), pp. 141–79.
65. G. Jones, *Merchants to Multinationals. British Trading Companies in the Nineteenth and Twentieth Centuries* (Oxford: Oxford University press, 2000), p. 295.
66. Kidron, *Foreign Investment*, p. 196.

67. R. Millward, 'The Rise of the Service Economy', in R. Floud and P. Johnson (eds), *The Cambridge Economic History of Modern Britain vol 3 Structural Change and Growth, 1939–2000* (Cambridge: Cambridge University Press, 2004), pp. 238–66.

68. 'Classics' of the genre include M. Shanks, *The Stagnant Society* (Harmondsworth: Penguin,1961); A. Shonfield, *British Economic Policy since the War* (Harmondsworth: Penguin, 1959); C. Barnett, *The Audit of War* (London: Macmillan,1986) – this followed up themes previously explored in *The Collapse of British Power* (London: Eyre Methuen, 1971); M. Wiener, *English Culture and the Decline of the Industrial Spirit 1850–1980* (Cambridge: Cambridge University Press, 1981). For commentary, J. Tomlinson, 'Inventing "Decline": The Falling Behind of the British Economy in the Post-War Years' *Economic History Review*, 49 (1996), pp. 734–60. D. Cannadine, 'Apocalypse When? British Politicians and British "Decline" in the Twentieth Century', in P. Clarke and C. Trebilcock (eds), *Understanding Decline: Perceptions and Realities of Britain's Economic Performance* (Cambridge: Cambridge University Press, 1997*)*, pp. 263–9; D. Edgerton, *Science and Technology and British Industrial 'Decline'* (Cambridge: Cambridge University Press, 1996); *Warfare State: Britain, 1920–1970* (Cambridge: Cambridge University Press, 2006).

69. A. Booth, 'The Manufacturing Failure Hypothesis and the Performance of British Industry during the Long Boom', *Economic History Review*, 56 (2003), pp. 1–33; Tomlinson, 'Thrice Denied: "Declinism" as a Recurrent Theme in British History in the Long Twentieth Century', *Twentieth Century British History*, 20 (2009), pp. 227–51.

70. D. Pilat, A. Cimper, K. Olsen, C. Webb, *The Changing Nature of Manufacturing in OECD Economies* (Paris: OECD, 2006), pp. 6–7.

71. Ibid., pp. 10–11.

72. S. Broadberry and N. F. R. Crafts, 'UK Productivity Performance from 1950 to 1979: a Restatement of the Broadberry-Crafts View', *Economic History Review*, 56 (2003), pp. 718–35; G. Owen, *From Empire to Europe* (London: Harper Collins, 2000). On the latter, see J. Tomlinson, 'Not "Decline and Revival": An Alternative Narrative on British Post-War Productivity' in R. Coopey and P. Lyth (eds), *Decline and Renaissance? Business in Britain in the Twentieth Century* (Oxford: Oxford University Press, 2009), pp. 153–67.

73. N. F. R. Crafts, 'The Golden Age of Economic Growth in Western Europe, 1950–1973' *Economic History Review* 48 (1995), pp. 429–47; C. Feinstein, 'Economic Growth Since 1870: Britain's Performance in International Perspective', *Oxford Review of Economic Policy*, 4 (1988), pp. 1–13; idem., 'Structural Change in the Developed Countries during the Twentieth Century' *Oxford Review of Economic Policy*, 15 (1999), pp. 35–55.

74. S. Broadberry and N. F. R. Crafts, 'British Economic Policy and Industrial Performance in the Early Post-War Period', *Business History*, 38 (1996), pp. 65–91; idem., 'Competition and Innovation in 1950s Britain', *Business History*, 43 (2001), pp. 97–118.

75. The top five firms in jute controlled 60 per cent of output in 1963: Broadberry and Crafts, 'Competition', p. 100.

76. C. Carter and B. Williams, *Industry and Technical Progress* (London: Oxford University Press, 1954), p. 187.

77. Howe, *The Dundee Textiles Industry*, pp. 130–7, 152.

78. T. Cox, 'Rationalisation and Resistance: The Imperial Jute Industries of Dundee and Calcutta, 1930–1940' (unpublished dissertation submitted for Trinity College Fellowship competition, Cambridge 1997), pp. viii, 9–10.

79. Working Party *Report*, pp. 85–9. For favourable comments on the industry's productivity performance in the interwar period, see Broadberry, *The Productivity Race*, pp. 193, 259–60.
80. Working Party, *Report*, pp. 55–61.
81. Carstairs and Cole, 'Recent Developments', pp. 132–3.

3 The Industry and Its Workforce

1. E. A. G. Robinson, 'The Economic Problems of the Transition from War to Peace, 1945–1949', *Cambridge Journal of Economics*, 10 (1985), pp. 165–85; J. Tomlinson, *Democratic Socialism and Economic Policy: The Attlee Years* (Cambridge: Cambridge University Press, 1997), pp. 68–93; N. Tiratsoo and J. Tomlinson, *Industrial Efficiency and State Intervention: Labour 1939–51* (London: Routledge, 1993). The Working Party *Report* is further discussed in Chapter 7.
2. J. Tomlinson, 'Productivity Policy', in H. Mercer, N. Rollings, J. Tomlinson (eds), *Labour Governments and Private Industry: The Experience of 1945–51* (Edinburgh: Edinburgh University Press, 1992), pp. 37–54.
3. Working Party, *Report*, p. ii.
4. The Jute Working Party had four jute employers, four jute trade unionists, an employer from the British Oxygen Company as chair, and four independent members.
5. Tomlinson, 'Productivity Policy', pp. 45–8; in jute the union side occasionally raised the issue of a Development Council, but the employers resisted this on the grounds that the Jute Trade Federal Council fulfilled the role – but without union involvement; see, for example, DDUJFW Minutes of Management Committee 7 February 1949 DCA/GD/JF/1/18 and 21 April 1954 DCA GD/JF/1/19.
6. FBI 'Meeting of Employer Members of Working Parties, 14 June 1946', p. 3, Modern Records Centre, Warwick University, MSS200/B/3/2/C487.
7. Working Party *Report*, p. 5.
8. 'Margaret Fenwick', in E. Ewan, S. Innes and S. Reynolds (eds), *The Biographical Dictionary of Scottish Women* (Edinburgh: Edinburgh University Press, 2006), pp. 116–17. She was Assistant General Secretary from 1960.
9. DDUJFW Minutes of Management Committee 17 April 1950, DCA GD/JF/1/20. There is no evidence that the union fought the management on this issue. On an earlier occasion when she saw herself as victimized by her employer she failed to gain the support of her union colleagues: ibid., minutes 27 October 1948 DCA GD/JF/1/18.
10. Working Party *Report*, p. 45.
11. Ibid., p. 46.
12. C. Morelli and J. Tomlinson, 'Women and Work after the Second World War: A Case Study of the Jute Industry, circa 1945–1954', *Twentieth Century British History*, 19 (2008), pp. 61–82.
13. *Scotsman*, 12 June 1948.
14. Ibid., 22 November 1948.
15. Ibid., 14 March 1950.
16. *Scotsman*, 21 March 1950.
17. Ibid., 19 April 1950.
18. Although it was decided that 'reasonable and economic expansion of existing new or old industries (including jute) will be approved, especially if such expansions are expected to contribute to increasing exports or saving dollar imports'. Ibid.

19. Sir Garnet Wilson provided evidence for the number of workers leaving jute for new industries, stating that one 'new' firm had 397 employees, of whom fifteen men and fifty-two women had left the jute industry. Ibid.
20. Morelli and Tomlinson, 'Women and Work', pp. 69–70.
21. Ibid., p. 70.
22. Discussions concerning the provision of nurseries for female workers at Jute Industries workplaces began in 1947. Camperdown nursery accommodated sixteen babies under one year, twelve children aged one to two years, and thirty-seven toddlers aged two to five years. Staff employed included a matron, deputy matron, three staff nurses, eight nursery helps, a cook and two part time cleaners. A yearly expenditure of £4,225 was anticipated. Employees were charged between 4/– and 7/6d per week. Jute Industries, general committee minute book, MS 66/10/1/4/5, 27 November 1947, 8 January 1948, 5 February 1948, 1 July 1948, 19 May 1949. Manhattan Nursery cost approximately £7,200 29 September 1949.
23. Jute Industries estimated, following a questionnaire to its female workforce that fifteen workers in the evening shift would work full time if a works nursery was provided and twenty-three persons not working would work full time if a works nursery was provided. Jute Industries, Ibid., 1 July 1948.
24. Ibid., 5 August 1948.
25. Ibid., 16 September 1948.
26. Jute Industries, industrial committee minute book, MS 66/10/1/4/5, 19 May 1949.
27. Gordon, *Women and the Labour Movement*, pp. 166–7.
28. Gordon, *Women and the Labour Movement*, p. 147.
29. Dundee Oral History Project (DOHP), Transcript 040/A/1, DCL: LHC, interview dated 1985.
30. Gordon, *Women and the Labour Movement*, p. 156. Also see DOHP, Transcript 021/A/2 and 040/A/1.
31. Ibid., Transcript 003/A/1.
32. DOHP, Transcript 022.
33. Jute Industries, ibid., 30 May 1946 and 9 September 1948.
34. Other companies involved included Caird Ltd, Scottish Co-operative Wholesale Society and James Scott & Sons. Ibid., 27 January 1949.
35. Ibid., 9 May 1946.
36. Discussions involved the need for further training on automatic devices and for day release classes for apprentices in order to 'help the congestion of night classes' at the Technical College. AJSM, Minutes of Joint Meetings with Workers' Representatives, 4 March 1952, 28 April 1952, 25 August 1952, 8 December 1952, 22 December 1952, 30 January 1952, 23 April 1953, 14 April 1954, 21 February 1955, 5 May 1955, 27 February 1956, 13 May 1959.
37. Ibid., 4 March 1954.
38. J. Arnott, 'Women Workers and Trade Union Participation in Scotland 1919–1939', (Unpublished PhD dissertation, University of Glasgow, 1999), p. 74.
39. Ibid., MS 66/10/1/4/4, 4 April 1946.
40. Jute Industries, Industrial Committee Minute Book, DUA MS 66/10/1/4/5, 6 May 1948.
41. Ibid., MS 66/10/1/4/5, 20 February 1947.
42. *Times*, 15 September 1947.
43. *Scotsman*, 17 March 1950.

44. A *Times* correspondent argued that the introduction of automatic and circular weaving was 'the first important developments of the loom for a century in this industry': *The Times*, 25 April 1952.

45. Jute Industries argued that this enabled the company to be 'one of the cheapest producers in the industry' as well as permitting 'higher wages', better working conditions, and a better quality of yarn: *Scotsman*, 15 March 1949 and *Times*, 30 March 1949.

46. *Scotsman*, 17 March 1949.

47. Howe, *The Dundee Textiles Industry*, p. 139.

48. DOHP, Transcript 044/A/1.

49. Ibid., Transcript 022/C/2.

50. AJSM, Minutes of Joint Meetings with Workers' Representatives 11 May 1961, DUA MS 84/7/1.

51. Ibid., 18 July 1962.

52. D. Simonton, *A History of European Women's Work* (London: Routledge, 1998), p. 263.

53. Jute Industries, General Committee Minute Book, MS 66/10/1/4/4, 27 February 1942 (installation of workers canteen at Stanley Mills – £750), 19 November 1943 (improved heating at Camperdown 'C' Range), 15 September 1944 (installation of eight drinking fountains – £50), 1 December 1944 (following the lead of Cairds Ltd tea was supplied in all works during working hours), 14 September 1945 (discussion of establishing a Central Canteen with van to transport meals to various works), 3 January 1946 (installation of wash basins and clothes pegs at Camperdown Works).

54. *The Times*, 10 March 1953.

55. Jute Industries, general committee minute book, 11 March 1955 DUA MS 66/10/1/4/4.

56. It was also argued that Douglasfield Works would 'help to satisfy the ever-increasing demand for yarn required to manufacture exports to the dollar markets, and thereby make an important contribution to the national economy'. Ibid., 12 March 1956.

57. Jute Industries argued that the shortage of labour meant that the company had 'been unable to make full use of our machinery potential' which resulted in a 'squeeze in profit margins'. Ibid., 1 February 1965, 17 January 1966.

58. Howe, *The Dundee Textiles Industry*, pp. 129–30. Jute Industries, General Committee Minute Book, 15 December 1944 DUA MS 66/10/1/4/4.

59. *Scotsman*, 15 March 1949.

60. *JIL News*, MS 66/10/15/1/1, June 1966.

61. Ibid., September 1966.

62. Ibid., 24 June 1965.

63. Ibid., 5 July 1965.

64. Howe, *The Dundee Textiles Industry*, pp. 128–9.

65. DDUJFW Minutes of Management Committee 15 December 1948 DCA GD/JF/1/18.

66. AJSM Minutes of Joint Meeting of General Committee and Wages and Hours Sub-Committee 8 June 1949 DUA MS 84/10/1; DDUJFW Minutes of Management Committee 21 October 1949, 21 November 1949 DCA GD/JF/1/19. Contrast the discussion in I. Gibson, 'The Revision of the Jute Wages-Structure', *Scottish Journal of Political Economy* 4 (1957) pp. 46–59 which overstates employers' enthusiasm for the change.

67. H. Clegg, *The System of Industrial Relations in Great Britain* (Oxford: Basil Blackwell, 1970), pp. 173–7.

68. AJSM Minutes of Joint Meeting of General Committee and Wages and Hours Sub-Committee 24 November 1949, 11 July 1950, 19 September 1950, 13 October 1950, DUA

MS 84/10/1. For a summary of the whole episode, National Board for Prices and Incomes, *Job Evaluation (Supplement)*, Cmnd. 3772–I (London: HMSO, 1968, pp. 15–17).

69. AJSM, Base Rate Analysis Working Committee, 15 November 1950, 5 March 1951, DUA MS84/10/1.

70. AJSM, Minutes of Joint Meetings with Workers' Representatives, 14 February 1952, DUA MS 84/10/1.

71. Ibid., 29 September 1956.

72. *The Times*, 10 March 1953.

73. AJSM, Minutes of Joint Meetings with Workers' Representatives, 11 May 1961.

74. The union employed Ian Mikardo, MP, an unusual Labour figure, on the left of the party, but also an industrial consultant and advocate of the benefits to the workers of higher productivity: DDUJFW Management Committee minutes, 11 September, 16 October, 20 November, 11 December 1950: DCA GD/JF/1/19.

75. *The Times*, 12 March 1956.

76. AJSM, Minutes of Joint Meetings with Workers' Representatives, 14 June 1957.

77. The union records only infrequently give membership data. In 1949 numbers were recorded as 3,450 but ten years later as only 2,000: DDUJFW Minutes of Management Committee 28 March 1949 DCA GD/JF/1/18, AGM minutes, 7 June 1959 DCA GD/JF/1/20.

78. Howe, *The Dundee Textiles Industry*, p. 129.

79. For example, by forty-nine votes to twelve at the AGM on 18 June 1961, forty-seven votes to seven at the AGM on 27 May 1962, sixty-nine to sixteen at the AGM on 26 May 1963 DDUJFW DCA GD/JF/1/20. Also in 1949, when the Dundee Trades Council was reorganized and became Communist dominated, there was talk of DDUJFW disaffiliating, though in the end this was rejected: Minutes of Management Committee 7 February 1949, 19 April 1949 DCA GD/JF/1/18.

80. DDUJFW Minutes of Management Committee 8 October 1961, 24 December 1961, 14 January 1962, 17 January 1962 DCA GD/JF/1/20.

81. Special Meeting of DDUJFW Management Committee, 14 July 1963 DCA GD/JF/1/20.

82. AJSM, Minutes of Joint Meetings with Workers' Representatives, 1 April 1954. Notably as well as the 'Negotiations Sub-committee' of the AJSM being present at this meeting, which included Robertson, representatives of Caird, James Scott and Sons and Jute Industries were also present. Given the labour shortage in the industry the presence of these individuals highlights the importance of the issue to employers.

83. Ibid.

84. Ibid.

85. Ibid., 3 June 1954.

86. Ibid., 24 September 1956.

87. Ibid.

88. Ibid., 4 February 1952, 6 March 1952.

89. Ibid., 26 January 1953.

90. Ibid., 3 February 1953.

91. Ibid., 28 December 1953. A similar request was made in the following April. 15 April 1954.

92. Ibid., 15 April 1955.

93. Ibid., 1 November 1957.

94. Ibid., 30 October 1958.

95. Ibid., 4 December 1961.
96. Ibid., 24 August 1959. The Unions represented included the Scottish Union of Power-loom Tenters, DDUJFW, AEU, National Union of General and Municipal Workers, Associated Blacksmiths' Forge and Smithy Workers' Society.
97. Macbeth suggested that in 1947, when the hours were reduced from forty-eight to forty-five, 'everyone was still under the strains of the war years' and 'the worker had returned from the army and had still to redevelop old skills'.
98. Macbeth supported this claim with evidence from the *Ministry of Labour Gazette* of July 1959 which stated that in the four weeks ended 30 May 680 operatives had been engaged in the industry while 844 operatives had left. This represented a loss of 204.
99. To support this statement Brown quoted the census of production of 1951 and 1954. In 1951 the production per operator was 422 lbs and the profit per operator was £252. The corresponding figure for 1954 were 585 lbs and £273.
100. Ibid., 6 November 1958.
101. Ibid. He argued that 'the grey, white and brown coats were only functional specialists and as always, the management managed, delegating responsibility to the foremen as before'.
102. Ibid., 9 April 1959.
103. Ibid. The questionnaire received thirty-six responses, nine establishments gave permission for the collection of dues, 6 made premises available to union officials and five provided 'other facilities' including notice boards.
104. Ibid., 30 June 1959.
105. DDUJFW Minutes of Management Committee 31 August 1962 DCA GD/JF/1/20.
106. AJSM, Minutes of Joint Meetings with Workers' Representatives 16 August 1962.
107. Ibid., 24 August 1962.
108. Ibid., 31 August 1962.
109. *Evening Telegraph*, 14 August 1981.
110. AJSM, *Annual Report*, 1979.
111. In 1964 the agreement was estimated to cover 45 per cent of the workers: Meeting of Wages Sub-Committee, 28 September 1964 DUA MS84/10/2.
112. Meeting of Employers on Joint Wages Structure Committee, 9 June 1966 DUA MS 84/10/3.
113. C. Craig, J. Rubery, R. Tarling and F. Wilkinson, 'Abolition and After: The Jute Wages Council', *Department of Applied Economics, University of Cambridge, Research Paper No. 15* (1980), p. 24.
114. Meeting of Wages Sub-Committee, 16 April 1964. DUA MS 84/10/2
115. Review Ad Hoc Committee, 7 December 1964, DUA MS 84/10/3.
116. Eventually the revised agreement reduced the number of male grades from thirty to thirteen, female from twenty-three to ten. A further revision in 1975 produced six grades with no gender differentiation: Craig, *et al.*, 'Abolition and After', p. 23.
117. Meeting of Joint Wage Structure Committee, 16 February 1966, 11 March 1966, 27 May 1966 DUA MS 84/10/3.
118. Meeting of Joint Wage Structure Committee, 14 July 1966 DUA MS 84/10/3.
119. Craig, *et al.*, 'Abolition and After', p. 1; 'Abolition of Jute Wages Council (GB) proposed', 3 June 1969, TNA: PRO LAB83/1373.
120. Craig, *et al.*, 'Abolition and After', p. 50.
121. The union unanimously endorsed the agreement, with no evidence at this date of concerns about the huge gender gap embodied within it – a male minimum of £10.2, and a

female minimum of £7.12 Minutes of management committee 23 October 1966 DCA GD/JF/1/20.

122. Meeting of Joint Wage Structure Committee, 30 August 1966, DUA MS 84/10/3.

123. Meeting of Joint Wages Structure Committee, 11 January 1968, MS 84/10/4.

124. Meeting Joint Wages Structure Committee, 11 January 1968. A Polypropylene Sub-Committee of the AJSM was established by 1969: DUA MS 84/9/2: Meeting of Polypropylene Sub-Committee 4 February 1969, DUA MS 84/10/4.

125. AJSM *Annual Report* 1972.

126. Craig, *et al.*, 'Abolition and After', pp. 35, 50–1. The union had inklings of the future when as early as 1948 it formally changed its name to the 'Dundee and District Union of Jute, Flax and other Fibre Workers' because it wished to accommodate those involved in rayon spinning: Minutes of Management Committee, 5 November 1948 GD/JF/1/18.

127. Craig, *et al.*, 'Abolition and After', pp. 22, 35.

128. The DDUJFW merged with the UJFKTO in 1966.

129. Craig, *et al.*, 'Abolition and After', p. 33.

130. Ibid., p. 43.

131. Ibid., p. 13.

132. AJSM, Meeting of Governing Committee, 1 December 1977 and 23 November 1976, DUA MS84/4/5.

133. AJSM, Meeting of Employers on Jute Wages Structure Board, 22 January 1970, DUA MS84/25/3.

134. Craig, *et al.*, 'Abolition and After', p. 23. Patriarchal attitudes remained in the jute industry, as indicated by an article discussing the implications of the forthcoming Equal Pay Act published in November 1969 in *JIL News*, the works newspaper of Jute Industries, entitled 'Money that's Strictly for the Birds'. The article outlined that the act would mean higher wages for women, changes in the terms of employment, the use of job evaluation and 'probably higher prices' throughout the industry.

135. Craig, *et al.*, 'Abolition and After', p. 49; see also C. Craig, J. Rubery, R. Tarling and F. Wilkinson, *Labour Market Structure, Industrial Organisation and Low Pay* (Cambridge, Cambridge University Press, 1982), p. 73 who argue 'it was the strength of the employers' association in jute and the traditions of female organization and relatively high female earnings that prevented jute firms from taking full advantage of the availability of 'marginal workers obtainable at low rates of pay'.

136. Craig, *et al.*, 'Abolition and After', p. 51.

137. The AJSM *Annual Report* 1981 reported 'eleven carpet companies under receivership by mid-1980'.

138. *Courier*, 9 January 1981.

139. AJSM, *Annual Report*, 1982. (This was the last published *Annual Report*). The Industrial Training Board for the industry was also abolished in 1981.

140. John McAllion, leader of the Labour group on Tayside Regional Council, and later a Dundee MP, was prominent in these efforts. *Courier*, 15 January 1987, *Evening Telegraph*, 11 June 1987, *Courier*, 12 February 1988.

141. *Courier*, 18 December 1986, 19 August 1992.

142. *Courier*, 1 September 1998, 29 September 1998, 28 June 1999.

4 Defending the Domestic Industry

1. M. Aoki, B. Gustaffson and O. E. Williamson, *The Firm as a Nexus of Treaties* (London: SAGE, 1990).
2. R. Evely and I. M. D. Little, *Concentration in British Industry: An Empirical Sudy of the Structure of Industrial Production 1935–51* (Cambridge: Cambridge University Press, 1960), Table 3.
3. Whatley, *Onwards from Osnaburgs* and *Stock Exchange Yearbook*, Guildhall Library London (hereafter GL),1950, p. 2449, 1961, p. 2649. and 1967, p. 2650.
4. *Stock Exchange Yearbook*, GL, 1950, p. 2449.
5. Ibid., 1949, p. 2330.
6. Board of Trade, Working Party *Report*, 1948, Recommendation 1 and 2, p. 4.
7. Working Party *Report*, 1948, p. 50
8. Note entitled 'Dundee', August 1943, TNA: PRO BT 64/2304, pp. 5–6.
9. Working Party *Report*, 1948, p. 51
10. D. Philips, *The Hungry Thirties: Dundee between the Wars* (Dundee: David Winter, 1981).
11. Working Party *Report*,1948, para. 13, p. 3.
12. G. Symeonidis, *The Effects of Competition: Cartel Policy and the Evolution of Strategy and Structure in British Industry* (London: MIT Press, 2002), table B1.
13. Working Party *Report*, 1948, p. 22 and Board of Trade, *Census of Production*, 1963, vol. 79, table 1.
14. Board of Trade, *Census of Production*, 1958, vol. 80, table 2 and 1963, vol. 79, table 1.
15. Gupta, 'Why Did Collusion Fail?'
16. D. Robertson and S. Dennison, *The Control of Industry* (Cambridge: Cambridge University Press, 1960); E. A. G. Robinson, *Monopoly* (Cambridge: Cambridge University Press, 1941), p. 268.
17. Ibid.
18. A. Cairncross, and N. Watts, *The Economic Section 1939–61: A Study in Economic Advising* (London: Routledge, 1989), pp. 83–4.
19. *The National Plan, Cmnd. 2764* (London: HMSO, 1965), Paragraph 21.
20. See for example S. N. Broadberry, and N. F. R. Crafts, 'British Economic Policy and Industrial Performance' and N. Tiratsoo and J. Tomlinson, *Industrial Efficiency and State Intervention: Labour 1939–1951* (London: Routledge, 1993).
21. Between 1934 and 1939 Indian production supplied on average 1.1m tons (58 per cent) of the average world consumption of 1.9m tons. Commonwealth Economic Committee, *Jute Manufactures: A Memorandum on Production, Prices and trade Prepared by the Intelligence Branch of the Commonwealth Economic Committee* (HMSO: London, 1955), table 5 and p. 7.
22. 'Protection of the UK Jute Industry', 1 May 1952 by R. M. Howell, TNA: PRO BT11/4879.
23. Working Party *Report*, 1948, table 2, pp. 24–5, *Census of Production*, 1951, table 4.
24. *Census of Production*, 1992, table 13.
25. M. E. Porter, *The Competitive Advantage of Nations* (London: Macmillan, 1990).
26. G. H. Boyce, *Information, Mediation and Institutional Development: The Rise of the Large-Scale Enterprise in British Shipping, 1870–1919* (Manchester: Manchester University Press, 1995).

27. See Dundee Chamber of Commerce, Directors minutes, DCA, GD/CC/4/11 1920–30 for an example.
28. The largest numbers of individuals involved, twenty-six of the seventy-three original subscribers, were solely engaged as 'merchants'. Comprising the second largest group were those identified as 'merchants and flaxspinners', with twenty-one subscribers. The next two largest groups were those of 'merchants and agents' and 'merchants and manufacturers', who together provided a further eighteen subscribers. The final nine subscribers, with the exception of one 'flaxspinner', one 'agent' and one 'flaxspinner and manufacturer', were again all involved in 'merchanting' and additional aspects of the trade as 'shipowners', 'insurers', 'bleachers' and 'manufacturers'. Chamber of Commerce, *Centenary Souvenir* 1936, DCA, pp. 41 & 62.
29. Chamber of Commerce *Yearbook 1937*, DCA, pp. 252–67.
30. Dundee City Corporation, *The City and Royal Burgh of Dundee: Survey & Plan, 1952* (Macclesfield: Dobson, Chapman & Partners, 1952), Appendix 2 and Chamber of Commerce, *Yearbook* 1937, DCA, p. 252–67.
31. Chamber of Commerce *Annual Report*, 20 March 1920, DCA.
32. Chamber of Commerce, Director's Stated Meetings Minutes 1960–4, 15 March 1960, Annual General Meeting, DCA, GD/CC.
33. Dundee Chamber of Commerce *Trade Directory and Buyers' Guide 1960–61*, DCA, p. 6
34. See Chapter 3 and *Scotsman*, 19 April 1950 and Letter from D. F. Eades Ministry of Materials to A. N. Halls Board of Trade, 8 October 1951, TNA: PRO BT177/522.
35. Chamber of Commerce, Director's Stated Meeting Minute, 22 September 1964, DCA, GD/CC.
36. In July 1968 the total membership of 1,141 was broken down as Dundee 806, Montrose 51, Forfar 45, Fife 58, Arbroath 90, Brechin 63 and Other members 28. Chamber of Commerce, Director's Stated Meeting Minute, 16 July 1968, DCA, GD/CC, p. 7.
37. S. K. Masrani, 'International Competition and Strategic Response in the Dundee Jute Industry during the Inter-War (1919–39) and Post-War (1945–60s): The Case of Jute Industries, Buist Spinning, Craiks and Scott & Fyfe' (unpublished PhD dissertation, University of St Andrews, 2007), pp. 121–66.
38. Jute Industries Minute Books, 9 December 1976, DUA, MS 66/10/1/12.
39. M. Olson, *The Rise and Decline of Nations* (New Haven, CT: Yale University Press, 1982).
40. A. Slaven, and S. Checkland (eds.), *Dictionary of Scottish Business Biography 1860–1960: Vol.1, The Staple Industries* (Aberdeen: Aberdeen University Press, 1986).
41. *Courier*, 30 April 1993.
42. *The Times*, 6 June 1954, p. 14.
43. London Jute Association, Minute Book, 13 February 1963, London Metropolitan Library Archive (hereafter LMA), MSS 16666, p. 2.
44. Report from Annual Dinner of the UK Jute Goods Assoc dinner by Board of Trade official D. N. Charlish, 31 May 1961, TNA: PRO BT 258/834.
45. *Times*, 11 September, 1970, p. 24.
46. *Guardian*, 3 December 2008, p. 37.
47. Commonwealth Economic Committee, *Jute Manufactures*, 1955, p. 4.
48. P. Sengupta, *The Indian Jute Belt* (Bombay: Orient Longmans, 1959), p. 92.
49. S. Pollard, *The Development of the British Economy 1914–80*, 3rd edn (London: Edward Arnold, 1983).
50. Revision of Anglo–Pakistan Trade Agreement: Jute 1950. TNA: PRO BT 64/1637

51. The only exceptions to this were special arrangements made for two large users of jute bags, Imperial Chemicals Industries and the British Sugar Corporation.

52. Restrictive Trade Practices Act 1956, the position of the jute industry, 21 November 1958, TNA: PRO BT 258/832, p. 2.

53. *Census of Production*, 1951, G, table 2 and 1958, 80, table 1.

54. Jute: Trading on Public Account, TNA: PRO BT 279/173.

55. Jute, note written by R. Esdale 28th December 1956, TNA: PRO, BT 258/6.

56. David Eccles MP was President of the Board of Trade from 1957–9. For his biography see Martin Pugh, 'Eccles, David McAdam, first Viscount Eccles (1904–1999)', *Oxford Dictionary of National Biography* (Oxford: Oxford University Press, 2004); online edn, May 2009 [http://www.oxforddnb.com/view/article/71965, accessed 17 Aug 2010].

57. Considerations on Conservative attitudes to control and state trading 29 August 1957, National Library of Scotland (hereafter NLS), Acc 11679 Series 1, 1–5, reference: Ref: btx.

58. London Jute Association, Minute Books, 18 October 1961, LMA.

59. J. N. Bartlett, *Carpeting the Millions: The Growth of Britain's Carpet Industry* (Edinburgh: John Donald Press, 1978), pp. 189–202.

60. Regional Report on Building Projects, 10 January 1950, TNA: PRO BT64/1641, p. 2

61. McDowall and Draper, *Trade Adjustment and the British Jute Industry*, p. 7.

62. Precognition Statement by Lewis F. Robertson to Restrictive Trade Practices Court (Scotland), DUA MS84/18/1/2, pp. 73–6.

63. Letter from Lewis Robertson to Directors (3), Mr Ireland & Mr Petrie 8/11/57, NLS, Acc 11679 Series 1 Correspondence & notes boxes 1–5, re: cai Commercial/General.

64. Ibid.

65. Letter 'Rove prices' from Lewis Robertson to Directors to Mr Ireland 31/10/57, NLS, Acc 11679 Series 1 Correspondence & notes boxes 1–5 re: bzi Yarn/Commercial.

66. Letter 'Rove prices' from Lewis Robertson to Directors to Mr Ireland 31/10/57, NLS, Acc 11679 Series 1 Correspondence & notes boxes 1–5 re: bzi Yarn/Commercial.

67. E. Fraser, *A Home by the Hooghly: A Jute Wallah's Wife* (Edinburgh: Mainstream, 1989).

68. Note of conversation with Mr W. G. N. Walker, NLS Acc 11679 Series 1 Correspondence & notes boxes 6–11, Box No.6, Ref: cso 10/1/58 Restrictive Trade Practices.

69. B. S. Yamey, *Resale Price Maintenance* (London: Weidenfield and Nicholson, 1966).

70. W. A. Brusse and R. T. Griffiths, 'The Incidence of Manufacturing Cartels in Post-War Europe' in C. J. Morelli (ed.), *Cartels and Market Management in the Post-War World* (London: Business History Unit London School of Economics, 1997), pp. 78–117.

71. Note of telephone conversation from Board of Trade's Miss Elizabeth Ackroyd to Restrictive Trade Practices Office, Mr. Ord Johnstone, 10 November 1959, TNA: PRO BT 258/6.

72. Correspondence between Mrs R. Esdale, Mr McGregor, Mr Ryder and Mr R. H. King, 4 January 1957–7 February 1957, TNA: PRO BT 258/832.

73. Advisory Committee Report by Sub Committee on Protection Methods, 1 October 1957, NLS Acc 11679 Series 1, 1–5, ref: bwa.

74. Note of Meeting with Sir Lewis Robertson and Mr Eccles of the Board of Trade, 29 August 1957, NLS Acc 11679 Series, ref: btx Considerations.

75. Jute, note written by R. Esdale, 28 December 1956, TNA: PRO BT 258/6.

76. Jute: Restrictive Trade Practices Court Hearing: preliminary information required by the Registrar, January 1961, TNA: PRO BT 258/834, p. 3.

77. Jute Restrictive Practices Court Hearing, TNA: PRO BT 258/1375 and Indian government request to remove the mark-up on imported jute goods 1961, TNA: PRO BT 256/8.
78. Meeting of Free Trade Area Working Party (Jute), 24 September 1957, NLS, Acc 11679 Series 1, 1–5, reference: bwe European.
79. Restrictive Trade Practices Notes, 3 September 1957, NLS, Acc 11679 Series 1 Correspondence & notes boxes 1–5, re: buj, 'p. 4.
80. Note of telephone conversation from Board of Trade's Mr E. Ackroyd to Restrictive Trade Practices Office, Mr Ord Johnstone, 10 November 1959, TNA: PRO BT 258/6.
81. Precognition Statement by Lewis F. Robertson to Restrictive Trade Practices Court (Scotland), 'The Jute References' November 1962, DUA MS84/18/1/2 pp. 52–7.
82. Ibid., p. 115.
83. Ibid., pp. 97–102.
84. Report of the Restrictive Trade Practices Court. April 1963.
85. *Economist,* 30 March 1963, 'Restrictive Practices Court: Jute Rejected', p. 1274.
86. Jute, 29 February 1960, DUA MS 84/12/7 (100 (1)).
87. Note of Meeting between Mr Hill, Hutton & Robertson, 17 September 1957, NLS, Acc 11679 Series 1 Correspondence & notes boxes 1–5, re: bvn.
88. Ibid.
89. Information Bureau letter, Jute, 26 March 1963, TNA: BT PRO 258/835.
90. Olson, *Rise and Decline.*
91. Note of Meeting with Sir Lewis Robertson and Mr. Eccles of the Board of Trade, August 1957. NLS Acc 11679 Series, ref: btx 29th Considerations.
92. Draft Cabinet Paper, Jute goods future policy, author Mr Ord Johnstone, 26 July 1963, TNA: PRO BT303/155.
93. Ibid., TNA: PRO BT303/155 p. 2.
94. Note by Mr A.L Burgess, 3 September 1963 and Working Group membership, TNA: PRO BT 258/1746, Jute Working Group correspondence and minutes, p. iii.
95. Jute Working Group correspondence and minutes. Final Report, TNA: PRO BT 258/1746, p. 1.
96. Jute Working Group Report, Press release, 1 September 1964, TNA: PRO BT 258/1832, p. 2.
97. M. W. Ord Johnstone to Mr Gregson, 28 July 1964, TNA: PRO BT 258/8.
98. K. E. Saunders writing to N. Bloom, 25 September 1969, TNA: PRO BT 258/2541.
99. *Census* (1968), 102, table 1 and (1971), PA415, table 1.
100. Howe, *The Dundee Textiles Industry*, p. 39.

5 Firms' Responses to the Decline of the Industry

1. N. Hood and S. Young, *Multinationals in Retreat. The Scottish Experience* (Edinburgh: University Press. 1982).
2. Sidlaw Industries, 'Background History of Sidlaw Industries Limited 1972', DUA, MS 66/10/1/12.
3. Ibid.
4. *Report on the UK Census of Production, Jute* (1963), 79 (London, HMSO), table 1.
5. *Census* (1963), 79, Table 5.
6. *Census* (1968), 102, table 1 and (1971), PA415, table 1.
7. *Census* (1972), PA415, table 1.

8. In moving from the *Census of Production* to an industrial survey under the *Business Monitor* series in 1970 government data changed the measurement of quantity data from output measured in weight to yardage making direct comparison impossible.

9. Polypropylene output in 1972 amounted to 196,681 square yards compared to total yarn and cloth output of 231,997 square yards, *Census* (1972), PA415, table 7.

10. *Census* (1958), 80, table 3 and (1971), PA415, table 3.

11. See Chapter 2 for further discussion of the formation and expansion of these two companies.

12. *Stock Exchange Yearbook*, 1961, p. 2649.

13. *Stock Exchange Yearbook*, 1950, p. 2449.

14. *Stock Exchange Yearbook*, 1967, p. 2650.

15. DUA, MS 66/10/1/12.

16. H. Corteen, 'Science at Work in the Jute Industry', *Dundee Chamber of Commerce Journal*, September 1958, pp. 143–5.

17. J. N. Bartlett, *Carpeting the Millions: The Growth of Britain's Carpet Industry* (Edinburgh: John Donald, 1978).

18. The management of Jute Industries argued that 'prior to 1939 carpet buying was very much a middle-class business', while 'the post-1945 situation opened up the market to a much wider cross-section of the populace'. DUA, MS 66/10/1/12.

19. A. Bagchi, *Private Investment in India* (Cambridge: Cambridge University Press, 1972) pp. 262–91.

20. The South African Canvas Co. Johannesburg was established in 1928 and interestingly this merchanting business traded in jute goods from Dundee and Calcutta, as well as flax and cotton goods and other articles. Low & Bonar company brochure, *c.* mid-1950s, DUA, MS 24/1/7/3/1.

21. Boyce, *Information, Mediation and Institutional Development*; O. E. Williamson, *The Economic Institutions of Capitalism: Firms, Markets, Relational Contracting* (London: Macmillan, 1985).

22. DUA, MS 66/10/1/12.

23. R. S. Tedlow, *New and Improved: The Story of Mass Marketing in America* (Oxford: Heineman, 1990).

24. *Stock Exchange Yearbook*, vol. 2 (annually from 1949 to 1969).

25. *Sidlaw News*, August 1973, DUA, MS 66/10/15/1/1.

26. DUA, MS 66/10/1/12, 9 December 1976.

27. Ibid.

28. Ibid.

29. Ibid.

30. In addition flax spinning at Garden Works, Dundee and the production of existing jute yarns and twines at Camperdown Works, Dundee, ceased in Spring 1977. Sidlaw Industries, 'News Release – Sidlaw Textiles to Modernise and Rationalise', Company Announcements, DUA, MS 66/10/15/2/1, 9 December 1976.

31. Ibid.

32. Ibid.

33. Ibid.

34. Ibid.

35. Ibid.

36. Ibid.

37. Ibid.

38. Sidlaw Industries, Historical records, DUA, MS 66/10/1/12, 9 December 1976.

39. 39.Sidlaw Industries, 'Interim Statement – Chairman's Statement', Company Announcements, DUA, MS 66/10/15/2/1, 31 March 1978.
40. Low & Bonar, Company Announcements, DUA, MS 24/1/7/1/1, 1 September 1977.
41. Ibid., 8 December 1977.
42. Ibid., 5 May 1978.
43. Low & Bonar, Company Press Releases, DUA, MS 24/1/7/1/1, 20 March 1977.
44. Ibid., 28 April 1977.
45. Low & Bonar, Company Announcements, DUA, MS 24/1/7/1/2, 2 May 1978.
46. *Census*, PA1002 (1977), table 2 and (1982), table 2.
47. *Sidlaw News*, DUA, MS 66/10/15/1/1, June 1978.
48. Ibid.
49. Sidlaw Industries, Company Announcements, DUA, MS 66/10/15/2/1, 7 December 1979.
50. Ibid.
51. Ibid., 28 March 1980.
52. *Sidlaw News*, 'Sidlaw in 78/79 – A Report to Employees', DUA, MS 66/10/15/1/1. A similar statement was issued by Low & Bonar. It argued that its carpet manufacturing companies had failed to earn the level of profits their well equipped plants should provide as too many carpet producers were chasing too few orders and also because of an inflow of cheaper imported carpeting, mainly from America. Low & Bonar, employee reports and newspapers, 'Report '79 – A Report for Everyone in the Low & Bonar Group', DUA, MS 24/1/8/5/1.
53. Sidlaw Industries, Company Announcements, DUA, MS 66/10/15/2/1, 28 March 1980.
54. Ibid., 16 October 1980.
55. Ibid.
56. Sidlaw Industries, 'Company Announcements', DUA, MS 66/10/1/12, 8 January 1981.
57. The entire share capital of Sidlaw of Scotland was sold on 27 March 1981, Ibid., 16 April 1981.
58. Ibid., 8 January 1981.
59. Ibid., 8 July 1982.
60. Ibid., 21 May 1986.
61. Sidlaw Industries, 'Company Announcements', DUA, MS 66/10/1/12, 18 January 1989 and 1 December 1988.
62. Sidlaw Industries, Company Announcements, DUA, MS 66/10/15/2/1, 31 May 1990.
63. Ibid., 29 November 1990.
64. Ibid., 11 November 1991.
65. *Courier*, 'Sidlaw to Sell Textiles Division', Wednesday 19 October 1994, p. 5, DUA, MS 66/10/15/4/13.
66. Low & Bonar, Company Announcements, DUA, MS 24/1/7/1/4, 29 August 1980.
67. Ibid., 10 October 1980.
68. Low & Bonar, Employee Reports and Newspapers, 'Report '80 – A Very Difficult Year', DUA, MS 24/1/8/5/1.
69. Within the UK polypropylene extrusion was later concentrated in Dundee with Low & Bonar's operation in Forfar being closed. Low & Bonar, Employee reports and newspapers, 'Bonar World – Results Extra, Supplement to Bonar World, May 1983', DUA, MS 24/1/8/5/1.
70. Low & Bonar, Company Announcements, DUA, MS 24/1/7/1/5, 8 July 1981.

71. See S. N. Broadberry, 'Unemployment', in N. F. R. Crafts and N. W. C. Woodward (eds), *The British Economy since 1945* (Oxford: Clarendon Press, 1991), pp. 212–35 and B. Eichengreen, 'Institutions and Economic Growth: Europe after World War II' in N. F. R. Crafts and G. Toniolo (eds), *Economic Growth in Europe since 1945* (Cambridge: Cambridge University Press, 1996), pp. 38–72.

72. A. Booth, *The British Economy in the Twentieth Century* (Basingstoke: Palgrave, 2001), p. 87.

73. Low & Bonar, Company Announcements, DUA, MS 24/1/7/1/5, 8 July 1981.

74. Low & Bonar, Company Brochure, DUA, MS 24/1/7/3/1, *c.* mid-1950s.

75. Howe, *The Dundee Textiles Industry*, p. 74.

76. Craig, *et al.*, 'Abolition and After', p. 9.

77. *Sidlaw News*, February 1972, DUA, MS 66/10/15/1/1.

78. Sidlaw Industries, 'Background history 1972', DUA, MS 66/10/1/12.

79. Sidlaw Industries, 'Sidlaw to handle Tenneco Tile business in UK', Company announcements, DUA, MS 66/10/15/2/1, 30 March 1977.

80. DUA, MS 24/1/7/1/3, 10 May 1979. Low & Bonar continued to invest in the Flotex carpeting company, which it stated was 'one of the few in the industry to have traded profitably'. 4 May 1982, DUA, MS 24/1/7/1/6.

81. Low & Bonar, Employee Reports and Newspapers, 'Report '79 – A Report for Everyone in the Low & Bonar Group' and 'Report '80 – A Very Difficult Year'. Also see *Bonar World*, 4:2 (May 1984), DUA, MS 24/1/8/5/1.

82. Low & Bonar, Employee Reports and Newspapers, '1978 – A Year of Improvements', DUA, MS 24/1/8/5/1.

83. Ibid.

84. *Bonar Business News*, 1:3 (June 1986), DUA, MS 24/1/8/5/1.

85. J. Bamberg, *British Petroleum and Global Oil 1950–75: The Challenge of Nationalism* (Cambridge: Cambridge University Press, 2000), pp. 350–70 and Figure 14.3.

86. See; G. Owen, *The Rise and Fall of Great Companies: Courtaulds and the Reshaping of the Man-Made Fibres Industry. Passold Studies in Textile History* (Oxford: Oxford University Press, 2010) and *Courier*, 19 November 1946 and *The Times*, 6 June 1972, p. 20.

87. http://www.unioncarbide.com/history/index.htm accessed 28 September 2010.

88. W. Lazonick, *Business Organisation and the Myth of the Market Economy* (Cambridge: Cambridge University Press, 1991).

89. This involved the sale of 240,000 'B' Ordinary Shares of £1.00 each (40 per cent) in Polytape Ltd, Dundee, 260,000 4.2 per cent Non-Cumulative Preference Shares of £1.00 each (50 per cent) in Synthetic Fabrics (Scotland) Ltd, Forfar, and 6,000 'A' Shares of B.Frs. 1000 each (25 per cent) N. V. Fibrilo S.A., Belgium. Sidlaw Industries, Company Announcements, 13 June 1977, DUA, MS 66/10/15/2/1. Also see Low & Bonar, Company press release, 13 June 1977, DUA, MS 24/1/7/1/1.

90. Ibid.

91. Ibid.

92. Ibid.

93. Sidlaw Industries, 'Stanley Mills', Company announcements, DUA, MS 66/10/15/2/1, 29 January 1979.

94. Ibid., 18 February 1985.

95. Low & Bonar, Company Announcements, DUA, MS 24/1/7/1/4, 29 January 1980.

96. Ibid., 22 August 1980.

97. Howe, *The Dundee Textiles Industry*, p. 96.

98. Ibid., pp. 65–100.
99. Sidlaw Industries, 'Background History, 1972' DUA, MS 66/10/1/12.
100. Low & Bonar, Company Brochure, c. mid 1950s, DUA, MS 24/1/7/3/1.
101. Ibid.
102. Low & Bonar, Company Announcements, DUA, MS 24/1/7/1/1, 26 August 1977.
103. Low & Bonar, Company Announcements, DUA, MS 24/1/7/1/3, 17 September 1979.
104. Low & Bonar, Company Announcements, DUA, MS 24/1/7/1/4, 7 January 1980.
105. Low & Bonar, Company Announcements, DUA, MS 24/1/7/1/5, 16 February 1981.
106. The investment amounted to $2.5 million. *Bonar Business News*, 1:1 (June 1985). DUA, MS 24/1/8/5/1.
107. *Bonar Business News*, 1:2, December 1985, DUA, MS 24/1/8/5/1.
108. Ibid.
109. Ibid., 3:1, Autumn 1988, DUA, MS 24/1/8/5/1.
110. http://www.lowandbonar.com/lwb/divisions/ accessed 29 September 2010.
111. Other possible choices were 'Meadowplace Industries Ltd' and 'Meadowside Industries Ltd', Jute Industries (Holding), General Committee Minute Book, 28 January 1971, DUA, MS 66/10/1/2/19.
112. *Sidlaw News*, DUA, MS 66/10/15/1/1, February 1972.
113. Ibid., April 1972.
114. Ibid., September 1974.
115. Sidlaw Industries, Company Announcements, DUA, MS 66/10/15/2/1, 22 June 1984.
116. Ibid., 1 February 1980.
117. Ibid., 28 March 1980.
118. Ibid., 25 June 1981.
119. Ibid., 2 October 1981. This was followed by the acquisition of S. B. Offshore Peterhead Base Ltd, which operated an oil service base in Peterhead similar to that of Aberdeen Service Company (North Sea) Ltd, DUA, MS 66/10/1/12, 13 February 1986.
120. Drexel also had a research and development facility at Montrose in Scotland to support a worldwide sales network and servicing and manufacturing facilities were also established in Dundee. Drexel employs some 250 people worldwide with 110 in the UK. DUA, MS 66/10/1/12, 3 April 1984.
121. Sidlaw Industries, Company Announcements, DUA, MS 66/10/15/2/1, 13 April 1984.
122. Sidlaw transferred to this Joint Venture the assets and undertakings of its Offshore Services Division, which was involved in providing skilled technical and general personnel offshore, the recruitment and placement of permanent and contractual staff and the provision of protective coatings and painting services. Sidlaw Industries, Company Announcements, 9 February 1987, DUA, MS 66/10/1/12.
123. In 1986 it was suggested that Oil Services have felt the impact of lower and more competitive North Sea activity most particularly in the supply of contract labour offshore. Sidlaw Industries, Company Announcements, 21 May 1986, DUA, MS 66/10/15/2/1.
124. Sidlaw Industries, Company Announcements, DUA, MS 66/10/15/2/1, 1 December 1988.
125. Ibid., 31 May 1990.
126. Ibid., 29 November 1990.
127. Ibid., 10 January 1991. ASCo had been providing similar support services from Peterhead for BP/Britoil's North Sea production operations for over 14 years.
128. Ibid., 30 April 1991. The 83 people employed in Dundee were redeployed, encouraged to take early retirement or made redundant.

129. Ibid., 11 November 1991.
130. Ibid., 9 February 1984.
131. Ibid., 21 May 1986.
132. HPC also produced items to customer specification for the health and pharmaceutical industries as well as the printing of high-quality firm for mail wrappers and printed bags for motor parts. The company was also a wholesaler of a wide range of workwear and protective clothing, including medical gloves, books, headwear and uniforms. Sidlaw Industries, Company Announcements, 18 January 1989, DUA, MS 66/10/1/12.
133. Sidlaw Industries, Company Announcements, DUA, MS 66/10/15/2/1.
134. Ibid., 9 November 1989.
135. Ibid., 9 November 1989.
136. Ibid., 12 January 1990.
137. Ibid., 12 January 1990.
138. Ibid., 29 November 1990.
139. Ibid. 29 November 1990. The main addition was its capacity for eight colour flexographic printing and cold sealing.
140. Ibid., 30 June 1991.
141. Ibid., 31 May 1990.

6 Influencing Government

1. These were the words of the 1944 White Paper on *Employment policy* (Cmnd 6527, 1944); Tomlinson, *Employment Policy*, ch. 3.
2. P. Addison, *The Road to 1945. British Politics and the Second World War*, 2nd edn (London: Pimlico, 1994).
3. R. Lowe, *The Welfare State in Britain since 1945*, 3rd edn (Basingstoke: Macmillan, 2005), chs 4–7.
4. Parsons, *The Political Economy of British Regional Policy*, ch. 3.
5. Board of Trade, Working Party, *Report* (London: HMSO, 1948), appendix A.
6. Morelli and Tomlinson, 'Women and Work'.
7. Working Party, *Report*, p. 1.
8. Ibid., 2.
9. 'Note of President's Talk with Chairman and Members of the Working Party', 10 June 1948 TNA: PRO BT64/3762. His predecessor, Stafford Cripps, had refused to give any undertaking to the industry on protection when he visited Dundee in late 1945, telling the employers and unions to await the Working Party report: AJSM Minutes of Working Party committee, 14 December 1945 DUA MS 84/6/1. The Association was the major employers organization, but its role had been supplemented as a spokesperson for the industry in 1947 by the creation of the British Jute Trade Federation, which seems to have come into existence in the face of worries that the Working Party report would presage a government sponsored re-organization of the industry – Dundee Chamber of Commerce minute book, 'Proposed Jute Federation', 25 March 1947 DCA DCC. The BJTF had no union representatives, and was therefore also aimed to pre-empt the idea of a Development Council.
10. 'Protection of the UK Jute Industry against Indian Imports', 12 February 1948 TNA:PRO BT64/3762.
11. On the issue of competition, H. Mercer, *Constructing a Competitive Order: The Hidden History of British Antitrust Policies* (Cambridge: Cambridge University Press, 1995).

12. Howe, *The Dundee Textiles Industry*, pp. 35–7, though see discussion in Chapter 5. This would be in sharp contrast to the case of cotton (returned to below),where the late 1940s saw strong government attempts, including the inducement of re-equipment subsidies, to get the industry to 'rationalize': see J. Singleton. 'Planning for Cotton, 1945–1951', *Economic History Review*, 43 (1990), pp. 62–78.

13. A. Cairncross, *Years of Recovery*, ch. 2; R. Toye, 'The Attlee Government, the Imperial Preference System, and the Creation of the GATT', *English Historical Review*, 118 (2003), pp. 912–39.

14. A. Ringe, N. Rollings and R Middleton, *Economic Policy under the Conservatives, 1951–65: A Guide to Documents in the National Archives of the UK* (London; Institute of Historical Research, 2004), ch. 2.

15. 'Jute Working Party Report: Main Recommendations-Protection and Re-Organization' 12 February 1948, TNA: PRO BT64/3761.

16. Cited in 'Jute Industry: Note on Future Level of Output' 21 August 1954, TNA: PRO BT64/5101.

17. The city authorities had produced a (jute-bound) booklet in 1931 entitled *Do it in Dundee,* extolling the virtues of the city. The wartime Lord Provost, Garnet Wilson. co-ordinated a joint Chamber of Commerce, Trades and Labour Council and City approach to the Board of Trade, based on a 'Memorandum on the post-war position of industry in the City of Dundee with special reference to past and future problems of unemployment' (Dundee: Dundee City Corporation, 1943). G. Wilson, *The Making of a Lord Provost* (Dundee: Winter, 1966), pp. 44–7.

18. R. Maclean to Prof G.C.Allen 'Dundee', 14 August 1943, TNA: PRO BT64/3204.

19. Ibid., 'Location of Industry'; G. Wilson, *Overspill. A Second Memory Book* (Dundee: Winter, 1970), pp. 56–7.

20. D. Eades to A. Halls 8 October 1951, TNA: PRO BT177/522.

21. I. Levitt, 'Scottish Papers Submitted to the Cabinet, 1945–1966: A Guide to Records held at the Public Record Office and National Archives of Scotland', *Scottish Economic and Social History*, 20 (2000), pp. 58–125.

22. There are large numbers of files on jute in the National Archives of Scotland (NAS), especially in the class SEP4 'Regional Industrial Development and Promotion'.

23. Scottish Council (Development and Industry) *Inquiry into the Scottish Economy, 1960–61: Report of a Committee under the Chairmanship of JN Toothill* (1961); Toothill Report: Scottish Council Meeting with Ministers, 1962 NAS SEP4/864. On the wider issues, see J. Phillips, *The Industrial Politics of Devolution* (Manchester: Manchester University Press, 2008).

24. D. Eades to A. Halls 8 October 1951, and Ibid., Note of Meeting with Secretary of Board of Trade, 6 June 1952 TNA: PRO BT177/522.

25. Lord Swinton to Churchill 22 July 1952 TNA: PRO PREM11/3141. Churchill had been a Liberal MP for Dundee between 1908 and 1922. The memo was occasioned by reports of the victory of the Labour candidate, George Thomson, in a Dundee by-election.

26. 'Working Party on Jute 1953/54' TNA: PRO T224/287.

27. Ibid., 'The Jute Industry', 1 July 1953.

28. Ibid., Report by officials 'Protection of the Jute Industry', 18 November 1953.

29. *Economist*, 21 November 1953, pp. 603–4.

30. Economic Policy Committee 'Protection of the Jute Industry', 30 December 1953 TNA: PRO T224/287.

31. K. MacGregor to Mr France 24 November 1953 TNA: PRO T224/287.

32. Ibid., K. McGregor, 'Protection of the Jute Industry', 14 August 1956. The relatively limited Indian interest in British policy on jute may be accounted for by the fact that while jute manufactures were hugely important to India, earning around a fifth of total foreign exchange in the 1950s and 60s, as a share of total Indian production, and even exports, Britain was quite a small market. IBRD, *Indian Exports of Jute Manufactures: Problems and Prospects* (Washington DC: International Bank for Reconstruction and Development, 1969).

33. Working Party on the Jute Industry, Meeting 20 March 1957 TNA: PRO T224/288; Board of Trade 'Jute' 7 March 1958 TNA: PRO BT224/289.

34. In 1960 Reginald Maudling, President of the Board of Trade, told industry representatives that 1960 was only the second occasion that India had formally objected to jute protectionism, 'but there was, of course, steady informal comment from Indian government officials and steady actual pressure from the Indian industry': AJSM 'Meeting on 11 January with Mr Maudling' DUA MS84/11/4. For pressures from Dundee, 'Note of a Meeting with the Dundee Jute Industry', 16 July 1957 TNA: PRO BT177/1743.

35. AJSM 'Record of Meeting at Board of Trade 2 December 1959' DUA 84/11/4. The Record explicitly states that the discussion, and the AJSM's acquiescence in a mark-up reduction, would not be made public, and that indeed at a planned meeting of the Jute Trade Federal Council the Board of Trade 'would not, of course, expect that the industry's representatives would abate their language in opposing the reduction'. See also 'Draft Letter President the Board of Trade to Secretary of State for Scotland', 15 December 1959 TNA: PRO BT258/6.

36. K. McGregor to A. Ogilvie-Webb, 6 November 1956 TNA: PRO T224/287; 'Working Party on Dundee: First Agreed Draft Report', 6 June 1957 TNA: PRO T224/288.

37. 'Specific Industries: Jute', 1959–61 NAS SEP4/1656; 'Jute Goods: RPC Hearing on Jute Industry Agreements', 1959–62 PRO BT258/6. Up to 1954 the Board of Trade had a 'gentleman's agreement' with the trade on prices, where after the industry developed its own 'Brown Book' – see Chapter 4.

38. Discussions within Board of Trade and consultations with the industry were almost continuous. For example Ministerial briefing Notes 'Note of Meeting with Sir William Walker', 12 January 1961 NAS SEP4/348.

39. Board of Trade 'Import Policy for Jute Goods', 30 July 1963 TNA: PRO CAB129/114.

40. Ibid. 'Since a violent reaction from the industry to any change in its present favoured position was to be expected, room for manoeuvre had been allowed for, and at a second meeting with the employers, unions and civic authorities in Dundee on July 18th, revised proposals were made by the Minister of State'.

41. Secretary of State for Scotland, 'Import Policy for Jute Goods' 29 July 1963 TNA: PRO CAB129/114.

42. Cabinet Conclusions 1 August 1963 TNA: PRO CAB128/37. For informal Ministerial discussion of the issues see 'Note of Meeting 24 July 1963' TNA: PRO PREM11/5076.

43. 'Report of Jute Working Party', 18 August 1964 TNA: PRO BT258/2002.

44. 'The Jute Industry: the Board of Trade's Proposed Dismantling of Protection' 18 July 1963 DUA AJSM84/21/1.

45. Ibid., Draft Letter J. Halley to *Statist*, 28 August 1963. See also Whatley, *Onward from Osnaburgs*, pp. 198–201.

46. J. McGuiness 'Jute', 21 August 1964 NAS SEP4/2094; A. Burgess 'Jute Industry Working Group', 5 May 1964 TNA: PRO BT258/8.

47. M. Ord Johnstone 'Jute Goods Import Policy', 22 April 1964 TNA: PRO BT258/8.

48. Private Secretary to Prime Minister, 31 August 1964 TNA: PRO PREM11/5076.
49. Heath to Prime Minister 'Protection for Jute', 27 August 1964 TNA: PRO PREM11/5076.
50. 'Jute Goods: Protection – The Next Step' April 1963 p. 7 TNA: PRO BT303/155. By contrast, in the 1957 discussions the Treasury had explicitly ruled out offering support for the Tay Bridge as part of a bargain to reduce protection of jute: A. Ogilvie-Webb, 'Dundee Jute Industry', 9 July 1957 TNA: PRO T224/287.
51. 'Report of Jute Working Party', pp. 53–5 TNA: PRO BT258/2002.
52. TNA: PRO BT230/474. The reference to EFTA reflected the fact that Portugal, an EFTA member, had recently emerged as a significant jute producer, though contrary to the EFTA agreements, its exports to Britain were subject to quotas: 'Review of Import Arrangements for Jute Goods', 27 November 1968 PRO BT241/815.
53. 'Review of Import Arrangements for Jute Goods', 15 March 1968 TNA: PRO BT241/815, 2; 'Review of Jute Industry Protection 1967' NAS SEP4/2027.
54. 'Review of Import Arrangements for Jute Goods', 27 November 1968 TNA: PRO BT2241/815.
55. 'Draft Submission to Ministers for Industry: Jute Import Quotas after May 1971', November 1970, pp. 1–2 TNA: PRO BT344/65.
56. 'Import Arrangements for Jute Textiles after April 1971 – Draft Submission', 15 December 1970, p. 2 TNA: PRO BT344/65.
57. 'Written PQ and Answer' by Secretary of State for Trade and Industry TNA: PRO BT241/1167.
58. Draft Press Notice 'EEC Jute Textiles Agreement with India' no date, but 1975 PRO BT303/724'; Notices to Importers: Arrangements for Imports to UK of Jute Goods, 1 January 1976–31 December 1979, 5 November 1976 TNA: PRO BT303/725.
59. On these two recessions see C. Dow, *Major Recessions: Britain and the World, 1920–1995* (Oxford: Oxford University Press, 1998).
60. Alex Fletcher, Scottish Office to Lord Trenchard, DTI 17 January 1980; Lord Mansfield, Scottish Office to Trenchard, 8 October 1979 TNA:PRO BT303/726.
61. AJSM to Lord Trenchard 1 June 1979 TNA: PRO BT303/726. In support of their case the AJSM enclosed a letter from the British Carpet Manufacturers Association saying their industry 'would suffer considerably if there was no longer a jute industry in the UK' because of the poor quality and irregularity of delivery of Calcutta yarns.
62. C. Parkinson, Department of Trade to Lord Trenchard, DTI, 17 January 1980 TNA: PRO BT303/726.
63. Ibid., N. Marten, ODA to Lord Trenchard, DTI, 21 September 1979.
64. Memorandum by D. Hellings, 28 September 1979 TNA: PRO BT303/726.
65. The prospect of any joint action in the city to address this plight was not helped by the 150 per cent rate rise in 1981, which the AJSM saw as another blow to the industry's fortunes, and was the immediate context for its radical slimming down in staff and giving up of its headquarters in Kandahar House: AJSM *Annual Report* 1982; *Courier*, 28 March 1981.
66. *Courier*, 6 November 1982.
67. *Courier*, 27 September 1986; 11 December 1986.
68. *Courier*, 18 March 1987; *Telegraph*, 11 June 1987.
69. In 1998, coinciding with the announcement of the closure of the last spinning mill, a local MP called for an enquiry into how far the final demise of the industry was due to

evasion of EU rules on access of jute yard from Bangladesh, but by that time the horse had well and truly bolted: *Courier*, 1 September 1998.

70. M. Rose, 'The Politics of Protection: An Institutional Approach to Government Industry Relations in the British and United States Cotton Industries, 1945–73', *Business History*, 3 (1997), pp. 128–50; M. Rose, *Firms, Networks and Business Values: The British and American Cotton Industries since 1750* (Cambridge: Cambridge University Press, 2000), ch. 8; also M. Dupree, 'Struggling with Destiny: The Cotton Industry, Overseas Trade Policy and the Cotton Board, 1940–1959', *Business History*, 32 (1990), pp. 106–28.

71. K. Anderson and R. Baldwin, 'The Political Market for Protection in Industrial Countries: Empirical Evidence' *World Bank Staff Working Paper no. 492* (Washington: World Bank, 1981).

72. The classic reference point for such discussions is M. Olson, *The Logic of Collective Action* (Cambridge, MA: Harvard University Press, 1965).

73. The number of AJSM members fell from thirty-nine in 1945 to fourteen in 1977, most of the fall coming after 1967: Howe, *The Dundee Textiles Industry*, p. 39.

74. Anderson and Baldwin, 'The Political Market for Protection', p. 8.

75. Rose, *Firms*, pp. 269–73.

76. Only six MPs seem to have been involved in lobbying for jute: Halley to Edward Heath, President of the Board of Trade 8 September 1964 PRO TNA: BT303/515.

77. Rose, *Firms*, p. 273.

78. Howe, *The Dundee Textiles Industry*, pp. 171–7 makes the point that whereas cotton was unable to get much protection from government, it got financial aid for restructuring, while the opposite was the case in jute, where no subsidy was paid.

79. Rose, 'The Politics of Protection', pp. 144–5. Note, however, that in the jute case, the link with Hong Kong, and sensitivity about that countries potential for responding to British protectionism by running down Sterling balances and disrupting the Sterling system did not apply.

80. Anderson and Baldwin, 'The Political Market for Protection', p. 12.

81. A. S. Brennan and G. Milward, *Britain's Place in the World* (London: Routledge and Kegan Paul, 1996), p. 190.

82. Though this process *pre-dated* protection; it had begun in the 1880s.

83. Working Party, *Report*, p. 71. The emphasis on Indian wage levels is interesting ideologically; from a union point of view it was problematic, because it made it harder to argue for wage increases.

84. Carstairs and Cole, 'Recent Developments in the Jute Industry'.

85. Craig *et al.*, 'Abolition and After', p. 8.

86. J. Odling-Smee, 'Introduction' to McDowall and Draper, *Trade Adjustment and the British Jute Industry*, p. xvii; chapter 5, above.

87. McDowall and Draper, *Trade Adjustment and the British Jute Industry*, 8; Howe, *The Dundee Textiles Industry*, pp. 54–5 suggests that in 1977 Dundee and district had 77 per cent of UK polypropylene manufacturing.

88. McDowall, *et al.* 'Protection', pp. 51–2.

89. Howe, *The Dundee Textiles Industry*, points out how different the cost structures of polypropylene are compared with jute – notably, much higher capital costs, very sensitive to activity levels and therefore tending to encourage concentration.

90. http://www.lowandbonar.com/lwb/divisions/; chapter 5, above.

91. http://www.themanufacturer.com/uk/detail.html?contents_id=5.

92. *Courier*, 25 November 1946; Chair of Regional Development of Industry Panel, quoted in ibid., 6 March 1947.
93. M. Lackey to K. Rogers, 14 June 1957 TNA: PRO BT77/1743.
94. For example, 'Jute Goods. Protection: The Next Step' April 1963, p. 4 TNA: PRO BT303/155. In 1979 the AJSM, seeking to prevent the 'extinction' of the industry stressed how serious this would be in employment terms, and responded to the idea of retraining by stressing that this would be of 'doubtful value since the labour force, being substantially female, is immobile and of an average age which makes retraining difficult', Letter from AJSM to Secretary of State for Industry, 1 June 1979 TNA: PRO BT303/726.
95. McDowall and Draper, *Trade Adjustment and the Jute Industry*, p. 10.
96. For example, AJSM 'Record of Meeting at Board of Trade', 2 December 1959 DUA MS84/11/4; 'Report of Working Party on Jute', 1964, pp. 29–32, TNA: PRO BT258/2002.

7 The Decline of Jute and the Economic Health of Dundee

1. Contemporary discussions emphasized 'decline' in this period, partly because growth rates fell below those in British' Western European neighbours. For 'decline' see Tomlinson, 'Thrice Denied'.
2. In output, and especially employment, terms the recessions of the early 1980s and 90s were much more serious than that of the mid-1970s: Dow, *Major Recessions*, pp. 308–9.
3. C. Lythe and M. Majmudar, *The Renaissance of the Scottish Economy?* (London: Allen and Unwin, 1982), pp. 157–62.
4. Tomlinson, 'The De-Globalization of Dundee'.
5. D. Blanchflower and A. Oswald, 'Well-Being Over Time in Britain and the USA', *Journal of Public Economics*, 88 (2004), pp. 1359–86; A. Clark and A. Oswald, 'Unhappiness and Unemployment' *Economic Journal*, 10 (1994), pp. 648–59.
6. Millward, 'The Rise of the Service Economy'.
7. *Scottish Economic Bulletin*, 22 (1981), p. 45; *Scottish Economic Bulletin*, 43 (1991), Table 51; on expenditure patterns over the long run, Tomlinson 'The De-Globalization of Dundee'.
8. C. Lee, *Scotland and the United Kingdom* (Manchester: Manchester University Press, 1995), pp. 109–17.
9. A. Carstairs, 'The Nature and Diversification of Employment in Dundee in the Twentieth Century', in S. Jones (ed.), *Dundee and District* (Dundee: British Association, 1968), pp. 318–36, p. 333.
10. M. Flinn, 'Overseas Trade of Scottish Ports', *Scottish Journal of Political Economy*, 13 (1966), pp. 220–37.
11. N. Beckles, 'Textiles and Port Growth in Dundee', *Scottish Geographical Journal*, 84 (1968), pp. 90–8. *Census 1951 Scotland Vol IV Occupations and Industries* Table 6 counts 828 'water transport workers' in 1951.
12. Dundee City Corporation (Dundee: Dundee City Corporation, 1931); J. Doherty, 'Dundee: A Post-Industrial City' in Whatley (ed.), *The Remaking of Juteopolis*, pp. 27–8.
13. R. Saville, 'The Industrial Background to the Post-War Scottish Economy', in R. Saville (ed.), *The Economic Development of Modern Scotland 1950–1980* (Edinburgh: John Donald, 1985), pp. 12–16.

14. Parsons, *The Political Economy of British Regional Policy*. An important part of this, nationally and in Dundee, was the provision of new state-financed factories to rent: P. Slows, *The Advance Factory in Regional Development* (Aldershot: Gower, 1981), pp. 15–24.

15. Scottish Council (Development and Industry) *Report of the Committee on Local Development in Scotland* (Edinburgh, 1952), p. 25.

16. Carstairs, 'The Nature and Diversification of Employment in Dundee', p. 335.

17. Scottish Council, *Report*, p. 25.

18. Morelli and Tomlinson, 'Women and Work'.

19. Hood and Young, *Multinationals in Retreat*, p. 9.

20. W. Knox and A. McKinlay, 'Working for the Yankee Dollar: US Inward Investment and Scottish Labour, 1945–1970' *Historical Studies in Industrial Relations* 7 (1999), pp. 1–26.

21. S. Young, N. Hood, and E. Peters, 'Multinational Enterprises and Regional Economic Development' *Regional Studies* 28 (1994), pp. 657–77; D. Forsyth, *US Investment in Scotland* (New York: Praeger, 1972); P. McDermott, 'Ownership, Organization and Regional Dependence in the Scottish Electronics Industry', *Regional Studies*, 10 (1976), pp. 319–35; Lee, *Scotland and the UK*, pp. 107–9, 115–17; J. Firn, 'External Control and Regional Policy' in G. Brown (ed.), *Red Paper on Scotland* (Edinburgh: Edinburgh University Student Publications Board).

22. There is a great deal of material on the early years of NCR in Dundee in the National Archives, TNA: PRO BT 177/857 and BT 177/1222, which show some hard bargaining between the company and the Board of Trade over the terms of support.

23. Hood and Young, *Multinationals in Retreat*, pp. 101–3. 1975 seems to have been the peak year for such employment across Scotland: 'Overseas Investment in Scottish Manufacturing Industry', *Scottish Economic Bulletin*, 20 (1980), p. 10.

24. 'Timex Corporation: Application for Treasury Financed Building on Estate or Site' 1965. The company gained significantly from import controls on watches, with these imports running at a quarter of the pre-war level in the late 1950s TNA: PRO BT177/1228: ibid., letter from J. Pimlott 20 October 1958. Like NCR, in the 1950s and 60s Timex fought hard for the maximum support from the British government.

25. Scottish Council (Development and Industry) *Toothill Inquiry into the Scottish Economy 1960–61* (Edinburgh, 1961) Cmnd. 2864. G. McCrone, *Regional Policy in Britain* (London: Allen and Unwin, 1969), pp. 208–22. J. Phillips, *The Industrial Politics of Devolution* (Manchester: Manchester University Press, 2008).

26. B. Moore and J. Rhodes, 'Regional Policy and the Scottish Economy', *Scottish Journal of Political Economy*, 21 (1974), pp. 215–35.

27. *Census 1951 Scotland Vol IV Occupations and Industries* Table 13.

28. R. Matthews, 'Why has Britain had Full Employment since the War?', *Economic Journal*, 78 (1968), pp. 555–69.

29. Census 1961, *Scotland Leaflet no 20 Occupation and Industry County Tables*, Table 1.

30. J. Tomlinson, 'A "Failed Experiment"? Public Ownership and the Narratives of Post-War Britain', *Labour History Review*, 73 (2008), pp. 228–43.

31. Census 1951, *Occupations and Industries* Table 6 records just over a thousand railway workers in 1951. How labour intensive railways were at this time is suggested by the fact that when the tiny and hardly used Dundee–Forfar branchline was closed in 1954 this ended the jobs of three stationmasters. 'Closure of Dundee East Forfar Railway Line', September 1954 PRO AN13/1790.

32. C. Feinstein, R. Matthews and J. Odling-Smee, *British Economic Growth 1856–1973* (Cambridge: Cambridge University Press, 1982), pp. 255–6.

33. Scottish Council, *Report*, p. 11.

34. Carstairs, 'The Nature and Diversification of Employment in Dundee', p. 333.

35. *Census 1951 Occupations and Industries*, p. xxvii; Scottish Council, *Report*, p. 16.

36. Lowe, *The Welfare State in Britain since 1945* pp. 147–54; K. Coates and R. Silburn, *Poverty: The Forgotten Englishman* (Harmondsworth: Penguin, 1970).

37. Poverty amongst the elderly in this period was in large part due to their inability to save during the interwar mass unemployment: I. Gazeley, *Poverty in Britain* (Basingstoke: Palgrave Macmillan 2004), p. 176.

38. Edgar *et al.*, 'Dundee's Housing: 1915–1974', in Whatley (ed.), *The Remaking of Juteopolis*.

39. R. A., Grant *et al.*, *Local Housing Needs and Strategies* (Edinburgh: HMSO, 1976), p. 23.

40. *Courier*, 14 March 1980. This corruption case involved an ex-Lord Provost, Tom Moore, and an ex-Councillor, James Stewart, alongside John Maxwell, a developer. The charges related to the period 1959–75. All three were sentenced to five years imprisonment, but both Moore and Stewart were freed on appeal. See *Courier*, 7 February 1980 to 14 March 1980, and 20 June 1980. Note that such corruption was not uncommon in this period, with parallels in the redevelopment of Newcastle, for example.

41. Secretary of State for Scotland, *The Scottish Economy 1965 to 1970: A Plan for Expansion*, Cmnd 2864 (1966), paras 196–7.

42. Ibid., para 199.

43. Carstairs, '"The Nature and Diversification of Employment in Dundee', p. 320.

44. Minutes of meetings of the directors of Dundee Chamber of Commerce, 12 June 1970 DCA. Optimistic views of the whole of Scotland's economic performance in the 1960s (and pessimistic ones about the 1970s) were common: see, for example, N. Buxton, 'The Scottish Economy, 1945–79: performance structure and problems', in Saville *Economic Development*, pp. 52–3, 55–7; Lythe and Majmudar, *The Renaissance of the Scottish Economy?* p. 188.

45. Phillips, 'The "Retreat to Scotland"'. On the University, K. Baxter, D. Rolfe and D. Swinfen, *A Dundee Celebration* (Dundee: University of Dundee, 2007).

46. AJSM *Annual Report* 1972; see also Peter Doig MP in House of Commons *Hansard* 18 February 1971, cols 2218–20.

47. *The Times*, 27 September 1971.

48. *The Times*, 18 June 1974.

49. Official unemployment reached seven per cent in 1976.

50. *The Times*, 14 June 1976, 7 May 1983, 9 May 1983, 9 July 1983; Hood and Young, *Multinationals in Retreat*, pp. 106–13.

51. Dow, *Major Recessions*, pp. 307–8; Tomlinson, 'Mrs Thatcher's Macroeconomic Adventurism'.

52. *Evening Telegraph*, 21 June 1983.

53. *Scotsman*, 17 April 1984; 19 November 1985.

54. On Timex, see W. Knox and A. McKinlay, 'The Union Makes Us Strong? Work and Trade Unionism in Timex, 1946–1983' in Tomlinson and Whatley (eds), *Jute No More* pp. 266–90.

55. E. Ross and J. Hardy, *Unemployment in Dundee* (Dundee: Dundee Labour Party, 1979), p. 3.

56. Official discussion of unemployment has recently focused more attention on the International Labour Office (ILO) survey figure, which is always higher than the claimant count, but this is not reliably available for local data, as it is based on a national sample.

57. C. Beatty, S. Fothergill, T. Gore and R. Powell, *The Real Rate of Unemployment 2007* (Sheffield: Sheffield Hallam University, 2007) calculate this real rate by benchmarking local incapacity benefit claimants amongst working age people by the claim level of the 'fully employed' South East, and adding the 'excess' to the official figure. (These calculations are returned to in the final section below).

58. These figures are for 1971–7: Scottish Development Agency, *Dundee: Labour Performance Study* (Glasgow: SDA, 1982), p. 2.

59. In September 1980 there were 2 registered vacancies for male manual workers, with 3,680 in that category registered as unemployed: ibid., p. 3.

60. R. Mitchison, 'The Hidden Labour Force: Women in the Scottish Economy since 1945', in Saville (ed.), *Economic Development*, p. 191.

61. 'Economic Review', *Scottish Economic Bulletin*, 21 (1980), p. 16.

62. Parsons, *The Political Economy of British Regional Policy*, pp. 239–78.

63. N. Hood, 'The Scottish Development Agency in Retrospect', *Three Banks Review*, 171 (1991), pp. 4–5.

64. *Courier*, 13 January 1981. Robertson had severed direct connections with the jute industry in 1970 after disagreements amongst the Directors of Scott Robertson, the company founded on a merger of his company, Unijute, and MydWynd Holdings, owned by Scotts, in 1965. William Walker retired around the same time as Robertson, Bonar in 1975. AJSM *Annual Report* 1971, 1975; *Evening Telegraph*, 19 August 1981.

65. Hood, 'The Scottish Development Agency', pp. 9–10.

66. Ibid., pp. 16, 18–20.

67. H. Morison, *The Regeneration of Local Economies* (Oxford: Clarendon, 1987), p. 180; for assessment of the impact of this partnership on the Whitfield area of Dundee, T. Begg, *Housing Policy in Scotland* (Edinburgh: John Donald, 1996), pp. 156–8.

68. Ibid., pp. 181–2.

69. I. Turok, 'Scottish Urban Policy: Continuity, Change and Uncertainty Post-Devolution' in C. Johnstone and M. Whitehead (eds), *New Horizons in British Urban Policy* (Aldershot: Ashgate 2004), pp. 114–16.

70. Department of the Environment, *Enterprise Zone Information 1989–1990* (London, 1993); Doherty, 'Dundee', p. 38.

71. Morison, *Regeneration*, pp. 178–82.

72. C. Di Domenico and M. Di Domenico 'Heritage and Urban Renewal in Dundee: Learning from the Past when Planning for the Future of a Post-Industrial City', *Journal of Retail and Leisure Property*, 6 (2007), pp. 327–39. In 2009 the 'City of Discovery' became 'One City: Many Discoveries'.

73. G. Duguid, 'Deprived Areas in Scotland: Results of an Analysis of the 1991 Census' (Edinburgh: Scottish Office Central Research Unit, 1995). Twenty of these ninety were in Whitfield.

74. G. Bramley, S. Lancaster and D. Gordon, 'Benefit Take-Up and the Geography of Poverty in Scotland' *Regional Studies*, 34 (2000), pp. 507–19.

75. H. Jones and D. Short, 'The "Pocketing" of Crime within the City: Evidence from Dundee Public-Housing Estates', in H. Jones (ed.), *Crime and the Urban Environment* (Aldershot: Avebury, 1993), pp. 85–98.

76. Doherty, 'Dundee', p. 34.

77. M. Savage and K. Williams (eds), *Remembering Elites* (Oxford: Blackwell, 2008), p. 1.
78. Dundee City Council, *About Dundee 2008* (Dundee: City Council, 2008), p. 14.
79. There is very little published material on DC Thomsons, though there is an informative website at www.londonfreelance.org/rates/owners/_dct.html. There is a great deal of material on the company's industrial relations in the 1950s to the 1970s in the National Archives, resulting from its strongly anti-union policies which date back to the aftermath of the 1926 general strike. TNA: PRO LAB 10/1508, PREM 11/556. The old-fashioned appearance of Thomson's had as early as the 1970s led to a visitor to the company to remark: 'I have seen the past, and it works'.
80. The figure released by the Department for Business, Skills and Innovation and the office of National Statistics in 2010 gave a figure of 29.8 per cent for public sector employment in Dundee City in 2008, but this seems likely to be an underestimate. On this basis the UK figure was 20.4 per cent. www.statistics.gov.uk.
81. J. Hills, T. Sefton, and K. Stewart (eds), *Towards a More Equal Society? Poverty, Inequality and Policy since 1997* (Bristol: Policy Press, 2009), pp. 6, 41.
82. 'NHS Tayside' at www.scotland.gov.uk NHS *Scotland Workforce Statistics*.
83. Hills, Sefton and Stewart, *Towards*, pp. 6, 41.
84. *About Dundee 2008*, p. 18.
85. K. Gannicott and M. Blaug, 'Manpower Forecasting since Robbins: A Science Lobby in Action', *Higher Education Review*, 2 (1969), pp. 56–74; Edgerton, *Science, Technology and the British Industrial 'Decline'*.
86. A re-amalgamation with St Andrews was raised as a serious possibility in this cutback period: 'University of Dundee , 1983' PRO UGC 7/1085.
87. Turok, 'Scottish Urban Policy', pp. 121–2.
88. Scottish Executive, '*The Framework for Economic Development in Scotland* (2004), p. 25, cited in Turok 'Scottish Urban Policy', p. 7
89. Turok, 'Scottish Urban Policy', pp. 123–4. Also that year, Dundee was one of three areas awarded money from the fund to develop vacant and derelict land.
90. Dundee City Council, *Dundee – A City Vision* (Dundee: City Council, 2003).
91. R. Florida, *The Rise of the Creative Class* (New York: Routledge, 2004); for sceptical views on this, for example E. Peck, 'Struggling with the Creative Class', *International Journal of Urban and Regional Research*, 29 (2005), pp. 740–70. G. Lloyd and J. McCarthy, 'Dundee: a City Discovering Inclusion and Regeneration', in C. Couch, C. Fraser and S. Percy (eds), *Urban Regeneration in Europe* (Oxford: Blackwell, 2003), pp. 66–7.
92. G. Lloyd, J. McCarthy and D. Peel, 'The Re-Constitution of a Small Scottish City: Re-Discovering Dundee', in D. Bell and M. Jayne (eds), *Small Cities. Urban Experience beyond the Metropolis* (Abingdon: Routledge, 2006), pp. 105–19.
93. 'Urban Policy In Scotland', p. 14.
94. *A City Vision,* especially pp. 16–18.
95. Beatty *et al.*, *The Real Level of Unemployment 2007*; C. Beatty, S. Fothergill, T.Gore and A. Green, *The Real Level of Unemployment 2002* (Sheffield: Sheffield Hallam University, 2002).
96. Scottish Executive, *Scottish Index of Multiple Deprivation* (Edinburgh, 2004)
97. Dundee City Council, *Scottish Index of Multiple Deprivation 2006: Dundee City Council Analysis* (Dundee: Dundee City Council, 2007), pp. 2–3.
98. S. Glynn, 'Home Truths: The Myth and Reality of Regeneration in Dundee' Edinburgh, Institute of Geography Online Paper Series: GEO-132.

99. J. Wadsworth. 'Eyes Down for a Full House: Labour Market Polarisation and the Housing Market in Britain' *Scottish Journal of Political Economy* 45 (1998), pp. 376–92.

100. City Corporate plan, cited in Dundee City Council, *Population Matters* (Dundee, 2004), p. 10.

101. *Population Matters*, p. 25.

102. S. Glynn, 'Getting Rid of the Ugly Bits: The Myth and Reality of Regeneration in Dundee, Scotland', ch. 5 in *Where the Other Half Lives* (London: Pluto, 2009).

103. Nationally, housing costs for average working-class households rose in the late twentieth century, but there is no local data on this: A Offer, 'British manual workers: from producers to consumers, *c.* 1950–2000' *Contemporary British History*, 22 (2008), p. 551.

104. C. McKean and P. Whatley, *Lost Dundee: Dundee's Lost Architectural Heritage* (Edinburgh: Birlinn, 2008), pp. 162–6, 182–9. B. Harris, '"City of the Future" James Thomson's Vision of the City Beautiful', in L. Miskell, C. Whatley and B. Harris (eds), *Victorian Dundee* (East Linton: Birlinn, 2000), pp. 169–84.

105. McKean and Whatley, *Lost Dundee*, Part III; Lloyd and McCarthy, 'Dundee: A City Discovering Inclusion and Regeneration', pp. 61–5.

106. Phillips, 'Retreat'.

107. *Population Matters*, p. 13: *Census 1951 Occupations and Industries* p. xl.

108. For the national pattern of redistribution, Hills, Sefton and Stewart, *Towards*, pp. 35–44.

Conclusions

1. 'The McDowall Report' AJSM Governing committee 9 May 1977 DUA MSS84/4/5; the published version is McDowall and Draper, *Trade Adjustment and the British Jute Industry*.

2. 'McDowall Report', p. 1.

3. Ibid., p. 1–2 and Annex A.

4. McDowall and Draper, *Trade Adjustment*, p. 35.

5. Ibid., p. 33.

6. Though the Communist Party, not a negligible force in Dundee politics, hung on to this position, with Dave Bowman, the CPGB candidate in Dundee West in 1945, arguing explicitly against protection because it would lead to the stagnation of the industry, and relying on higher wages in independent India to increase Dundee's competitiveness: *Future of Jute* (Dundee: Dundee Communist Party, 1945), pp. 9–11.

7. Dundee City Corporation, 'Do it at Dundee' (Dundee: City Corporation, 1931)

8. J. Tomlinson, 'City of Discovery? Dundee since the 1980s', in Tomlinson and Whatley (eds), *Jute No More*, pp. 301–2.

9. 'Dundee: In the Balance between Boom and Doom', *The Times*, 27 September 1971.

10. 'Report of Meeting of Jute Trade Federal Council with Harold Wilson' Dundee, 16 June 1948, DUA MS 84/11.

11. Mercer, *Constructing a Competitive Order*, p. 89.

12. Ringe, Rollings and Middleton, *Economic Policy under the Conservatives*, p. 28.

13. Parsons, *The Political Economy of British Regional Policy*, pp. 135–69; P. Scott, 'Regional Development and Policy', in R. Floud and P. Johnson (eds), *The Cambridge Economic History of Modern Britain volume 3 Structural Change and Growth, 1939–2000* (Cambridge: Cambridge University Press, 2004), pp. 345–57.

14. Carter and Williams, *Industry and Technical Progress*, p. 225.

15. BJTRA *Third Annual Report 1948/9* DUA MS/86/XXIV/1.
16. BJTRA *Twenty Second Annual Report 1967/8* MS/86/XXIV/20.
17. F. Figgures to A. France 24 November 1953 TNA: PRO T224/287.
18. For example, Peter Doig in *Hansard* House of Commons, 18 February 1971 cols. 2218–20.
19. Cabinet Conclusions 1 August 1963 TNA: PRO CAB 128/37.
20. Craig *et al.*, 'Abolition and After', Down to the 1970s there was a separate Forfar and Kirriemuir Manufacturers Association, almost all of whose members also belonged to the AJSM: L. Robertson, 'The Restrictive Practices Court (Scotland). The Jute References. Precognition' (Dundee: Park Mill, 1962), p. 18.
21. Robertson, 'Precognition', p. 9.
22. Slaven and Checkland (eds), *Dictionary of Scottish Business Biography*. Robertson went on to become the Chief Executive of the Scottish Development Agency and a member of the Monopolies and Merger Commission. See *Courier*, 13 January 1981 and Obituary, *Guardian*, 3 December 2008.
23. There was hostility to Robertson based partly on a 'feeling that he is not only too clever, but rather too anxious to show he is', but also on the fact that his family firm had twice gone bankrupt and that he had established a paper bag factory in Hull: D. Charlish, report from the Annual dinner of the UK Jute Goods Association 31 May 1961 TNA:PRO BT258/834.
24. Robertson, 'Precognition', pp. 7–8. This producer/importer distinction is oversimplified, as some Dundee producers were also importers, but the structure of decision-making within the UKJGA tended to give greater weight to the non-Dundee, 'pure importer' members: Robertson, 'Precognition', pp. 13–14.
25. Robertson, 'Precognition', p. 12.
26. Morelli and Tomlinson, 'Women and Work'.
27. Dundee Chamber of Commerce, *Trade Directory and Buyer's Guide 1975*, p. 75, DCA.
28. D. Bowman letter to Board of Trade 27 March 1950 TNA: PRO BT177/522.
29. Dundee ceased to be a dual-member constituency in 1950. Dundee East was lost by Labour for the first time in 1974, when the seat was won by Gordon Wilson for the SNP.
30. For the case of Timex, see Knox and McKinlay, 'The Union Makes Us Strong?'
31. Miss M. Lackey to K. Rogers 14 June 1957 TNA:PRO BT177/1743.

WORKS CITED

Archival sources

Dundee City Archives: Dundee and District Union of Jute and Flax Workers;

Dundee Chamber of Commerce

Dundee City Library: Local History Collection: Dundee Oral History Project, Transcripts.

Dundee University Archives: Low and Bonar Papers; Jute Industries/Sidlaws papers;

Association of Jute Spinners and Manufacturers Papers; British Jute Trade Research Association Papers.

Graham, O., 'The Dundee Jute Industry 1828–1928', unpublished manuscript, Dundee, 1929.

Lennox, D., 'Working Class Life in Dundee for 25 years 1878 to 1903' (unpublished manuscript, St Andrews, 1928).

London School of Economics Archives: Tariff Commission papers TC1 2/7

Scottish National Archives: Economic Development Papers

The National Archives: Public Record Office: Board of Trade papers; Ministry of Labour Papers; Treasury Papers.

Official Publications

Board of Trade, *Hours and Earnings Enquiry* (London, HMSO, 1906)

—, *Departmental Committee on Textile Trades after the War* (London: HMSO, 1918).

—, *Census of Production* (HMSO: London, various years).

—, *Jute Working Party Report* (London: HMSO, 1948).

Census 1951, *Scotland Vol IV. Occupations and Industries.*

Census 1961, *Scotland Leaflet no 20, Occupation and Industry, County Tables.*

Commonwealth Economic Committee, *Jute Manufactures: A Memorandum on Production, Prices And Trade Prepared by the Intelligence branch of the Commonwealth Economic Committee* (HMSO: London, 1955).

Department of the Environment, *Enterprise Zone Information 1989–1990* (London: HMSO, 1993).

Dundee Chamber of Commerce *Centenary Souvenir* (Dundee: DCC,1936).

Dundee Chamber of Commerce *Yearbook 1937.* (Dundee: DCC, 1937).

Dundee Chamber of Commerce, *The Jute Industry and India* (Dundee: DCC, 1937).

Dundee Chamber of Commerce, *Critical Position of the Jute Industry* Address by the President 2 September 1937 (Dundee: DCC, 1937).

Dundee Chamber of Commerce *Annual Reports.*

Dundee Chamber of Commerce *Trade Directory and Buyers' Guide 1960–61* (Dundee: DCC, 1961).

Dundee City Corporation, *Do it in Dundee* (Dundee: Dundee City Corporation, 1931).

Dundee City Corporation, *Memorandum on the Post-War Position of Industry in the City of Dundee with Special Reference to Past and Future Problems of Unemployment* (Dundee: Dundee City Corporation, 1943).

Dundee City Corporation, *The City and Royal Burgh of Dundee: Survey & Plan, 1952* (Macclesfield: Dobson, Chapman & Partners, 1952).

Dundee City Council, *Population Matters* (Dundee: Dundee City Council, 2004).

Dundee City Council, *Scottish Index of Multiple Deprivation 2006: Dundee City Council Analysis* (Dundee: Dundee City Council, 2007).

Dundee City Council, *About Dundee 2008* (Dundee: Dundee City Council, 2008).

Employment Policy Cmnd 6527 (London: HMSO, 1944).

FAO, 'The Competitive Position of Jute Manufacture in Western Europe and the Far East' *Monthly Bulletin of Agricultural Economics and Statistics* 11 (1962), pp. 3–4.

—, *Impact of Synthetics on Jute and Allied Fibres* (Rome: FAO, 1969).

—, *Impact of Changing Technological and Economic Factors on Markets for Natural Industrial Fibres* (Rome: FAO, 1989).

Government of India, *Report of the Jute Committee* (New Delhi: Ministry of International Trade, 1963).

Government of Pakistan, *Report of Jute Enquiry Commission* (Karachi: Ministry of Commerce, 1961).

Government of Pakistan, *The Growth of Jute Industry in Pakistan* (Rawalpindi: Bureau of National Research and Reference, 1968).

IBRD, *Indian Exports of Jute Manufactures: Problems and Prospects* (Washington DC: IBRD, 1969).

The National Plan, Cmnd. 2764 (London: HMSO, 1965).

Report on the UK Census of Production (London: HMSO, various years).

Scottish Council (Development and Industry) *Report of the Committee on Local Development in Scotland* (Edinburgh, 1952).

Scottish Council (Development and Industry*) Inquiry into the Scottish Economy, 1960–61: Report of a Committee under the Chairmanship of JN Toothill* (Edinburgh, 1961).

Scottish Development Agency, *Dundee: Labour Performance Study* (Glasgow: SDA, 1982).

Scottish Executive, *Scottish Index of Multiple Deprivation* (Edinburgh, 2004).

Secretary of State for Scotland, *The Scottish Economy 1965 to 1970: A Plan for Expansion*, Cmnd 2864 (London: HMSO, 1966).

UNCTAD, International Agreement on Jute and Jute Products, 1989 (New York: UNCTAD, 1996).

Newspapers and Journals

Courier

Economist

Evening Telegraph

Guardian

IJMA, Annual Report

Indian Jute News

Scotsman

Scottish Economic Bulletin

Stock Exchange Yearbook

The Times

Other Sources

http://www.lowandbonar.com/lwb/divisions/ accessed 29 September 2010

A SWOT Analysis of Indian Jute industry' at www.indiantextilejournal.com/articles/FAdetials.asp?id+1929 accessed 12 October 2010.

http://www.unioncarbide.com/history/index.htm accessed 28 September 2010.

'NHS Tayside' at www.scotland.gov.uk accessed 23 November 2009.

Theses

Arnott, J., 'Women Workers and Trade Union Participation in Scotland 1919–1939' (unpublished PhD dissertation, University of Glasgow, 1999).

Cox, T., 'Rationalisation and Resistance: The Imperial Jute Industries of Dundee and Calcutta, 1930–1940' (unpublished dissertation submitted for Trinity College Fellowship competition, Cambridge 1997).

Masrani, S. K., 'International Competition and Strategic Response in the Dundee Jute Industry during the Inter-War (1919–1939) and Post-War (1945–1960s): The Case of Jute

Industries, Buist Spinning, Craiks and Scott & Fyfe' (unpublished PhD dissertation, University of St Andrews, 2007).

Watson, N., 'Daughters of Dundee, Gender and Politics in Dundee: The Representation of Women 1870–1997' (unpublished PhD dissertation, Open University, 2000).

Secondary Sources

Addison, P., *The Road to 1945. British Politics and the Second World War*, 2nd edn (London: Pimlico, 1994).

Aldcroft D., and Richardson, H., *The British Economy 1870–1939* (London: Macmillan, 1969).

Aoki, M., B. Gustaffson and O. E. Williamson, *The Firm as a Nexus of Treaties* (London: SAGE, 1990).

Anderson K. and R. Baldwin, 'The Political Market for Protection in Industrial Countries: Empirical Evidence' *World Bank Staff Working Paper no. 492* (Washington DC: World Bank, 1981).

Bagchi, A., *Private Investment in India* (Cambridge: Cambridge University Press, 1972).

Bamberg, J., *British Petroleum and Global Oil 1950–75: The Challenge of Nationalism* (Cambridge: Cambridge University, 2000).

Barnett, C., *The Collapse of British Power* (London: Eyre Methuen, 1971).

—, *The Audit of War* (London: Macmillan, 1986).

Bartlett, J. N., *Carpeting the Millions: The Growth of Britain's Carpet Industry* (Edinburgh: John Donald, 1978).

Baxter, K., D. Rolfe and D. Swinfen, *A Dundee Celebration* (Dundee: University of Dundee, 2007).

Beatty, C. Fothergill, S., Gore, T. and Green, A., *The Real Level of Unemployment 2002* (Sheffield: Sheffield Hallam University, 2002).

Beatty, C. Fothergill, S., Gore, T. and Powell, R., *The Real Level of Unemployment 2007* (Sheffield: Sheffield Hallam University, 2007).

Beckles, N., 'Textiles and Port Growth in Dundee', *Scottish Geographical Journal*, 84 (1968), pp. 90–8.

Begg, T., *Housing Policy in Scotland* (Edinburgh: John Donald, 1996).

Beveridge, W., *Full Employment in a Free Society* (London: Allen and Unwin, 1944).

Blanchflower, D., and A. Oswald, 'Well-being Over Time in Britain and the USA', *Journal of Public Economics*, 88 (2004), pp. 1359–86.

Bonar, G., *The Industrial Outlook*, Lecture by George Bonar, 19 January 1929 (Dundee: Dundee Chamber of Commerce, 1929).

Booth, A., *British Economic Policy, 1931–1949: Was there a Keynesian Revolution?* (London: Harvester Wheatsheaf, 1989).

—, *The British Economy in the Twentieth Century* (Basingstoke: Palgrave, 2001).

—, 'The Manufacturing Failure Hypothesis and the Performance of British Industry During the Long Boom', *Economic History Review*, 56 (2003), pp. 1–33.

Bowman, D., *Future of Jute* (Dundee: Dundee Communist Party, 1945).

Boyce, G. H., *Information, Mediation and Institutional Development: The Rise of the Large-Scale Enterprise in British Shipping, 1870–1919* (Manchester: Manchester University Press, 1995).

Boyce, J., *The Globalization of Market Failure? International Trade and Sustainable Agriculture* (Amherst, MA: Political Economy Research Institute, 1999).

Bramley, G., S. Lancaster and D. Gordon, 'Benefit Take-Up and the Geography of Poverty in Scotland', *Regional Studies*, 34 (2000), pp. 507–19.

Brennan, A. S., and G. Milward, *Britain's Place in the World* (London: Routledge and Kegan Paul, 1996).

British Association, *A Scientific Survey of Dundee and District* (London: British Association, 1939).

Broadberry, S. N., 'Unemployment', in N. F. R. Crafts and N. W. C. Woodward (eds), *The British Economy Since 1945* (Oxford: Clarendon Press, 1991), pp. 212–35.

—, *The Productivity Race* (Cambridge: Cambridge University Press, 1997).

Broadberry, S. N. and Crafts, N. F. R., 'British Economic Policy and Industrial Performance in the Early Post War Period' *Business History* 38 (1996), pp. 65–91.

Broadberry, S. N. and Crafts, N. F. R., 'Competition and Innovation in 1950s Britain' *Business History* 43 (2001), pp. 97–118.

—, 'UK Productivity Performance from 1950 to 1979: A Restatement of the Broadberry-Crafts View', *Economic History Review*, 56 (2003), pp. 718–35.

Brusse W. A., and R. T. Griffiths, 'The Incidence of Manufacturing Cartels in Post-War Europe', in C. J. Morelli (ed.), *Cartels and Market Management in the Post-War World* (London: Business History Unit, 1997), pp. 78–117.

Burn, D., *The Economic History of Steelmaking, 1867–1939* (Cambridge: Cambridge University Press, 1940).

Buxton, N., 'The Scottish Economy, 1945–79: performance structure and problems', in R. Saville, *The Economic Development of Modern Scotland* (Edinburgh: John Donald, 1985), pp. 52–7.

Capie, F., *Depression and Protectionism: Britain between the Wars* (London: Allen and Unwin, 1983).

Cairncross, A., *Years of Recovery: British Economic Policy 1945–51* (London: Methuen, 1986).

Cairncross, A., and Watts, N., *The Economic Section 1939–61: A Study in Economic Advising* (London: Routledge, 1989).

Cannadine, D., 'Apocalypse When? British Politicians and British "Decline" in the Twentieth Century', in P. Clarke and C. Trebilcock (eds), *Understanding Decline: Perceptions and Realities of Britain's Economic Performance* (Cambridge: Cambridge University Press, 1997), pp. 261–84.

Carstairs, A., 'The Nature and Diversification of Employment in Dundee in the Twentieth Century', in S. Jones (ed.), *Dundee and District* (Dundee: British Association, 1968), pp. 318–36.

Carstairs A. and A. Cole, 'Recent Developments in the Jute Industry', *Scottish Journal of Political Economy*, 7 (1960), pp. 117–33.

Carter, C. and B. Williams, *Industry and Technical Progress* (London: Oxford University Press, 1954).

Chapman, D., 'The Establishment of the Jute Industry. A Problem in Location Theory', *Review of Economic Studies*, 6 (1938), pp. 33–55.

Clark, A., and A. Oswald, 'Unhappiness and Unemployment' *Economic Journal*, 10 (1994), pp. 648–59.

Clegg, H., *The System of Industrial Relations in Great Britain* (Oxford: Basil Blackwell, 1970).

Coates, K. and R. Silburn, *Poverty: The Forgotten Englishman* (Harmondsworth: Penguin, 1970).

Coleman, D. C., *Courtaulds. An Economic and Social History – vol. III: Crisis and Change 1940–1965* (Oxford: Clarendon, 1980).

Corteen, H., 'Science at Work in the Jute Industry', *Dundee Chamber of Commerce Journal*, September 1958, pp. 143–5.

Crafts, N. F. R., 'The Golden Age of Economic Growth in Western Europe, 1950–1973' *Economic History Review* 48 (1995), pp. 429–47.

Craig, C., J. Rubery, R. Tarling and F. Wilkinson, 'Abolition and After: The Jute Wages Council', *Department of Applied Economics, University of Cambridge, Research Paper No. 15* (1980).

—, *Labour Market Structure, Industrial Organisation and Low Pay* (Cambridge, Cambridge University Press, 1982).

Cutler, T., K. Williams and J. Williams, *Keynes, Beveridge and Beyond* (London: Routledge and Kegan Paul, 1986).

Daunton, M., 'Britain and Globalization since 1850: I Creating a Global Order 1850–1914', *Transactions of the Royal Historical Society*, 16 (2006), pp. 1–38.

Di Domenico, C., and M. Di Domenico, 'Heritage and Urban Renewal in Dundee: Learning from the Past when Planning for the Future of a Post-Industrial City' *Journal of Retail and Leisure Property* 6 (2007), pp. 327–39.

Doud, G., 'Tom Johnston in India' *Scottish Labour History Journal* 19 (1984), pp. 6–21.

Dow, C., *Major Recessions: Britain and the World, 1920–1995* (Oxford: Oxford University Press, 1998).

Duguid, G., 'Deprived Areas in Scotland: Results of an Analysis of the 1991 Census' (Edinburgh: Scottish Office Central Research Unit, 1995).

Dundee Social Union, *Report on Housing and Industrial Conditions in Dundee* (Dundee: John Leng, 1905).

Dupree, M., 'Struggling with Destiny: The Cotton Industry, Overseas Trade Policy and the Cotton Board, 1940–1959', *Business History*, 32 (1990), pp. 106–28.

Eastham, J., 'Economic Survey' in R. Mackie (ed), *A Scientific Survey of Dundee and District* (Dundee: British Association, 1939), pp. 94–101.

Eastham, J. (ed), *Economic Essays in Commemoration of the Dundee School of Economics 1931–1955* (Dundee: School of Economics, 1955).

Economist Intelligence Unit, *World Jute Study* (London: EIU, 1956).

Edgerton, D., *Science, Technology and the British Industrial 'Decline' 1870–1970* (Cambridge: Cambridge University Press, 1996).

—, *Warfare State: Britain, 1920–1970* (Cambridge: Cambridge University Press, 2006).

Eichengreen, B., 'Institutions and Economic Growth: Europe after World War II' in N. F. R. Crafts and G. Toniolo (eds), *Economic Growth in Europe since 1945* (Cambridge: University Press, 1996), pp. 38–72.

Evely, R., and I. M. D. Little, *Concentration in British Industry: An Empirical Study of the Structure of Industrial Production 1935–51* (Cambridge: Cambridge University Press, 1960).

Ewan, E., Innes, S. and Reynolds, S. (eds), *The Biographical Dictionary of Scottish Women* (Edinburgh: Edinburgh University Press, 2006).

Feinstein, C., 'Economic Growth since 1870: Britain's Performance in International Perspective' *Oxford Review of Economic Policy*, 4 (1988), pp. 1–13.

—, C., 'Structural Change in the Developed Countries during the Twentieth Century' *Oxford Review of Economic Policy*, 15 (1999), pp. 35–55.

Feinstein, C., R. Matthews and J. Odling-Smee, *British Economic Growth 1856–1973* (Cambridge: Cambridge University Press, 1982).

Firn, J., 'External Control and Regional Policy', in G. Brown (ed.), *Red Paper on Scotland* (Edinburgh: Edinburgh University Student Publications Board).

Flinn, M., 'Overseas Trade of Scottish Ports', *Scottish Journal of Political Economy*, 13 (1966), pp. 220–37.

Florida, R., *The Rise of the Creative Class* (New York: Routledge, 2004).

Fogarty, M., *Prospects of the Industrial Areas of Great Britain* (London: Methuen, 1945).

Forsyth, D., *US Investment in Scotland* (New York: Praeger, 1972).

Frank, H., *Polypropylene* (London: Macdonald, 1969).

Fraser, E., *A Home by the Hooghly: A Jute Wallah's Wife* (Edinburgh: Mainstream, 1989).

Gannicott, K., and M. Blaug, 'Manpower Forecasting since Robbins: A Science Lobby in Action', *Higher Education Review*, 2 (1969), pp. 56–74.

Gazeley, *Poverty in Britain* (Basingstoke: Palgrave Macmillan 2004).

Glynn, S., 'Home Truths: The Myth and Reality of Regeneration in Dundee' Edinburgh, Institute of Geography Online Paper Series: GEO-132.

—, *Where the Other Half Lives* (London: Pluto, 2009).

Gordon, E., *Women and the Labour Movement in Scotland 1850–1914* (Oxford: Oxford University Press, 1991).

Goswami, O., 'Co-operation and Conflict. European and Indian Capitalists and the Jute Economy of Bengal, 1919–1939', *Indian Economic and Social History Review*, 19 (1982), pp. 141–79.

Grant R., B. Thomson, J. Dible and J. Randa., *Local Housing Needs and Strategies* (Edinburgh: HMSO, 1976).

Greaves, J., *Industrial Reorganization in Interwar Britain* (Aldershot: Ashgate, 2005).

Gupta, B., 'Why Did Collusion Fail? The Indian Jute Industry in the Interwar Years', *Business History*, 47 (2005), pp. 532–52.

Hannah, L., *The Rise of the Corporate Economy* 2nd edn (London: Methuen, 1976).

Hargreaves, E. and M. Gowing, *Civil Industry and Trade*. History of the Second World War. (London: HMSO, 1952).

Harris, B., '"City of the Future" James Thomson's Vision of the City Beautiful', in L. Miskell, C. Whatley and B. Harris (eds), *Victorian Dundee* (East Linton: Birlinn, 2000), pp. 169–84.

Hills, J., T. Sefton and K. Stewart (eds), *Towards a More Equal Society? Poverty, Inequality and Policy since 1997* (Bristol: Policy Press, 2009).

Hood, N., 'The Scottish Development Agency in Retrospect', *Three Banks Review*, 171 (1991), pp. 3–21.

Hood, N,. and S. Young, *Multinationals in Retreat: The Scottish Experience* (Edinburgh, 1982).

Howe, W. S., *The Dundee Textile Industries, 1960–77: Decline and Diversification* (Aberdeen: University Press, 1982).

Kidron, M., *Foreign Investment in India* (London: Oxford University Press, 1965).

Jackson, J., 'Leading Industries', in J. Jackson (ed.), *The Third Statistical Account of Scotland: the City of Dundee* (Arbroath: Herald Press, 1979).

Johnman, L., and H. Murphy, *British Shipbuilding and the State since 1918* (Exeter: Exeter University Press, 2002).

Johnston, T., *Memories* (London: Collins, 1952).

Jones, D., J. Duncan and H. Conacher, *Rural Scotland during the War* (London: Oxford University Press, 1926).

Jones, G., *Merchants to Multinationals. British Trading Companies in the Nineteenth and Twentieth Centuries* (Oxford: Oxford University Press, 2000).

Jones, H. and D. Short, 'The "Pocketing" of Crime within the City: Evidence from Dundee Public-Housing Estates', in H. Jones (ed), *Crime and the Urban Environment* (Aldershot: Avebury, 1993), pp. 85–98.

Knox, W. and McKinlay, A., 'Working for the Yankee Dollar: US Inward Investment and Scottish Labour, 1945–1970', *Historical Studies in Industrial Relations*, 7 (1999), pp. 1–26.

—, 'The Union Makes us Strong? Work and Trade Unionism in Timex, 1946–1983' in J. Tomlinson and C. Whatley, *Jute No More,* pp. 266–90.

Lazonick, W., *Business Organisation and the Myth of the Market Economy* (Cambridge: Cambridge University Press, 1991).

Lee, C., *Scotland and the United Kingdom* (Manchester: Manchester University Press, 1995).

Lenman, B., *Economic History of Modern Scotland 1660–1976* (London: Batsford, 1977).

Lenman, B. and K. Donaldson, 'Partners' Incomes, Investment and Diversification in the Scottish Linen Area 1850–1921', *Business History,* 13 (1971), pp. 1–18.

Lenman, B., C. Lythe, and E. Gauldie, *Dundee and its Textile Industry* (Dundee: Abertay Historical Society, 1969).

Levinson, M., *The Box. How the Shipping Container Made the World Smaller and the World Economy Bigger* (Princeton, NJ: Princeton University Press, 2006).

Levitt, I., 'Scottish Papers Submitted to the Cabinet, 1945–1966: A Guide to Records Held at the Public Record Office and National Archives of Scotland', *Scottish Economic and Social History,* 20 (2000), pp. 58–125.

Lloyd, G. and J. McCarthy, 'Dundee: A City Discovering Inclusion and Regeneration' in C. Couch, C. Fraser and S. Percy (eds), *Urban Regeneration in Europe* (Oxford: Blackwell, 2003), pp. 56–68.

Lloyd, G., McCarthy, J. and Peel, D., 'The Re-Constitution of a Small Scottish City: Re-Discovering Dundee' in D. Bell and M. Jayne (eds), *Small Cities. Urban Experience Beyond the Metropolis* Abingdon: Routledge, 2006), pp. 105–19.

Lowe, R., *The Welfare State in Britain since 1945,* 3rd edn (Basingstoke: Macmillan, 2005).

Lythe, C. and M. Majmudar, *The Renaissance of the Scottish Economy?* (London: Allen and Unwin, 1982).

McCrone, G., *Regional Policy in Britain* (London: Allen and Unwin, 1969).

McDermott, 'Ownership, Organization and Regional Dependence in the Scottish Electronics Industry', *Regional Studies,* 10 (1976), pp. 319–35.

McDowall, S., and Draper, P., *Trade Adjustment and the British Jute Industry: A Case Study* (Glasgow: Fraser of Allander Institute, 1978).

McDowall, S., Draper, P. and McGuinness, T., 'Protection, Technological Change and Trade Adjustment: The Case of Jute in Britain' (St. Andrews: University Department of Economics Reprint series no 14, 1976).

McKean, C. and Whatley, P., *Lost Dundee. Dundee's Lost Architectural Heritage* (Edinburgh: Birlinn, 2008).

Marrison, A., *British Business and Protection 1903–1932* (Oxford: Clarendon, 1996).

Matthews, R., 'Why has Britain had Full Employment since the War?', *Economic Journal,* 78 (1968), pp. 555–69.

Menzies I., and D. Chapman, 'The Jute Industry', in H. Silverman (ed), *Studies in Industrial Organization* (London: Methuen, 1946), pp. 235–63.

Mercer, H., *Constructing a Competitive Order The Hidden History of British Antitrust Policies* (Cambridge: Cambridge University Press, 1995).

Millward, R., 'The Rise of the Service Economy', in R. Floud and P. Johnson (eds), *The Cambridge Economic History of Modern Britain, volume 3 – Structural Change and Growth, 1939–2000* (Cambridge: Cambridge University Press, 2004), pp. 238–66.

Mitchison, R., 'The Hidden Labour Force: Women in the Scottish Economy since 1945' in R. Saville (ed.), *The Economic Development of Modern Scotland* (Edinburgh: John Donald, 1985), pp. 183–94.

Moore, B. and Rhodes, J., 'Regional Policy and the Scottish Economy' *Scottish Journal of Political Economy* 21 (1974), pp. 215–35.

Morelli, C., and J. Tomlinson, 'Women and Work after the Second World War: A Case Study of the Jute Industry, circa 1945–1954', *Twentieth Century British History*, 19 (2008), pp. 61–82.

Morison, H., *The Regeneration of Local Economies* (Oxford: Clarendon, 1987).

Offer, A., 'British Manual Workers: From Producers to Consumers, *c.* 1950–2000', *Contemporary British History,* 22 (2008), pp. 537–71.

Ollerenshaw, P., 'Textile Business in Europe during the First World War: The Linen Industry, 1914–18' *Business History*, 41 (1999), pp. 63–87.

—, P., 'Stagnation, War and Depression: The UK Linen Industry, 1900–1930', in P. Ollerenshaw and B. Collins (eds), *The European Linen Industry in Historical Perspective* (Oxford: Oxford University Press, 2003), pp. 285–307.

Olson, M., *The Logic of Collective Action* (Cambridge, MA: Harvard University Press, 1965).

—, *The Rise and Decline of Nations* (Connecticut: New Haven, 1982).

Owen, G., *From Empire to Europe* (London: Harper Collins, 2000).

—, *The Rise and Fall of Great Companies: Courtaulds and the Reshaping of the Man-Made Fibres Industry.* (Oxford: Oxford University Press, 2010).

Oxford Dictionary of National Biography (Oxford: University Press, 2004); online edn, May 2009 [http://www.oxforddnb.com/view/article/71965, accessed 17 Aug 2010].

Parker, M., *Thatcherism and the Fall of Coal* (Oxford: Oxford University Press, 2000).

Parsons, W.A., *The Political Economy of British Regional Policy* (Beckenham: Croom Helm,1986).

Peck, E., 'Struggling with the Creative Class', *International Journal of Urban and Regional Research*, 29 (2005), pp. 740–70.

Philips, D., *The Hungry Thirties: Dundee Between the Wars* (Dundee: David Winter, 1981).

Phillips, J., *The Industrial Politics of Devolution* (Manchester: Manchester University Press, 2008).

—, 'The "Retreat" to Scotland: The Tay Road Bridge and Dundee's Post-1945 Development' in J. Tomlinson and C. Whatley (eds), *Jute No More*, pp. 246–65.

Pilat, D., A. Cimper, K. Olsen, and C. Webb, *The Changing Nature of Manufacturing in OECD Economies* (Paris: OECD, 2006).

Pollard, S., *The Development of the British Economy 1914–80*, 3rd edn (London: Edward Arnold, 1983).

—, *Britain's Prime and Britain's Decline. The British Economy 1870–1914* (London: Edward Arnold, 1994).

Porter, M. E., *The Competitive Advantage of Nations* (London: Macmillan, 1990).

Reeder D., and R. Rodger, 'Industrialization and the City Economy' in M. Daunton (ed), *The Cambridge Urban History of Britain, vol 3 – 1840–1950* (Cambridge: Cambridge University Press, 2000), pp. 553–92.

Ringe, A., N. Rollings and R. Middleton, *Economic Policy under the Conservatives, 1951–65: A Guide to Documents in the National Archives of the UK* (London; Institute of Historical Research, 2004).

Robertson, D., and S. Dennison, *The Control of Industry* (Cambridge: Cambridge University Press, 1960).

Robinson, E. A. G., *Monopoly* (Cambridge: Cambridge University Press, 1941).

—, 'The Economic Problems of the Transition from War to Peace, 1945–1949' *Cambridge Journal of Economics* 10 (1985), pp. 165–85.

Rose, M., 'The Politics of Protection: An Institutional Approach to Government Industry Relations in the British and United States Cotton Industries, 1945–73' *Business History*, 3 (1997), pp. 128–50.

—, *Firms, Networks and Business Values: The British and American Cotton Industries Since 1750* (Cambridge: Cambridge University Press, 2000), pp. 250–95.

Ross, E. and Hardy, J., *Unemployment in Dundee* (Dundee: Dundee Labour Party, 1979).

Savage, M. and K. Williams (eds), *Remembering Elites* (Oxford: Blackwell, 2008).

Schmit, C., 'The Nature and Dimensions of Scottish Foreign Investment, 1860–1914', *Business History*, 39 (1997), pp. 42–68.

Scott, P., 'Regional Development and Policy', in R. Floud and P. Johnson (eds), *The Cambridge Economic History of Modern Britain, vol 3 – Structural Change and Growth, 1939–2000* (Cambridge: Cambridge University Press, 2004), pp. 332–67.

Sengupta, P., *The Indian Jute Belt*, Orient (Bombay: Orient Longmans, 1959).

Sethia, T., 'The Rise of Jute Manufacturing in Colonial India: A Global Perspective', *Journal of World History*, 7 (1996), pp. 71–99.

Shanks, M., *The Stagnant Society* (Harmondsworth: Penguin, 1961).

Shonfield, A., *British Economic Policy since the War* (Harmondsworth: Penguin, 1959).

Singleton, J., 'Planning for Cotton, 1945–1951', *Economic History Review*, 43 (1990), pp. 62–78.

—, *Lancashire on the Scrapheap* (Oxford: Oxford University Press, 1991).

Slaven, A., and S. Checkland (eds), *Dictionary of Scottish Business Biography 1860–1960: Vol.1. The Staple Industries* (Aberdeen: Aberdeen University Press, 1986).

Slows, P., *The Advance Factory in Regional Development* (Aldershot: Gower, 1981).

Stewart, G., *Jute and Empire* (Manchester: Manchester University Press, 1998).

—, 'End Game for Jute: Dundee and Calcutta in the Twentieth Century' in J. Tomlinson and C. Whatley (eds), *Jute No More*, pp. 29–51.

Supple, B., *The History of the British Coal Industry, iv 1913–1946: The Political Economy of Decline* (Oxford: Clarendon, 1987).

Symeonidis, G., *The Effects of Competition: Cartel Policy and the Evolution of Strategy and Structure in British Industry* (London: MIT Press, 2002).

Tedlow, R. S., *New and Improved: The Story of Mass Marketing in America* (Oxford: Heinemann, 1990).

Thigpen, M., P. Marongiu, and S. Lasker, *World Demand Prospects for Jute* (Washington DC: World Bank, 1982).

Thigpen, M. and T. Akiyama, *Prospects for the World Jute Industry* (Washington DC: World Bank, 1986).

Tiratsoo, N., and J. Tomlinson, *Industrial Efficiency and State Intervention: Labour 1939–1951* (London: Routledge, 1993).

Tolliday, S., *Business, Banking and Politics: The Case of British Steel* (Cambridge, MA: Harvard University Press, 1987).

Tomlinson, B. R., *The Political Economy of the Raj, 1914–1947* (Basingstoke: Macmillan,1979).

—, 'Colonial Firms and the Decline of Colonialism in Eastern India 1914–1947' *Modern Asian Studies* 15 (1981), pp. 455–86.

—, 'British Business in India, 1860–1970' in G. Jones and R. Davenport-Hines (eds), *British Business in Asia since 1860* (Cambridge: Cambridge University Press, 1989), pp. 92–116.

—, *The Economy of Modern India 1860–1970* (Cambridge: Cambridge University Press, 1993).

Tomlinson, J., *Employment Policy: The Crucial Years, 1939–1955* (Oxford: Oxford University Press, 1986).

—, 'Productivity Policy' in H. Mercer, N. Rollings and J. Tomlinson (eds), *Labour Governments and Private Industry: The Experience of 1945–51* (Edinburgh: Edinburgh University Press, 1992), pp. 37–54.

—, 'Inventing "Decline": The Falling Behind of the British Economy in the Post-War Years' *Economic History Review* 49 (1996), pp. 734–60.

—, *Democratic Socialism and Economic Policy: The Attlee Years* (Cambridge: Cambridge University Press, 1997).

—, 'Mrs. Thatcher's Macroeconomic Adventurism, 1979–1981, and its Political Consequences' *British Politics*, 2 (2007), pp. 3–19.

—, 'A "Failed Experiment"? Public Ownership and the Narratives of Post-War Britain', *Labour History Review*, 73 (2008), pp. 228–43.

—, 'Not "Decline and Revival": An Alternative Narrative on British Post-War Productivity' in R. Coopey and P. Lyth (eds), *Decline and Renaissance? Business in Britain in the Twentieth Century* (Oxford: Oxford University Press, 2009), pp. 153–67.

—, 'Thrice Denied: Declinism and the Narrative of British History in the Long Twentieth Century', *Twentieth Century British History*, 20 (2009), pp. 227–51.

—, 'The Deglobalization of Dundee, *c.* 1900–2000', *Journal of Scottish Historical Studies*, 29 (2009), pp. 123–40.

—, 'Responding to Globalization? Churchill and Dundee in 1908', in *Twentieth Century British History*, 21 (2010), pp. 257–80.

Tomlinson, J., and Whatley, C. (eds), *Jute No More: Transforming Dundee* (Dundee: Dundee University Press, 2011).

Toye, R., 'The Attlee Government, the Imperial Preference System, and the Creation of the GATT' *English Historical Review*, 118 (2003), pp. 912–39.

Trentmann, F., *Free Trade Nation* (Oxford: Oxford University Press, 2008).

Turok, I., 'Scottish Urban Policy: Continuity, Change and Uncertainty Post-Devolution', in C. Johnstone and M. Whitehead (eds), *New Horizons in British Urban Policy* (Aldershot: Ashgate 2004), pp. 111–28.

van der Steen, B., 'The Jute Industry a Statistical Overview' www.iisg.nl/research/jute-industry.pdf, accessed 19 October 2010

Wadsworth, J., 'Eyes Down for a Full House: Labour Market Polarisation and the Housing Market in Britain' *Scottish Journal of Political Economy* 45 (1998), pp. 376–92.

Wainwright, E. M., 'Dundee's Jute Mills and Factories: Spaces of Production, Surveillance and Discipline', *Scottish Geographical Journal*, 121 (2005), pp. 121–40.

—, 'Constructing Gendered Workplace "types": The Weaver-Millworker Distinction in Dundee's Jute Industry, *c.* 1880–1910', *Gender, Place & Culture*, 14 (2007), pp. 467–82.

Walker, W., *Juteopolis: Dundee and its Textile Workers 1885–1923* (Edinburgh: Scottish Academic Press, 1979).

Wallace, D., *The Romance of Jute: A Short History of the Calcutta Jute Mill Industry 1855–1909* (Calcutta: Empire Press, 1909).

Wass, D., *Decline to Fall, the Making of British Macro-Economic Policy and the 1976 IMF Crisis* (Oxford: Oxford University Press, 2008).

Whatley, C. (ed), *The Remaking of Juteopolis: Dundee circa 1891–1991* (Dundee: Abertay Historical Society, 1992).

—, *Onwards from Osnaburgs: The Rise and Progress of a Scottish Textile Company: Don and Low of Forfar, 1792–1992* (Edinburgh: Mainstream, 1992).

Wiener, M., *English Culture and the Decline of the Industrial Spirit 1850–1980* (Cambridge: Cambridge University Press, 1981).

Wilkinson, E., *The Town that was Murdered; The Life-Story of Jarrow* (London: Left Book Club, 1939).

Williamson, O. E., *The Economic Institutions of Capitalism: Firms, Markets, Relational Contracting* (London: Macmillan, 1985).

Wilson, G., *The Making of a Lord Provost* (Dundee: Winter, 1966).

—, *Overspill. A Second Memory Book* (Dundee: Winter, 1970).

Wright, V., 'Juteopolis and After. Women and Work in Twentieth Century Dundee' in J. Tomlinson and C. Whatley (eds), *Jute no more*, pp. 132–62.

Yamey, B. S., *Resale Price Maintenance* (London: Weidenfield and Nicholson, 1966).

Young, S., N. Hood and E. Peters, 'Multinational Enterprises and Regional Economic Development', *Regional Studies*, 28 (1994), pp. 657–77.

INDEX